Elias Sime

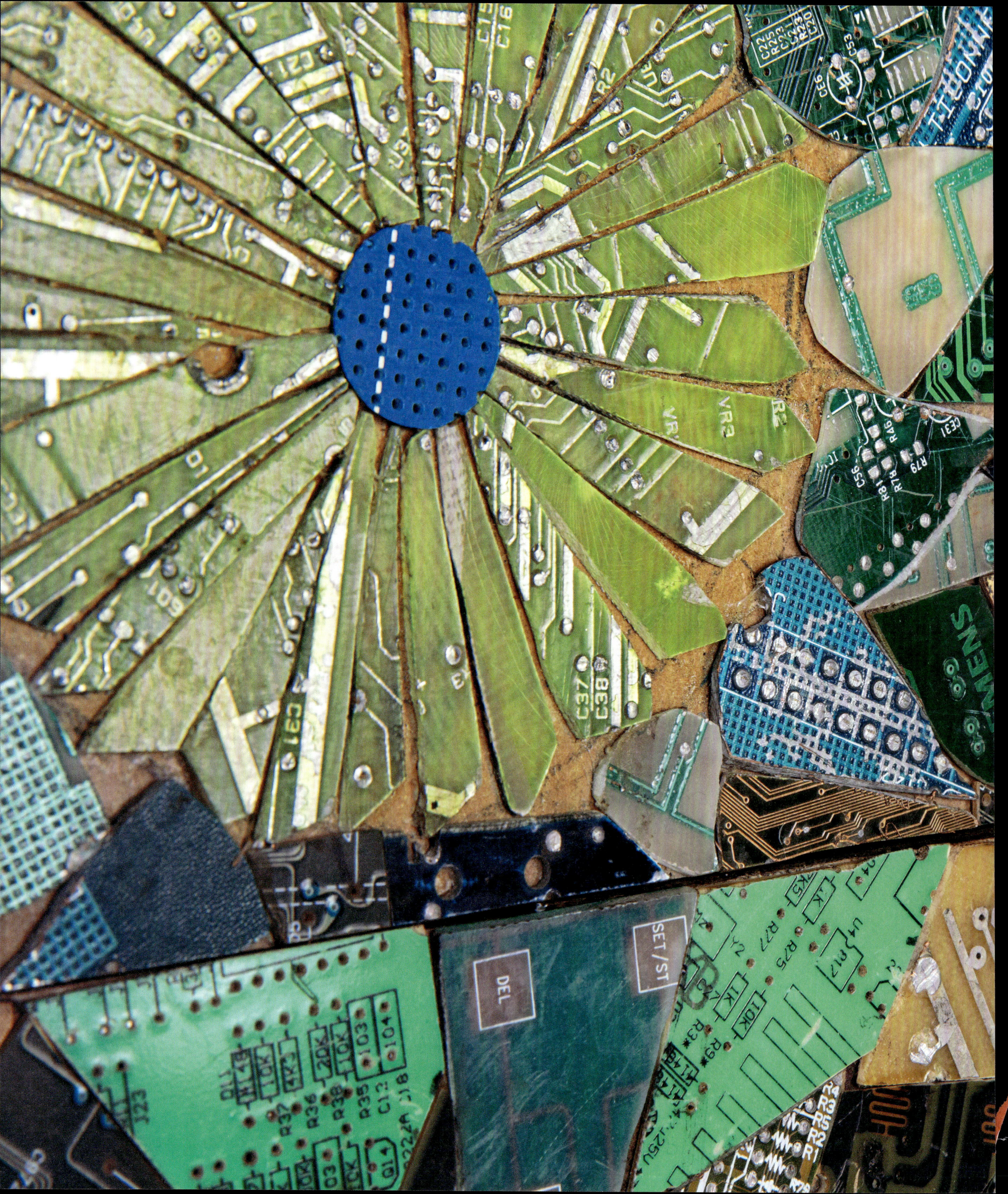

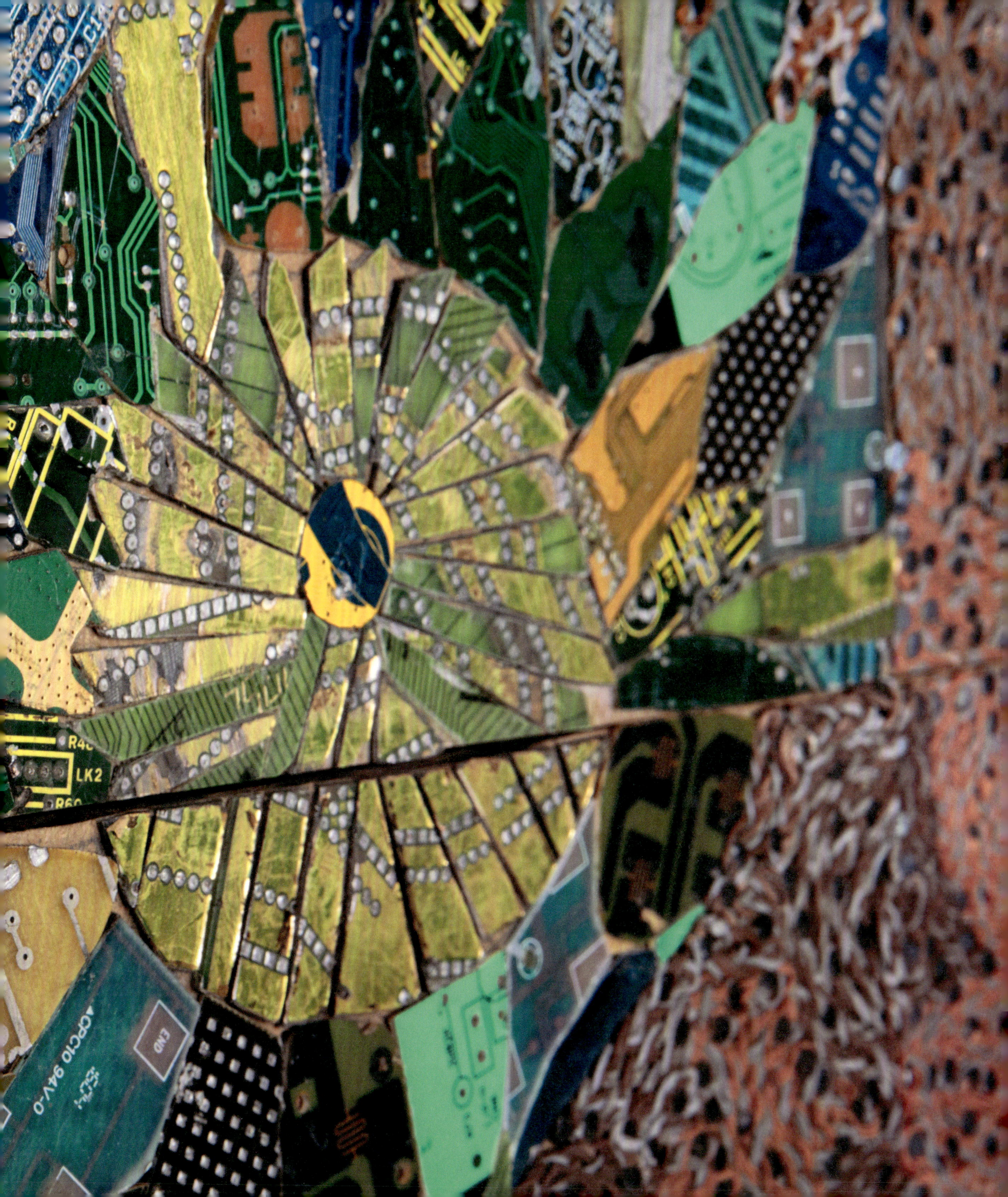
LK2
ACPC10 94V-0

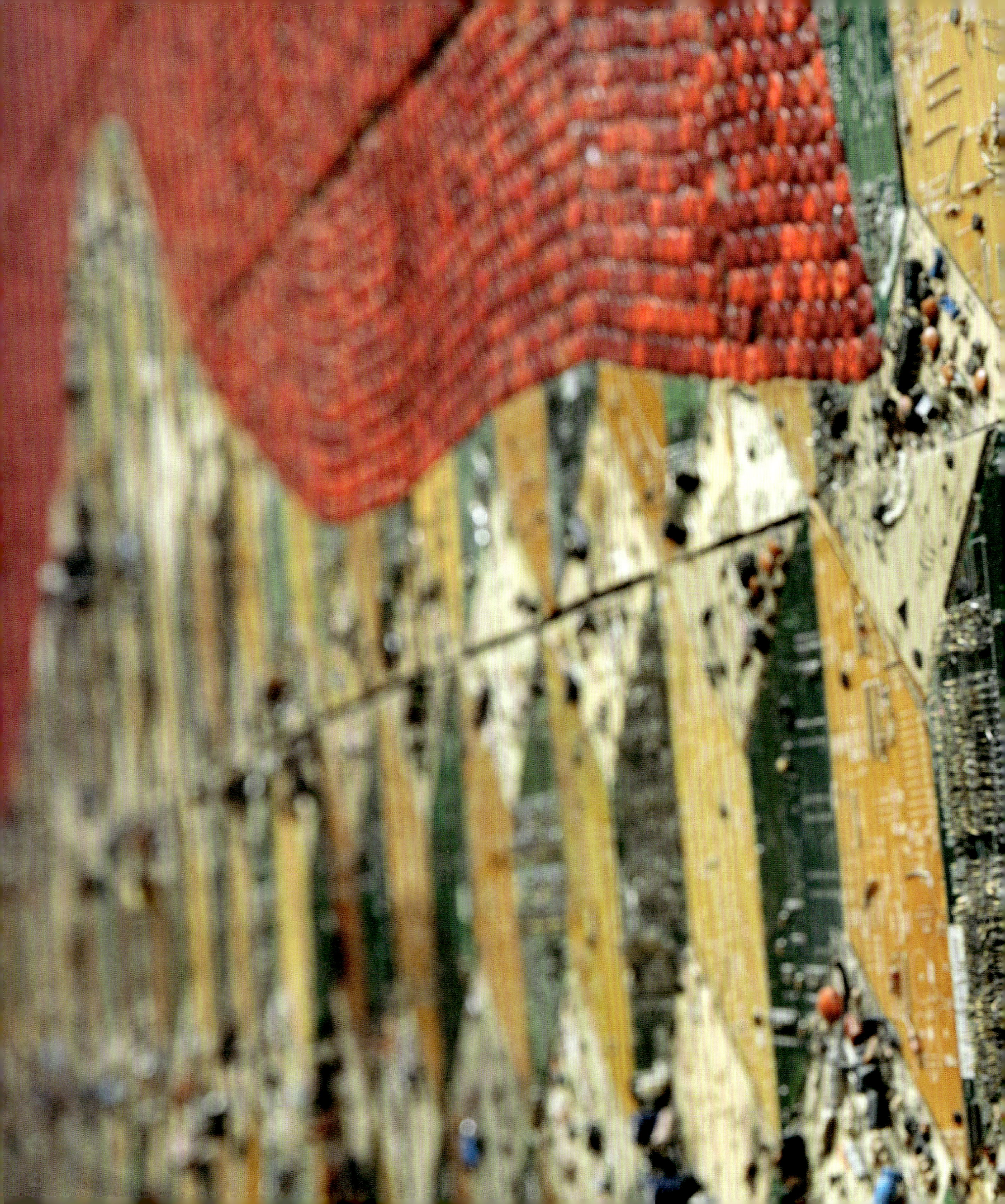

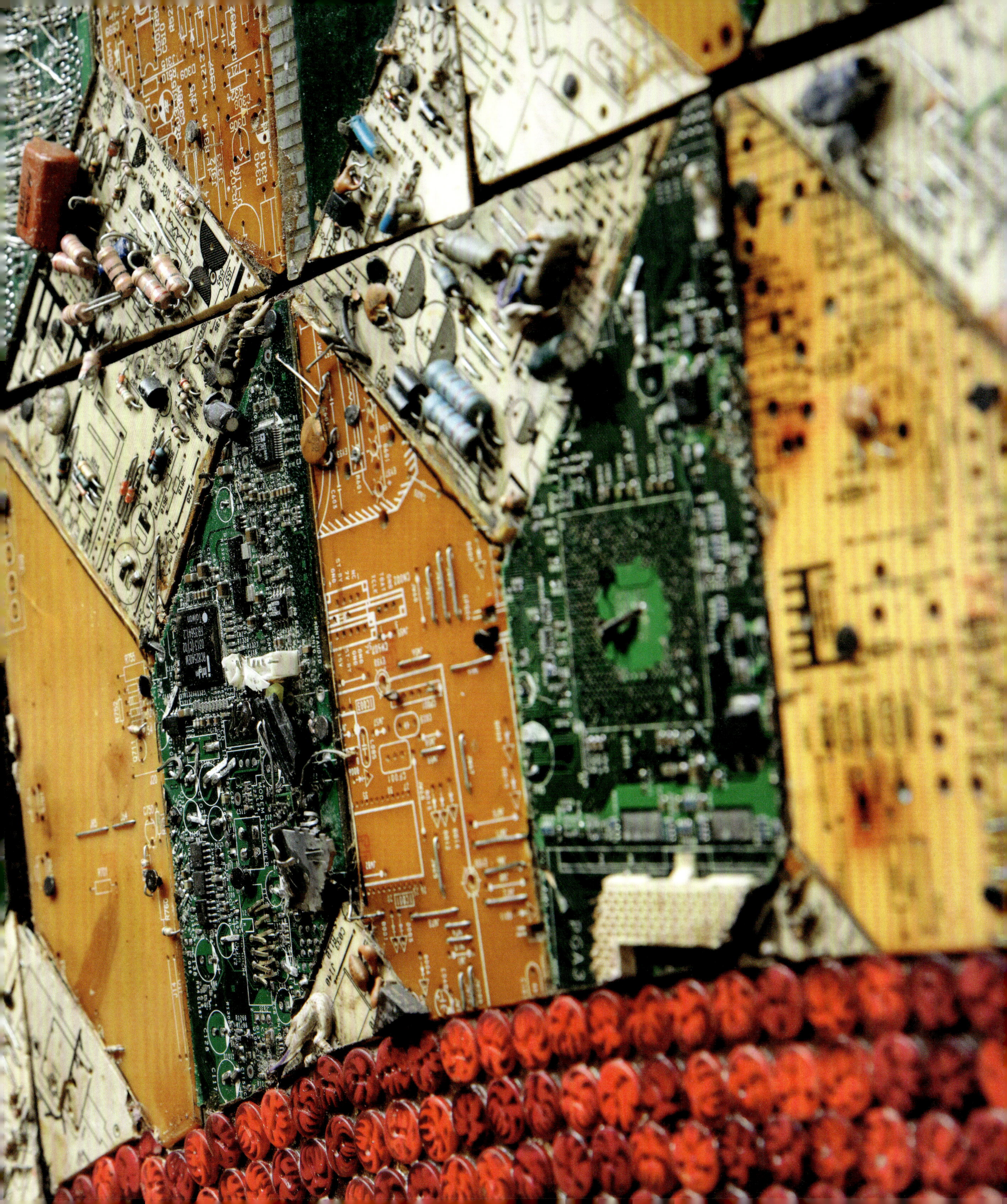

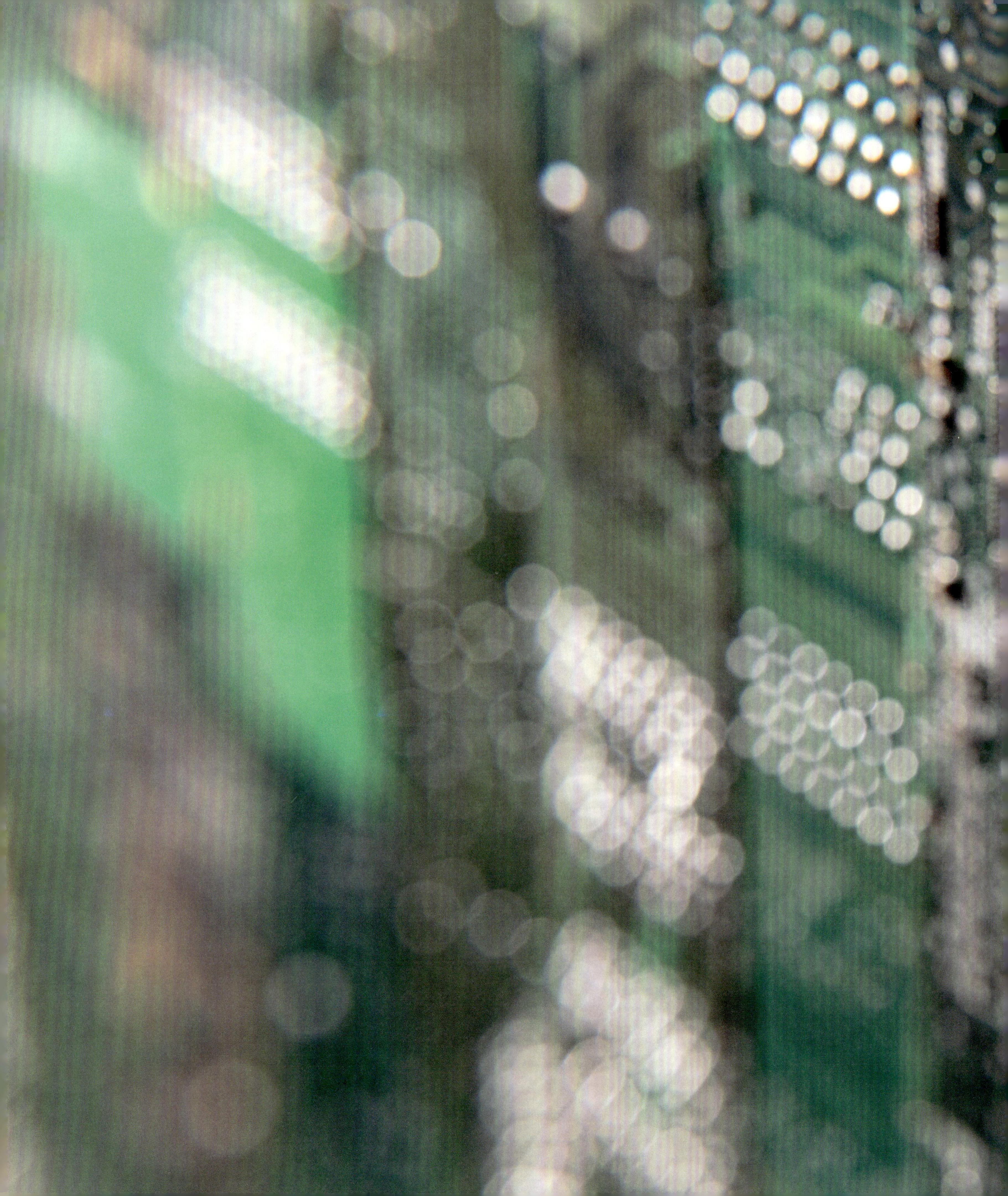

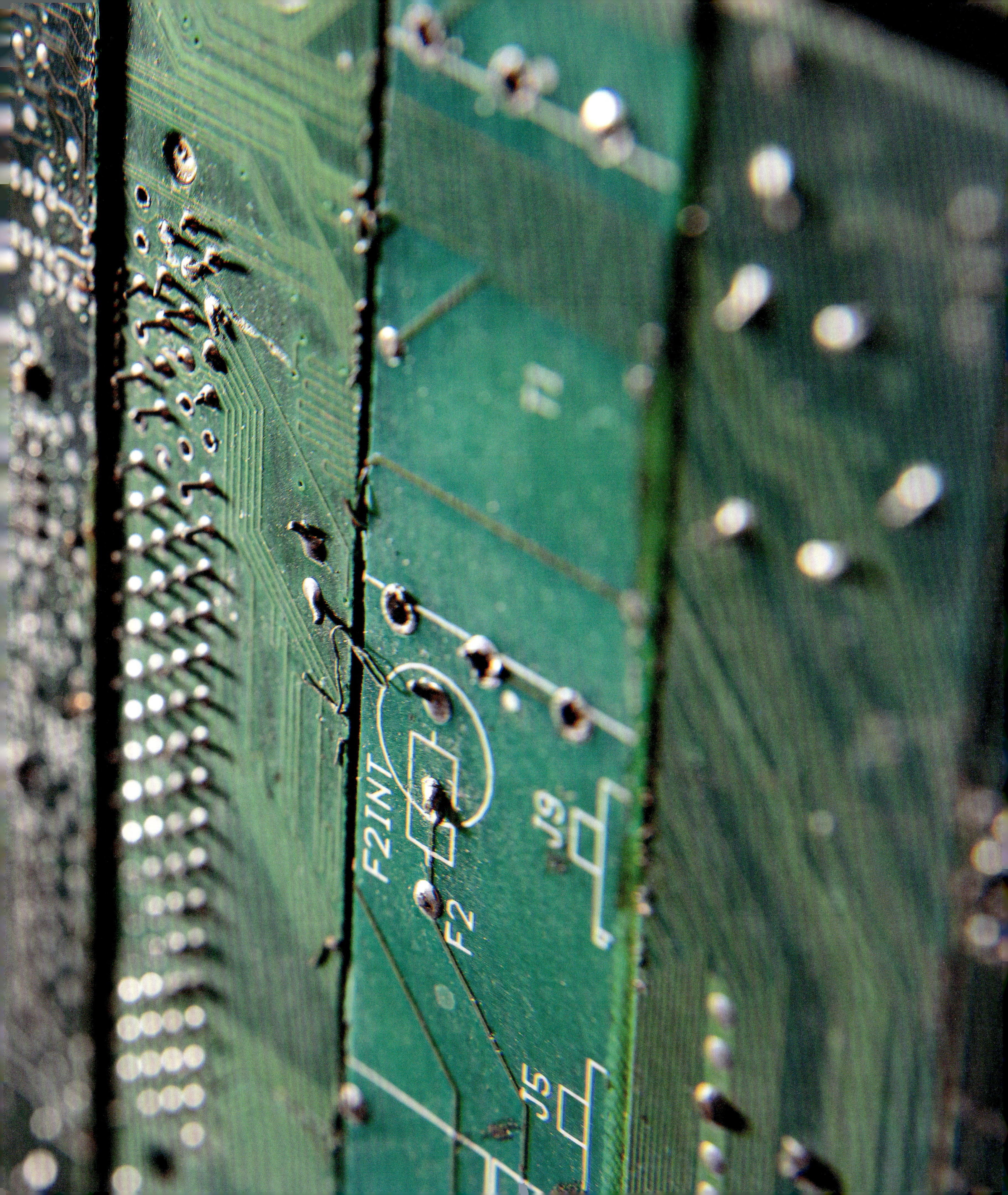
F2INT
J9
F2
J5

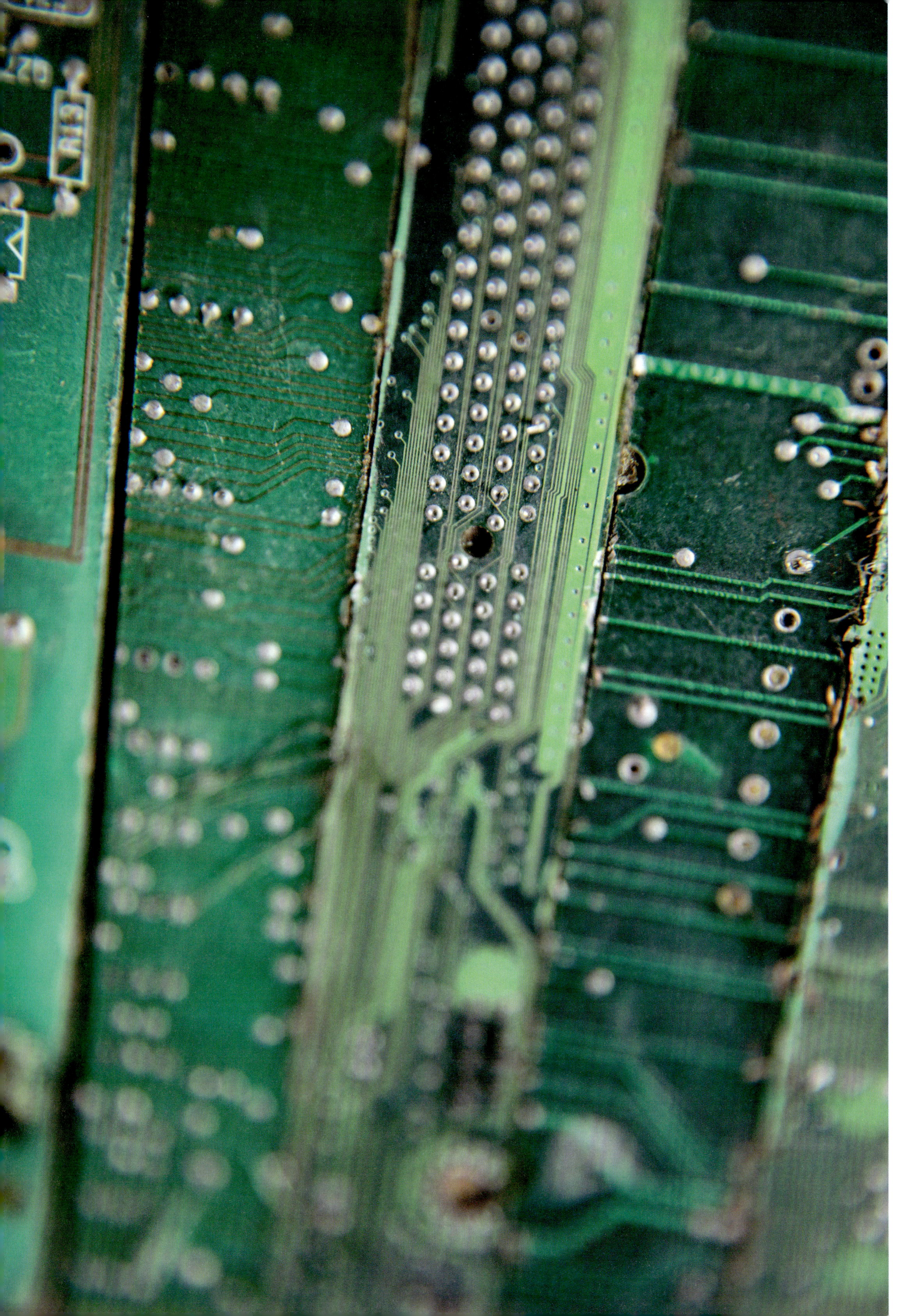

Elias Sime

TIGHTROPE

Edited by Tracy L. Adler

DelMonico Books • Prestel
Munich London New York

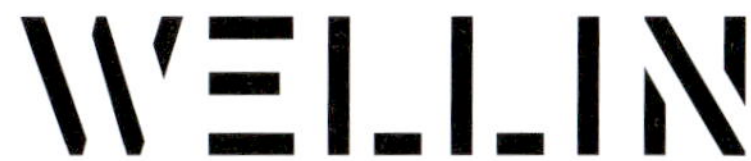

Ruth and Elmer Wellin Museum of Art
Hamilton College

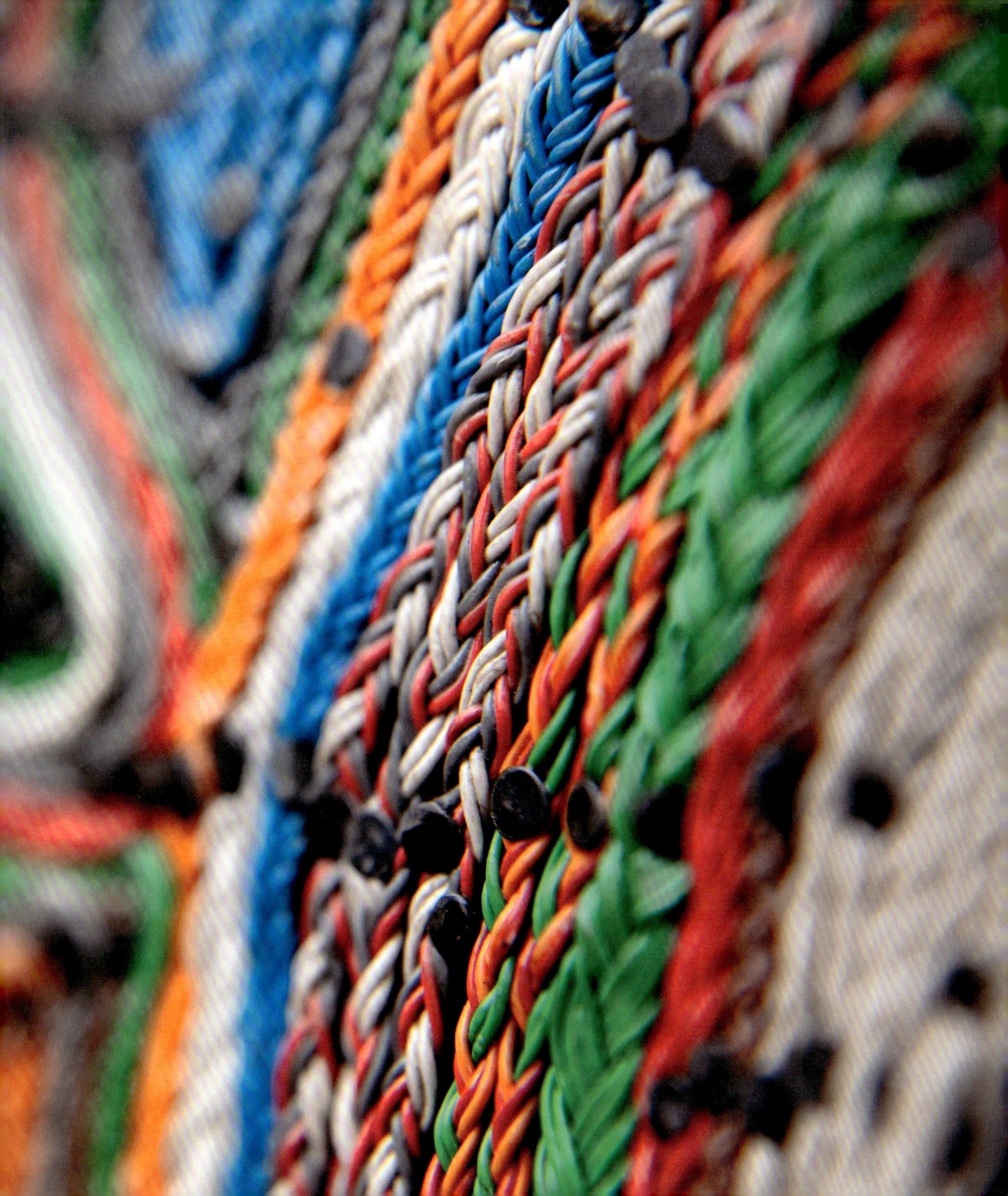

CONTENTS

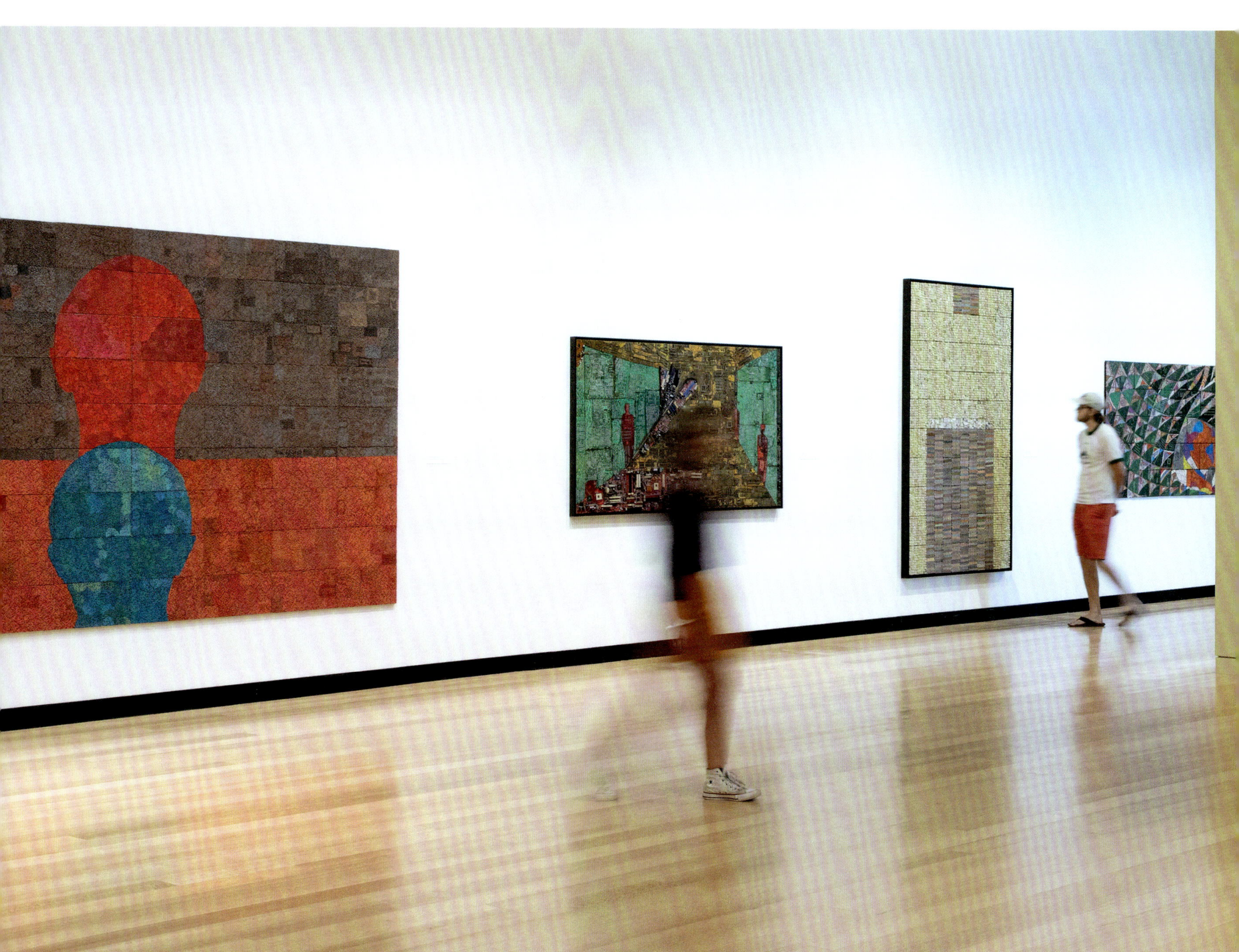

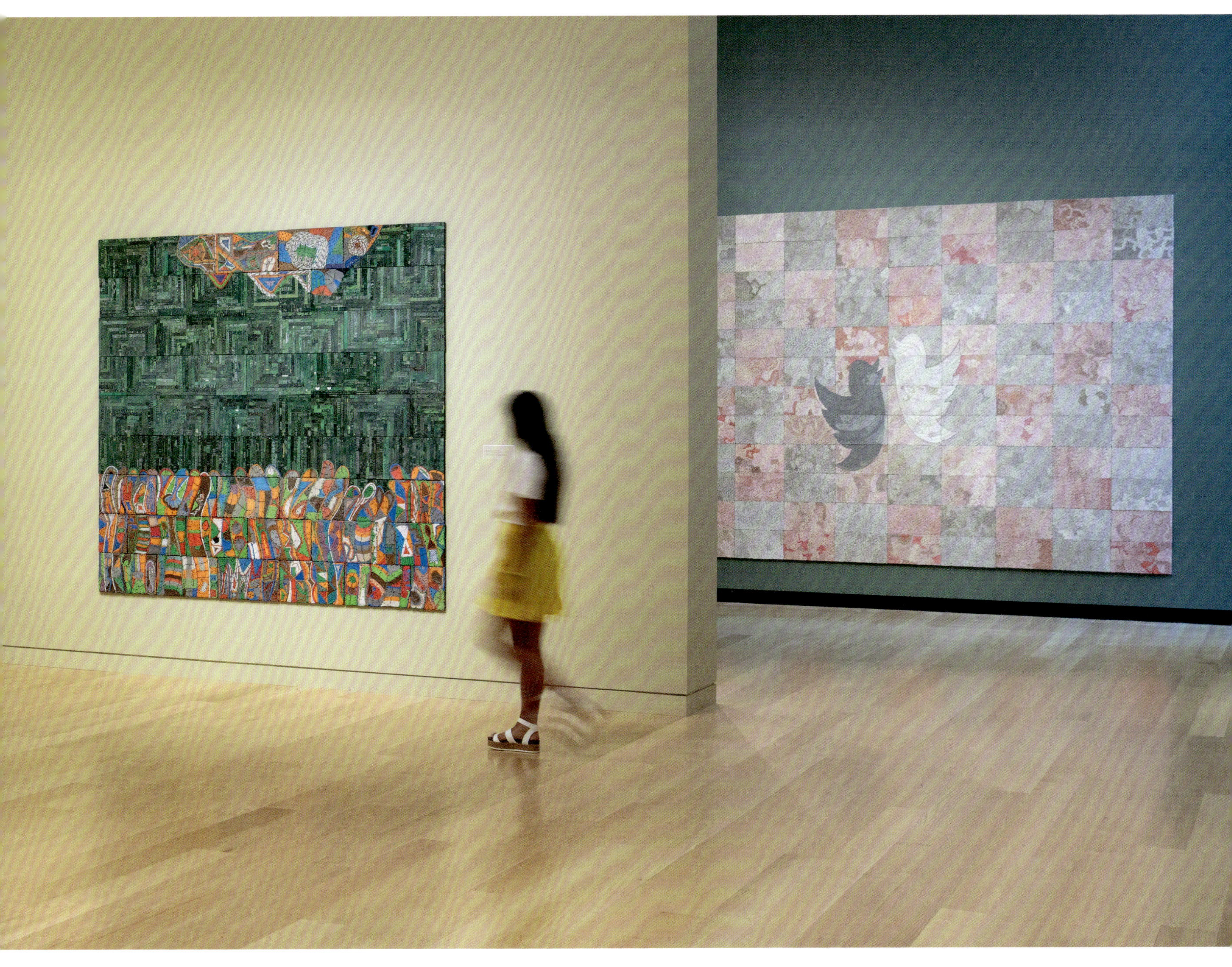

Installation view of *Elias Sime: Tightrope*, Ruth and Elmer Wellin Museum of Art at Hamilton College, Clinton, NY (September 7–December 8, 2019)

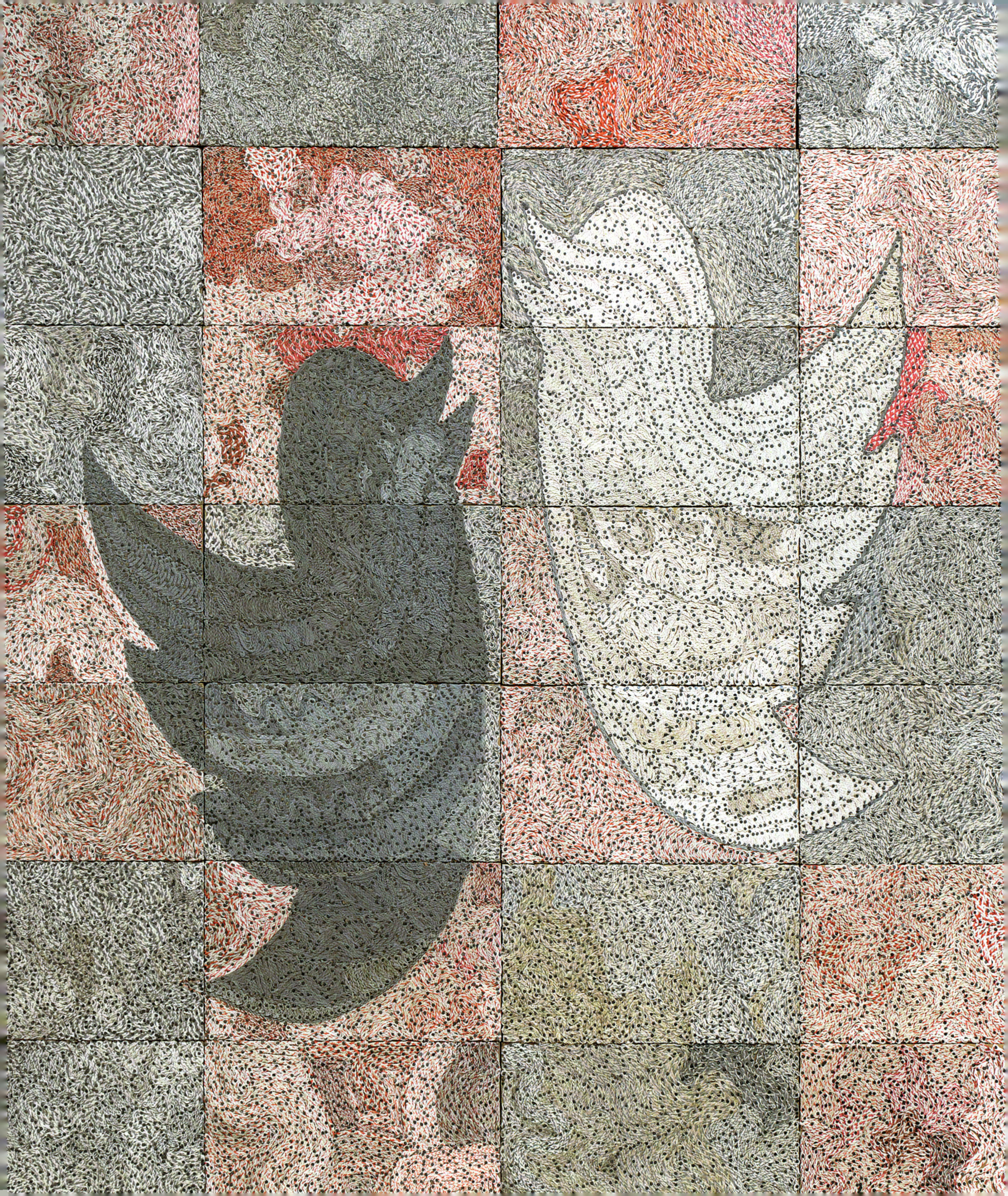

DIRECTOR'S FOREWORD AND ACKNOWLEDGMENTS

TRACY L. ADLER

As director of the Wellin Museum, I aim to generate and support programs that have multiple vantage and access points, particularly when it comes to developing the institution's long-term exhibition strategy. The Wellin is a teaching museum deeply engaged with Hamilton College's liberal arts mission, and our intention is to present exhibitions that can act as a catalyst for scholarly innovation and an extension of the classroom experience, providing teaching opportunities in a range of disciplines across divisions and fields of study. Through the lens of a particular artist or theme, these exhibitions create opportunities for our students, faculty, and community to forge unexpected connections and expand the dialogue around art into subjects relevant to their studies, areas of expertise, and everyday lives. In the case of *Elias Sime: Tightrope*, themes such as ecological sustainability, the resilience and complexity of nature, social responsibility, and the global impact of technology are well positioned to foster numerous critical conversations about and around the work of a single contemporary artist.

Beyond its role in the formal curriculum, the Wellin provides experiential learning opportunities through its docent program, comprising thirty to forty current Hamilton students who are involved in all aspects of the museum's activities. The Wellin's docents have diverse interests and backgrounds and are at the very heart of its programs. We hope to empower them to feel agency and ownership and to advance their skills in areas such as research, oral and written communication, aesthetic discernment, creative thinking, and problem solving—qualities that will serve them throughout their lives, both personally and professionally. For *Elias Sime: Tightrope*, a group of seven students worked with the artist and his collaborator, Meskerem Assegued, to create a site-specific sculpture on the Wellin's Selch Terrace over the summer of 2019. We have found that such opportunities to work alongside practicing artists on large-scale projects at the museum contribute greatly to students' growth, enrich their college experience, and offer practical insight into the process of realizing a project from conception through completion that is invaluable and irreplaceable.

This type of interactivity distinguishes the Wellin both for Hamilton's students and for the artists who are engaged by the museum to create new works, exploring uncharted creative directions and connecting both parties to the museum in ways that cannot be quantified. Sime's sculpture *Flower & Roots* (2019; pl. 1), supported through the Daniel W. Dietrich '64 Fund for Innovation in the Arts, constituted our first commission outside the walls of the museum. Safa Ahmed '21, Alexander Fergusson '20, Olivia Fuller '19, Elias Griffin '20, Anika Huq '19, Lila Reid '20, and Henry Andrew Watson '19 worked full-time for three weeks with Sime and Assegued to make the work a reality. I am grateful to the artist and his collaborator for envisioning such an ambitious project, to the students for their enthusiastic participation, and to the Wellin's outstanding Building Manager and Preparator, Christopher Harrison, for producing the project with me. Harrison's positive attitude and professionalism are unparalleled, and the project would not have been possible without his

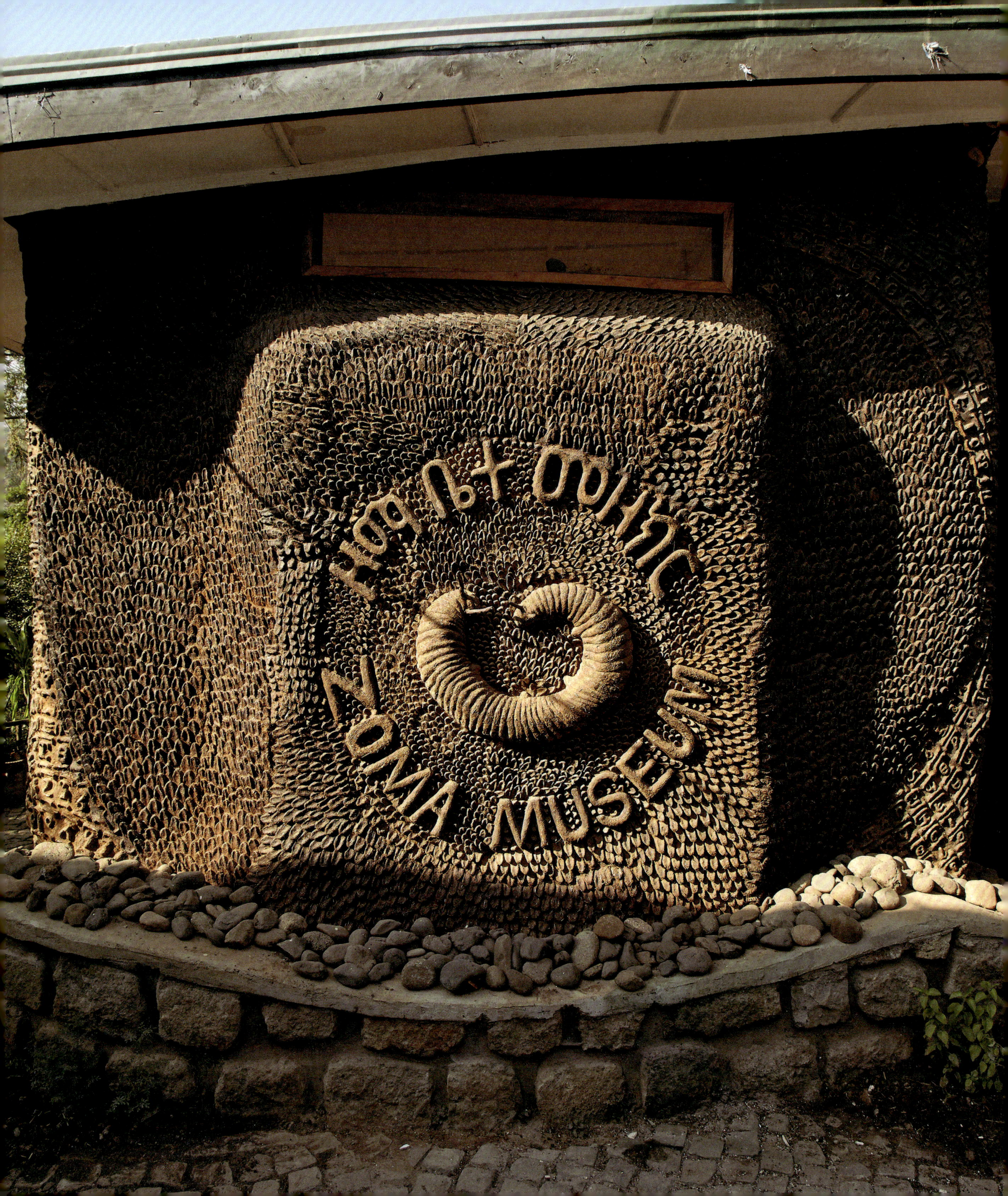
ዞማ ቤተ መዘክር
ZOMA MUSEUM

expertise, generosity, and leadership. His team of preparators, led by Brian Baker, managed both the site-specific project and the exhibition installation with efficiency and aplomb.

My curatorial process involves working closely with artists and spending time with them in their studios. Understanding an artist's practice and approach is a critical part of doing justice to the work in the resulting exhibition. For this project, a particularly propitious opportunity arose. In spring 2019, through the Johnson-Pote Museum Director Fund, I was able to travel to Ethiopia with a group of distinguished international museum and art-world professionals, collectors, and gallerists, some of whom are partners in *Elias Sime: Tightrope*, notably Bill and Christy Gautreaux, lenders to the exhibition; Erin Dziedzic, Director of Curatorial Affairs at the Kemper Museum of Contemporary Art, Kansas City, Missouri; Silvia Forni, Senior Curator, Arts and Cultures of Africa, at the Royal Ontario Museum, Toronto; and the organizers of the trip, Jane and James Cohan and Annie Stuart of the New York–based gallery James Cohan.

Arriving ahead of the group to spend dedicated time with the artist in his studio, I encountered an unforgettable scenario. I have often felt as though spending time in artists' studios is like stepping inside their world, but at the recently opened Zoma Museum, cofounded by Sime and Assegued, this experience was magnified. Zoma is the manifestation—made concrete—of the founders' ideas about art's ability to impact society. Comprising an elementary school, a working farm, herb and flower gardens, a library, and exhibition and project spaces on four acres of land in the Mekanisa neighborhood of Addis Ababa, Zoma presents an opportunity for reimagining the role of art in a sustainable and ecologically conscious society. The buildings, constructed in the vernacular wattle-and-daub technique, have elaborately decorated surfaces designed by Sime that include references to butterflies (the transformational symbol of Zoma), roots, fingerprints, and numerals in the ancient Ge'ez script, among other abstract forms and inspirations. These patterns bring movement and energy to the structures and reinvigorate an ancient Ethiopian building tradition. The entire environment offers something new; there is nothing comparable to Zoma anywhere in the world. Each building, of which there are many, is immersed in nature: a variety of indigenous plants, a patch of flowers, a copse of trees, plots of fruits and vegetables, are all linked by stone pathways. The ensemble is verdant, fragrant, and tactile—a full sensory experience. Zoma is the museum reimagined.

Among the buildings and greenery is Sime's studio, and his work is installed throughout the grounds. Behind the studio, assistants sort through heaps of salvaged e-waste bought at the Merkato, the large open-air market in Addis Ababa where the artist sources much of his raw material. All the items amassed—be they computer keyboards, circuit boards, electrical wires, buttons, or bottle caps—were once purposeful, and it is this trace of a former existence, of a life lived, that appeals to Sime. While the sorting continues, other helpers work under the artist's direction to create his intricate tableaus. It's a kind of controlled chaos. The concentration required to realize Sime's complex constructions creates a hush in the studio, which contrasts with the lively sounds and vibrant energy that pervade the surrounding grounds. The studio is a place of busy contemplation, a quiet site of inspiration.

I am extremely grateful for the partnership I have been able to develop with Sime and Assegued over the past few years as we embarked on this exhibition project together. Full of heart and sincerity, they work from a position of integrity and openness that I hope will become a model for other creative producers. I am honored that they welcomed me into their lives and shared their creative world with me. The experience of working and spending time with

Entrance to Zoma Museum, Addis Ababa

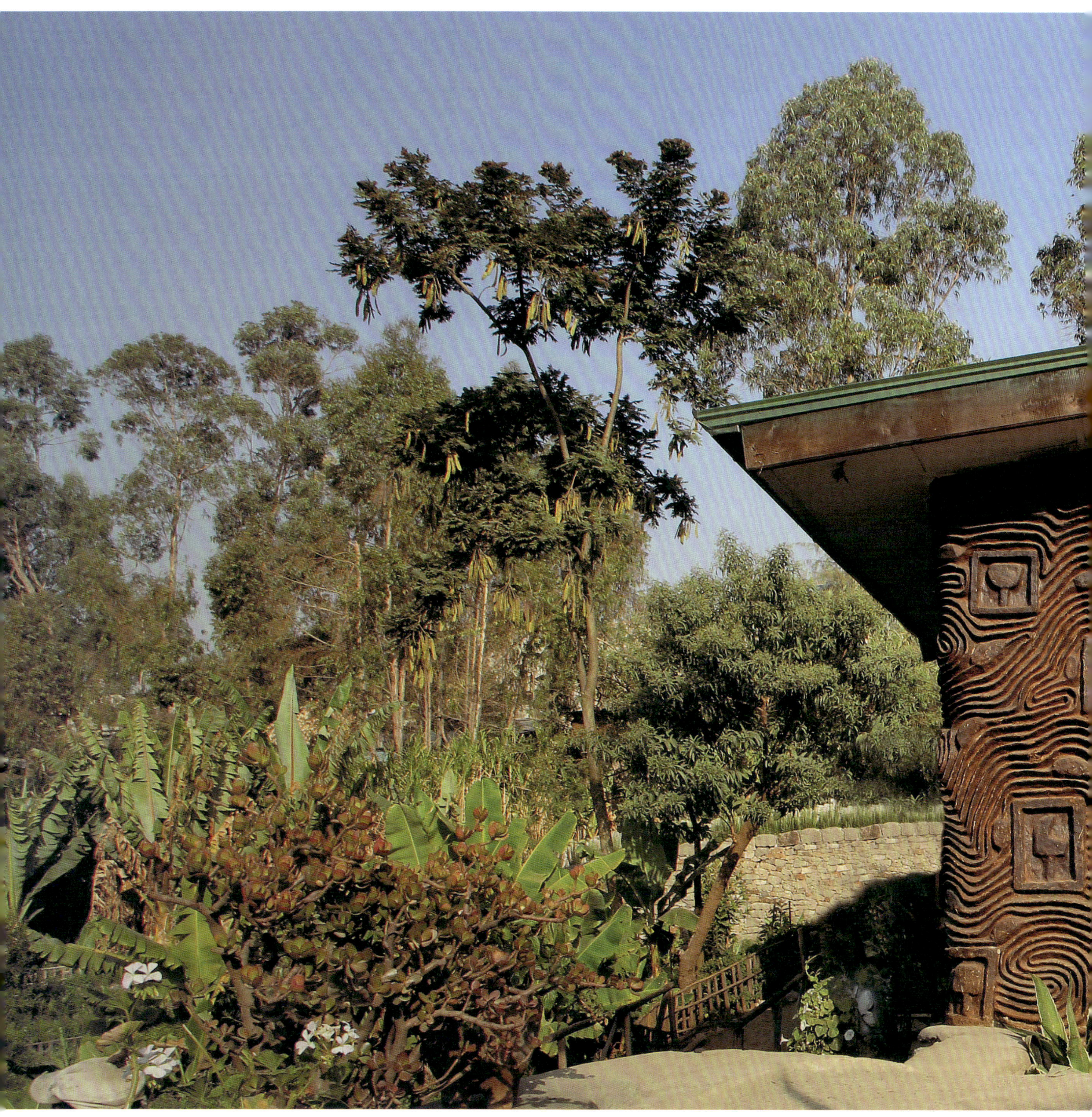

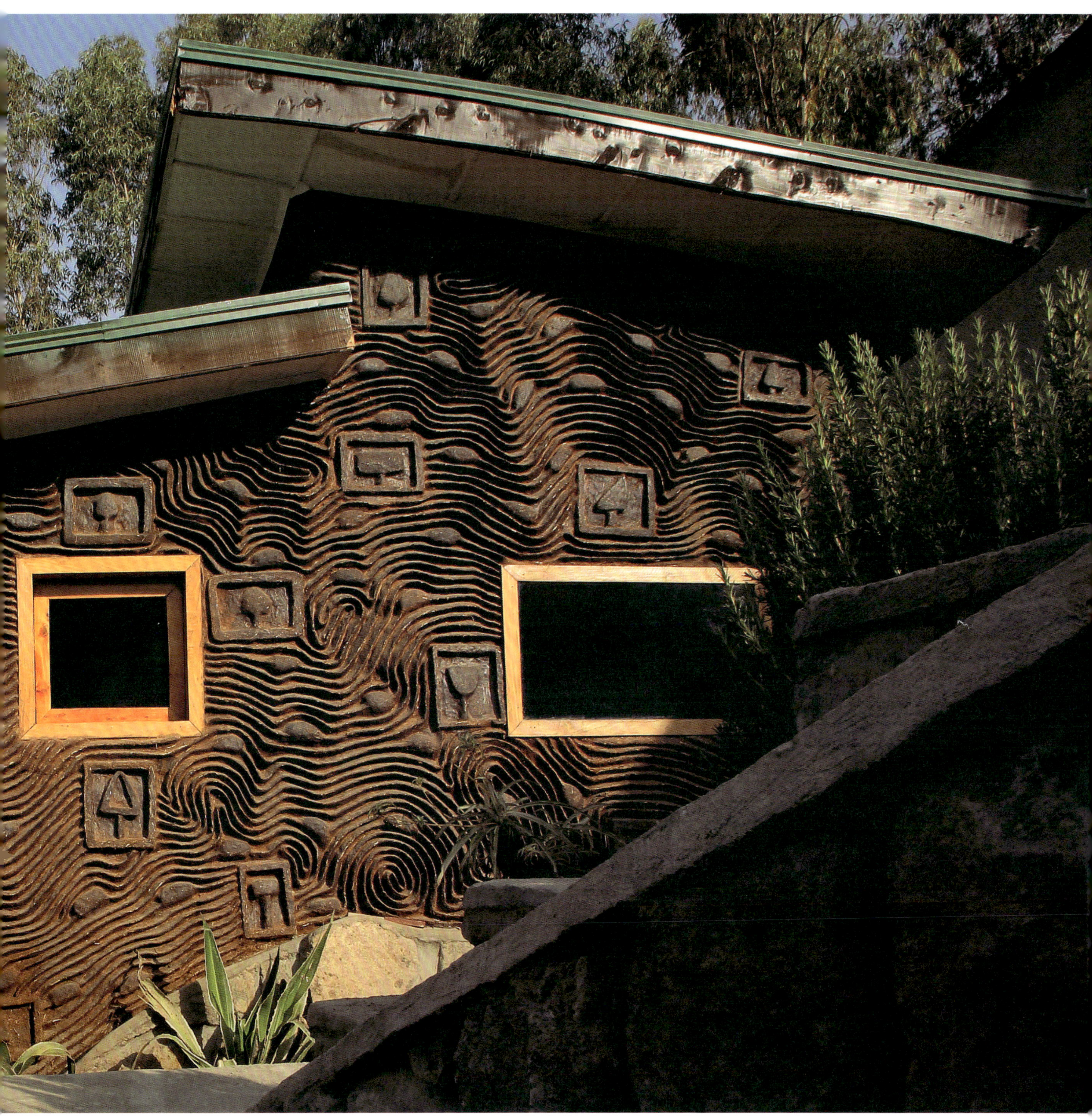

them in Ethiopia greatly impacted my approach to curating this exhibition. During my visit, Assegued, who is both an experienced curator and a trained anthropologist, said to me, “As curators, we are the artist’s artist”—which highlights the creative partnership and symbiotic role enjoyed by some artists and curators. The working relationship Sime and Assegued have established as artistic and curatorial partners is driven by a shared vision and belief in the power of art to effect change. Through Sime’s work and the development of Zoma Museum, they have proved that this goal is not merely theoretical but practical and possible.

I am equally indebted to James Cohan, who first introduced me to Sime’s work in 2015. Through shows at the gallery and art fairs in which the gallery participated, I continued to observe the artist’s evolution and deepen my understanding of his work, resulting in an acquisition by the Wellin Museum in 2017. James Cohan has been an extraordinary advocate for Sime, Assegued, and Zoma Museum. I am also grateful to Jane Cohan, the gallery’s co-owner, and Annie Stuart, Director, Art Fairs, for facilitating this project. Without their efforts, support, and partnership, the exhibition would not have been possible.

In Ethiopia, I would like to thank Michael Raynor, the United States Ambassador, for offering his assistance, hosting us at his residence in Addis Ababa, and visiting the Wellin Museum at Hamilton College. A special note of appreciation goes to Teddy Berhanu of Acacia Tours Ethiopia for expertly and thoughtfully navigating our trip, providing new insights, and making connections and introductions for us. At Zoma Museum, I would like to thank Benedetta Castrioto for helping to coordinate our visit as well as numerous details of the exhibition, and at Addis Fine Art, Mesai Haileleul and Rakeb Sile for hosting us for an afternoon at the gallery with their artists.

For the exhibition, I am grateful to the following private lenders: Charles Banta, Nancy and Joseph Chetrit, Jane and James Cohan, Beth Rudin DeWoody, Robert and Karen Duncan, Bill and Christy Gautreaux, Chris and Heather Kempczinski, Scott Mueller, the Pizzuti Collection, Tony and Sandra Tamer, Erica Tennenbaum and Alex Friedman, and James Zang, along with those who elected to remain anonymous. I am also grateful to the exhibition’s institutional lenders, the Des Moines Art Center, Kemper Museum of Contemporary Art, Royal Ontario Museum, and Carl & Marilynn Thoma Art Foundation. Thanks to their generosity, the works in those collections will be appreciated by new audiences.

On behalf of the museum, I wish to thank the Akron Art Museum, the Kemper Museum of Contemporary Art, and the Royal Ontario Museum for participating in the exhibition tour. *Elias Sime: Tightrope* is the Wellin Museum’s largest traveling show to date. It is a proud moment to collaborate with such outstanding institutions and to find our first international partner in the Royal Ontario Museum. At that institution, I would like to thank Josh Basseches, Director and CEO; Silvia Forni, Senior Curator, Arts and Cultures of Africa; and Tamara Onyschuk, Head, Exhibitions and Interpretive Planning. At the Akron Art Museum, I offer my thanks to Theresa Bembnister, Curator of Exhibitions; Mark Masuoka, John S. Knight Director and CEO; and former Chief Curator Ellen Rudolph. At the Kemper Museum, I thank Erin Dziedzic, Director of Curatorial Affairs, and Sean O’Harrow, Executive Director.

I am very appreciative of Hamilton’s faculty, staff, and students as well as the broader community for their engagement with the museum and the artist. Thanks to Suzanne Parker Keen, Vice President of Academic Affairs and Dean of Faculty, for her commitment to the museum and its programming. For their support and ongoing advocacy for the museum, I am very grateful to Hamilton College’s administration: President David Wippman, the Offices of the President and the Dean of Faculty, and my colleagues in the Advancement Office.

Much appreciation is also due to the Trustees of Hamilton College for their continued support of the museum. The professional development that augmented this curatorial effort was made possible through the Johnson-Pote Museum Director Fund. Funding for the Wellin Museum’s programs has been provided by the Daniel W. Dietrich '64 Arts Museum Programming Fund, the John B. Root '44 Exhibition Fund, the Edward W. and Grace C. Root Endowment Fund, and the William G. Roehrick '34 Lecture Fund. Additional support for *Elias Sime: Tightrope* has been provided by the Daniel W. Dietrich '64 Fund for Innovation in the Arts, the Carl & Marilynn Thoma Art Foundation, the Gautreaux Family Foundation, and private contributions. The William G. Roehrick '34 Acquisition and Preservation Fund made possible the purchase in 2017 of Sime's *Tightrope: Familiar Yet Complex 2* (2016; pl. 13). The work was exhibited for the first time in fall 2017 in *Innovative Approaches, Honored Traditions*, the expansive collection exhibition marking the museum's five-year anniversary, which was curated by Katherine D. Alcauskas, then the Wellin's Collections Curator and Exhibitions Manager. The overwhelmingly positive response to the work in that exhibition laid the groundwork for *Elias Sime: Tightrope*, the first major traveling survey of Sime's work to be organized in North America.

I wish to thank the members of the Wellin Museum's Advisory Committee for their invaluable support and advice: Theodore Altman '15, Peter B. Fischer '63, Linda E. Johnson '80, Kevin W. Kennedy '70, William E. Williams '73, and Michael E. Shapiro '71, who serves as chair of the group and to whom I am particularly grateful. I would like to add a note of personal thanks to Wendy Wellin for her sustained engagement with the museum.

This exhibition and the related programming would not have been possible without the dedicated staff at the Wellin Museum of Art: the aforementioned Katherine D. Alcauskas and Christopher Harrison; Alexander D'Acunto, Security Manager; Marjorie Johnson, Museum Educator and Docent Program Supervisor; Emma Pfeifer, Office Assistant; Michelle Reynolds, Curatorial and Academic Programs Specialist; and Amy Sylvester, Office Administrator. I am fortunate to work with such a committed group of outstanding museum professionals.

For this publication, particular thanks are owed to Karen E. Milbourne, Senior Curator, National Museum of African Art, Smithsonian Institution, Washington, DC, and Ugochukwu-Smooth C. Nzewi, Steven and Lisa Tananbaum Curator, Department of Painting and Sculpture, The Museum of Modern Art, New York, for their outstanding essays and to our talented graphic designers, Tim Laun and Natalie Wedeking; our committed editor, Jennifer Bernstein; photographers John Bentham, Christopher Burke Studios, Phoebe d'Heurle, Brian Pinkley, Adam Reich, Janelle Rodriguez, and Michel Temteme; and, for her partnership in copublishing the book, Mary DelMonico of DelMonico Books • Prestel. I am grateful to videographer Brett Novak for journeying to Ethiopia to make the thoughtful and visually arresting exhibition trailer and video. I offer a special note of thanks to the team at Golden Artist Colors, particularly chemist Ulysses Jackson, for developing custom pigments used to make the site-specific work *Flowers & Roots* for *Elias Sime: Tightrope*. Additional thanks are due to Rebecca Murtaugh, Professor of Art at Hamilton College, for consulting on the construction of *Flowers & Roots*; to Sarah Windham for coordinating the shipping of artworks to the exhibition; and to Valerie Kane for assisting with the incoming loans.

Over the next two years, it will be exciting to see the responses the exhibition elicits in central New York, Akron, Kansas City, and Toronto. I am sure that the partnering institutions will adapt and reconfigure the show to highlight different aspects of the artist's multifaceted work, and I look forward to being a part of each museum's interpretation and approach.

Elias Sime brings life, color, energy, and a fresh outlook to global contemporary art. Through his creative output, he extends the conversation beyond biography to embrace themes significant to all our lives: our shared humanity, an appreciation for the beauty of human production and nature alike, and the potential to create a confluence between art, education, and nature. His artwork and the shared vision with Assegued in founding Zoma Museum invite us to consider the world anew and envision how art can effect change beyond what we thought possible.

Editorial Note: The official language of Ethiopia is Amharic, the second-most widely spoken Semitic language in the world, after Arabic. There are multiple systems for transcribing written Amharic into the Latin alphabet, and no particular system of romanization is in widespread use. In this book, spellings of names, titles, and terms reflect the preferences of individual stakeholders or the editorial choices made in various secondary sources.

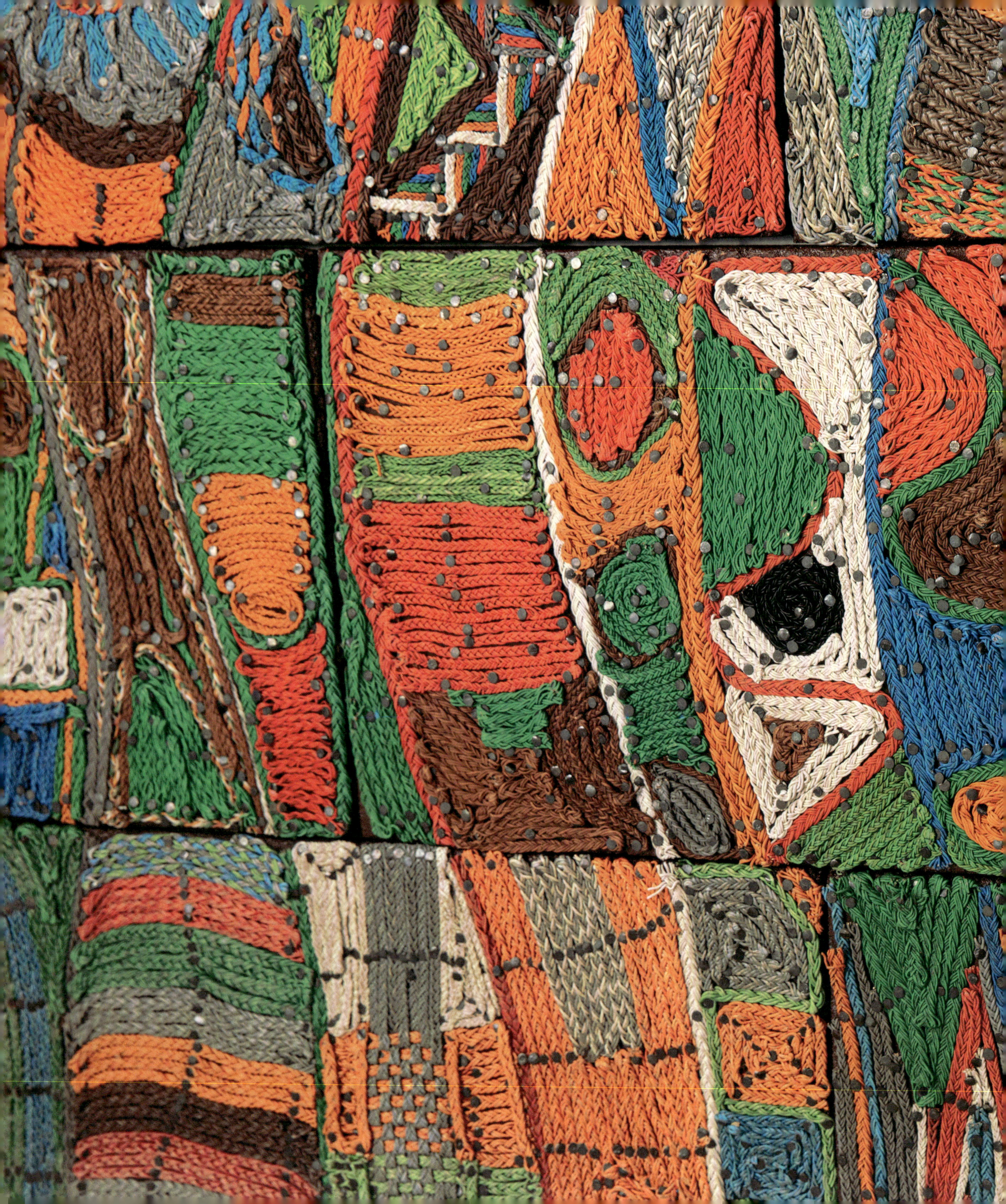

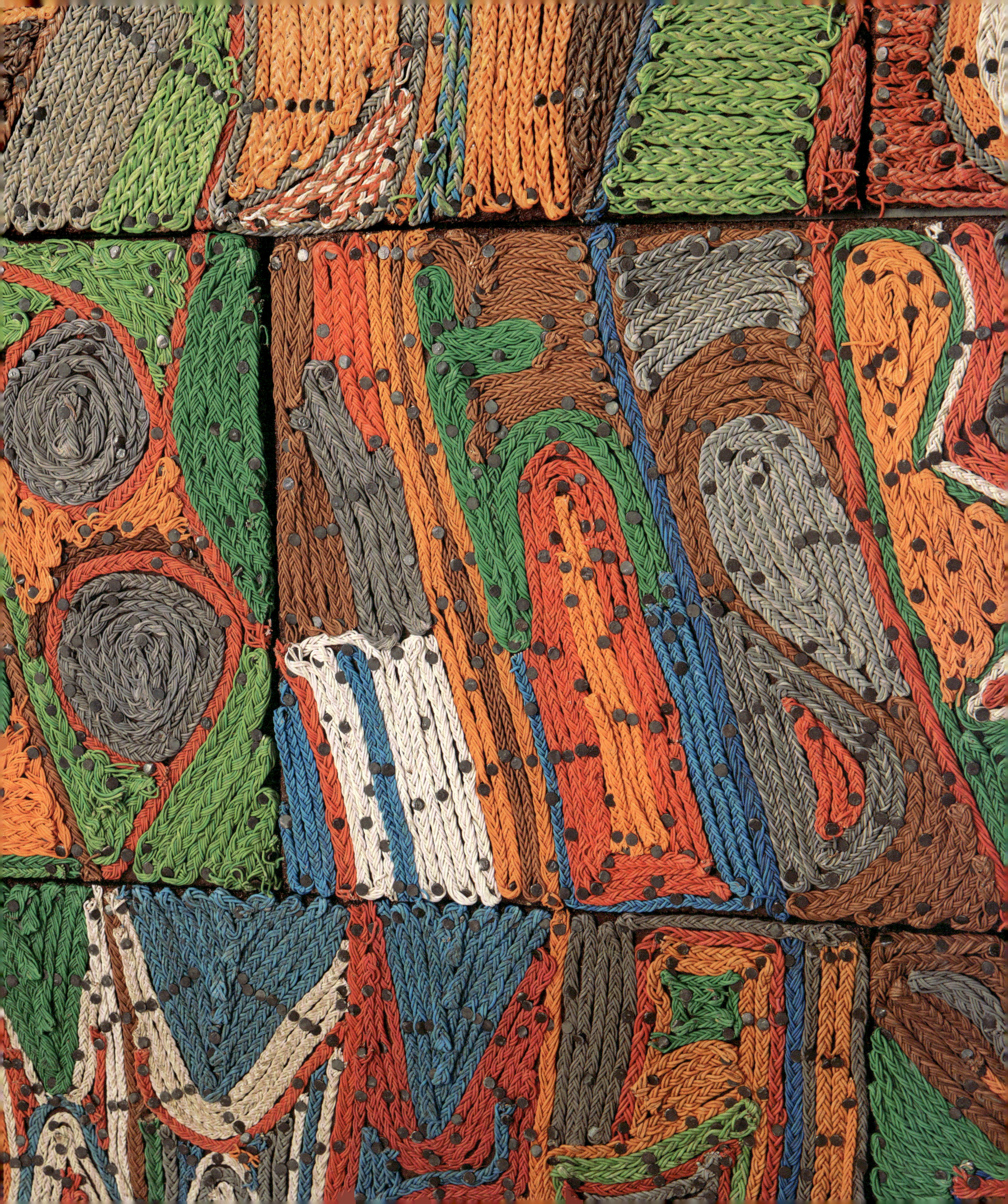

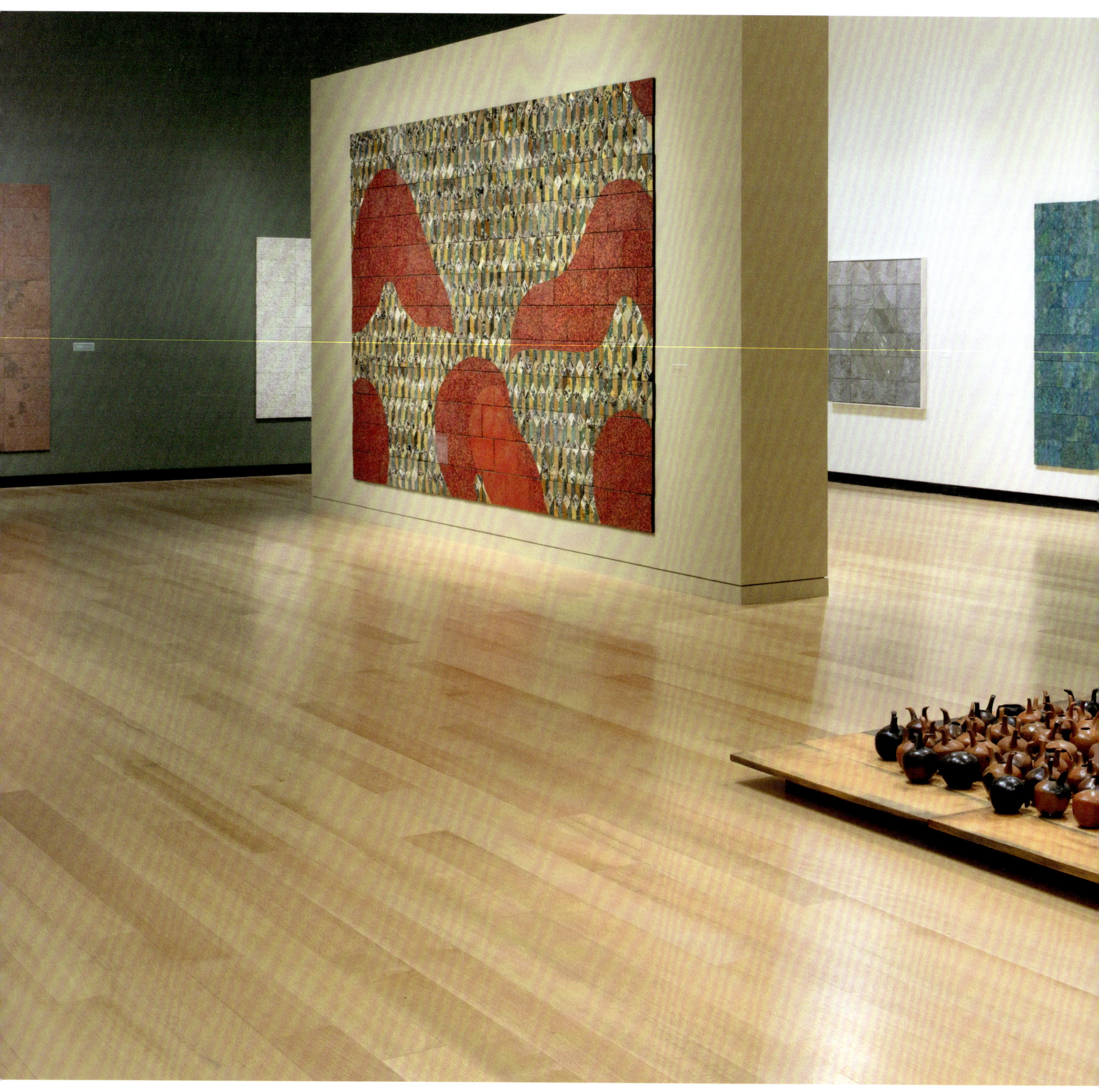

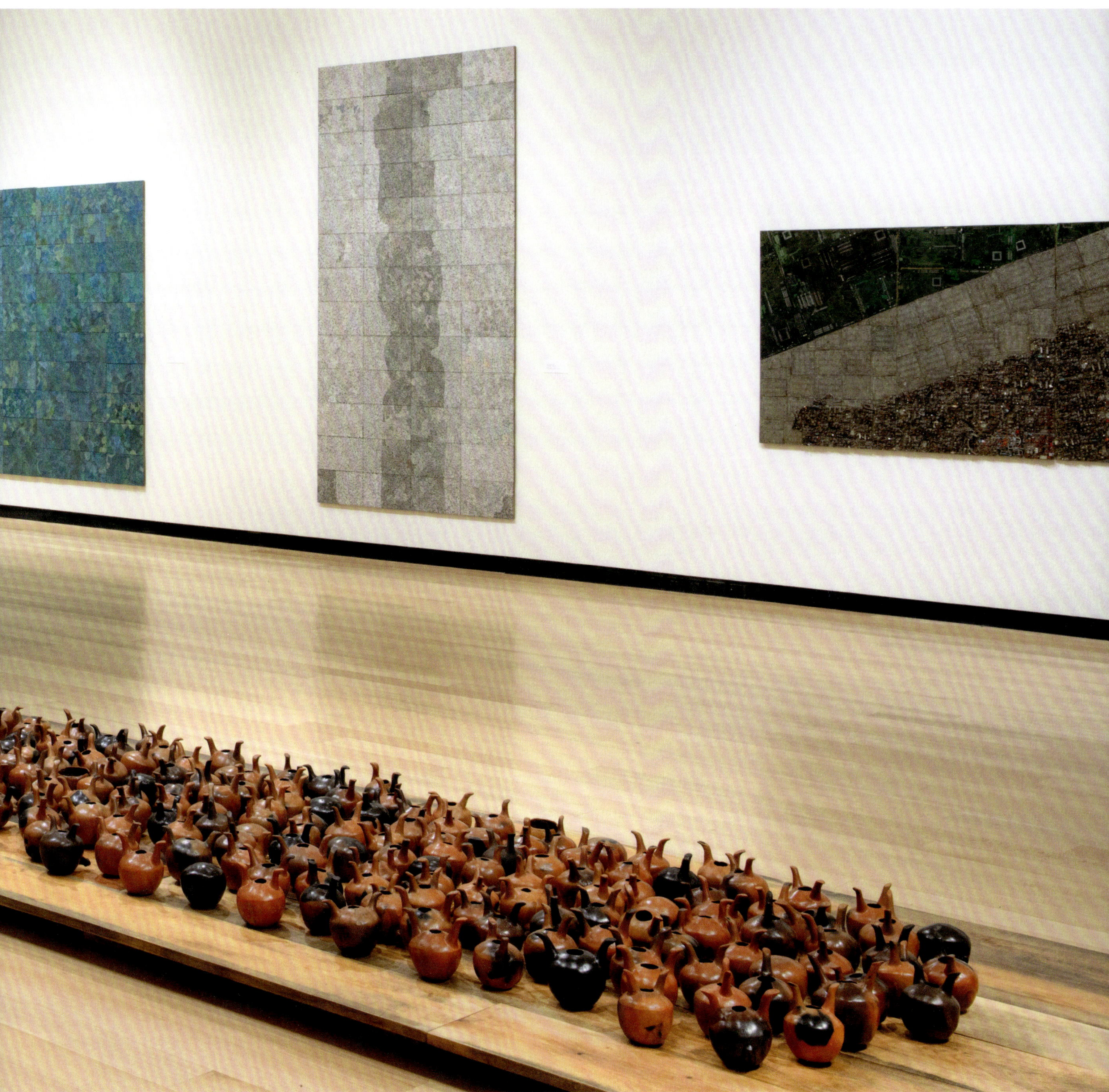

Installation view of *Elias Sime: Tightrope*, Ruth and Elmer Wellin Museum of Art at Hamilton College, Clinton, NY (September 7–December 8, 2019)

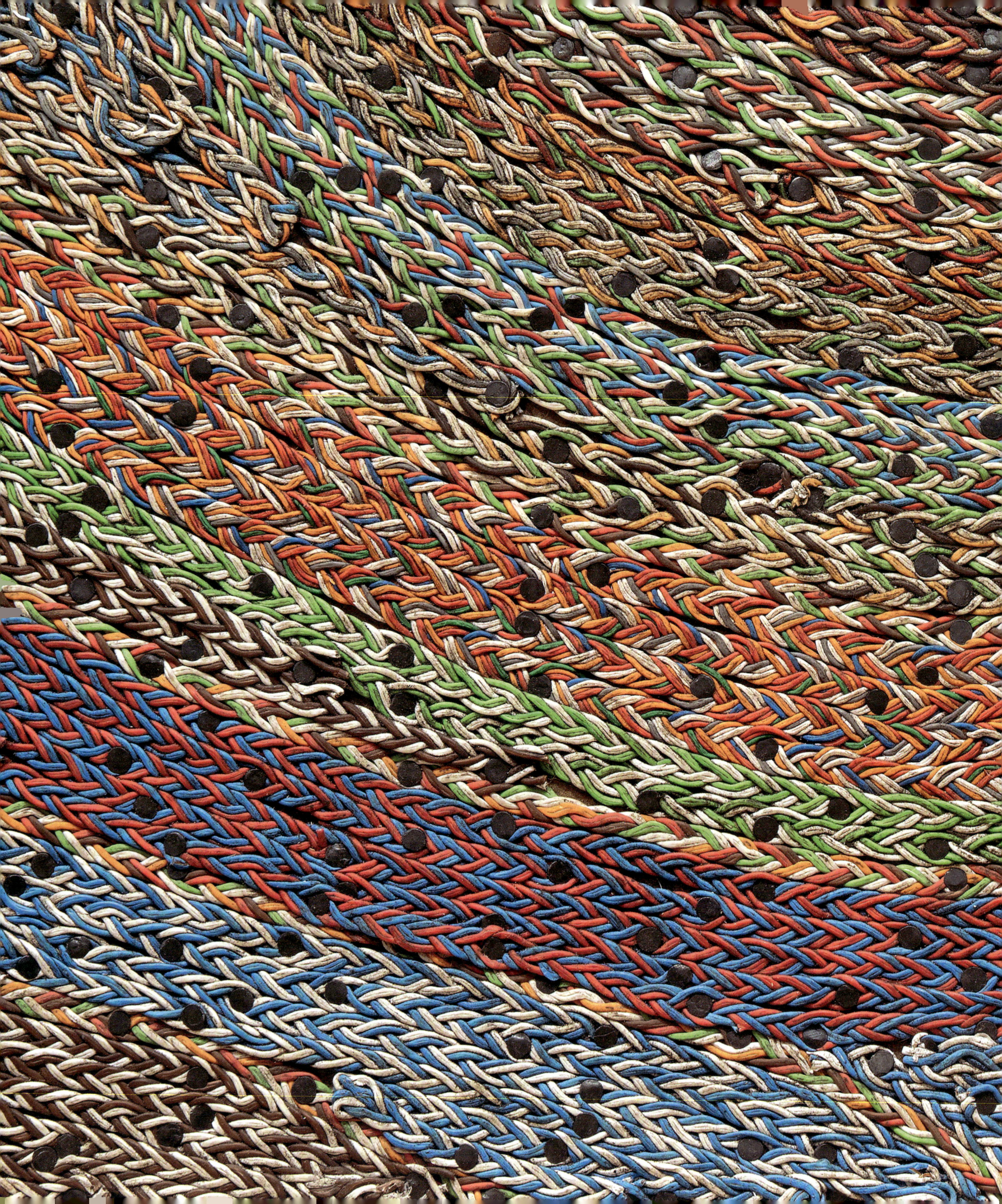

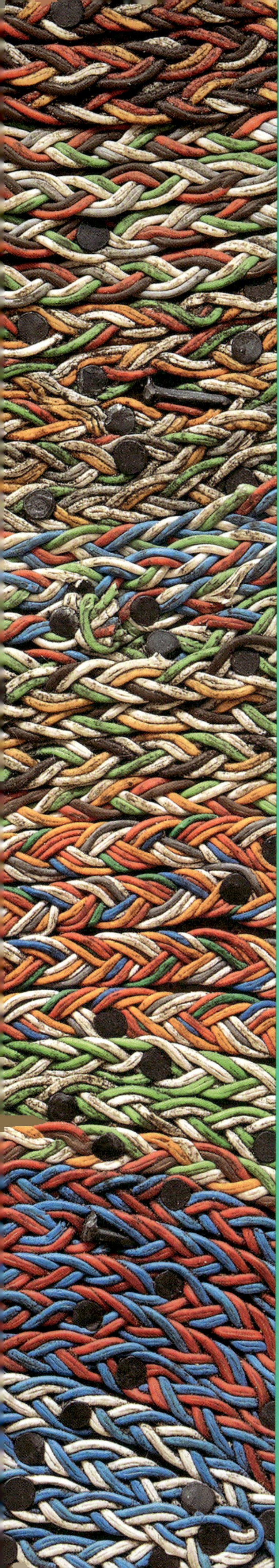

INTRODUCTION

TRACY L. ADLER

Under the trees light
has dropped from the top of the sky,
light
like a green
latticework of branches,
shining
on every leaf,
drifting down like clean
white sand.

A cicada sends
its sawing song
high into the empty air.

The world is
a glass overflowing
with water.

La luz bajo los árboles
la luz del alto cielo.
La luz
verde
enramada
que fulgura
en la hoja
y cae como fresca
arena blanca.

Una cigarra eleva
su son de aserradero
sobre la transparencia.

Es una copa llena
de agua
el mundo.

—**Pablo Neruda**
"Ode to Enchanted Light" / "Oda a la luz encantada"

We learn about the beauty of nature as a matter of course. Throughout time and across cultures, artists, poets, musicians, writers, and other creative thinkers have reflected on the beauty of the natural world as a featured subject of their work. From the arabesque forms and brilliant colors of flowers in bloom, to the limbs of trees flourishing with leaves and laden with fruits, to the awe-inspiring biodiversity of insects and animals, the variations that have evolved over time, with and without human intervention, are both functionally and visually remarkable. We marvel at the uniqueness and dynamism of natural forms but rarely apply similar aesthetic criteria to man-made objects and machines. Is a button, an electrical wire, a bottle cap, or a computer keyboard worthy of such aesthetic contemplation? If we consider evolution broadly, do not both nature and technology share the same evolutionary trajectory—adaptation brought about by responsiveness to an environment and by changing needs? We do not automatically weigh technology's beauty beyond the sleekness of its overall design; its inner workings—its interior world—remain a mystery. Instead, could we approach the communication inherent in technological innovation on the same terms as we do nature? While we think of ecosystems as a balance of environment, animals, and plant life, could we also consider trees as a society in mutual communication, or a community of animals as a network endowed with a kind of syncopation similar to that of modern technology? Don't both nature and technology consist of a series of relayed signals? Could there be a fluid way to conceptualize the systems of nature and technology alike, or would this lead to an aporia?

For Ethiopian artist Elias Sime (born 1968), these worlds are not as oppositional as we might think. He employs the material aspects of technology—electrical wires and transistors, cell-phone components, computer keyboards, and motherboards, for example—in ways that often suggest natural forms, such as landscapes and figures. The artist remarks, "Humans are the bridge between the natural and built environments. We cannot be separated from either one." (Unless otherwise noted, all quotations are from the interview with Sime and Meskerem Assegued reproduced on pp. 173–80 of the present volume.) Expertly braiding and twisting electrical wires into textile-like surfaces with gestures akin to brushstrokes, Sime creates a sense of movement and energy that evokes various organic phenomena—a rising wisp of smoke, clouds in the sky, light reflecting off the surface of water, a bird's-eye view of a landscape. His works are an exercise in patience: sometimes he searches for materials for years to complete a tableau in a specific palette. To realize *Tightrope: Noiseless 2* (2019; pl. 25), the artist collected rust-colored wire, a color not often found in cable bundles, for over a decade. The vast, variegated brown surface recalls scorched earth, but in the lower left corner, a cluster of flowers bursts forth angularly, demonstrating that even barren terrain can produce new, dynamic life. And that life fights to endure.

So, there is hope, and Sime's art brims with it. In the context of his work, hope is a humanist endeavor, a philosophy, and an ideology. Understanding the complicated political and social history of Ethiopia in Sime's lifetime—from Communism and ethnic federalism to today's democracy—helps one to appreciate the value and complications of the notion. Hope is not simplistic; it requires commitment, perseverance, and constant nurturing. Sime has proved that the concept has real weight, both in his art and with Zoma Museum, which he and anthropologist and curator Meskerem Assegued cofounded in Addis Ababa. Begun on a more intimate scale in 2002 as Zoma Contemporary Art Center, the museum's expanded permanent quarters in Mekanisa opened in 2019 on the former site of a garbage dump. Comprising a school, a working farm, a garden of indigenous plants, a library, a café, and exhibition and project spaces, Zoma offers a holistic conception of how community, sustainability, and art can be merged into a unified vision—one that posits a way forward toward a future in which nature, society, and creativity thrive together. Hope abounds at Zoma. Sime and Assegued have fought hard for that to be the case.

Then, there is the intensive labor required to make the artworks themselves, whose complex materiality and intricate fabrication are a testament to the artist's commitment to his chosen means of expression. Sime drafts and sketches constantly, often on scraps of paper, to capture an idea when it strikes, considering the medium and composition simultaneously. A team of assistants works under his direction to assemble the tableaus as he has envisioned them. Creating the works requires the kind of enduring patience a gardener or a farmer must possess to wait for flowers to bloom or crops to mature. This temporal element in both the making and the viewing of Sime's works cannot be overstated: a braid of wire appears to wend endlessly, or, at least, the implication of the infinite is there. The meshed strands point to a continuum and a connectedness that takes time to unfold. From afar, many of his compositions contain fundamentally graphic forms, but closer inspection reveals an intricacy that belies that initial impression.

This notion of slow looking is integral to Sime's approach. In our fast-paced world, he reminds us that we must take the time to observe closely, to follow each thread. Once we allow ourselves to do so, we can get lost in the details of Sime's surfaces. His work initiates a meditative process that encourages engaged study and reflection. As we investigate and interrogate the work, we also learn about our own process of viewing it.

For Sime, the materials he selects, whether repurposed or new, have biographies of their own. They carry associations that, in the artist's hands, are reimagined, gaining a new existence beyond their intended use—one that values their formal qualities, recognizes their latent beauty, and honors the work they were created to perform. In the case of reused materials, the idea that signals have been sent through these wires, that these buttons have had a bodily relationship, that these keyboards have been touched and tapped by human fingers, nods to their previous existence and to an unexpected reinvention. Sime brings the aesthetics and meanings of the materials into alignment as an analogy for the potential of imagination, inviting us to appreciate the beauty of an object's efficiency and purpose.

The artist's ongoing series of the past decade, "Tightrope," begun in 2009, acknowledges the tensions among technology, society, and nature without elevating one over the other or implying a particular hierarchy. The densely woven and layered surfaces draw upon their materiality to comment on ecological sustainability, the resilience of nature, our social responsibility, and the beauty of the utilitarian. Through the title "Tightrope," Sime recognizes the uneasy balance between the advances made possible by technology and the impact they have had on our humanity and environment, exploring how devices intended to connect us have mediated our interactions and lived experiences while creating massive amounts of e-waste. He deconstructs these modern means of communication to expose and demystify their internal dynamics, allowing a new lyricism and energy to emerge. Sime's work also points to the fact that the natural pathways that exist in humans, flora, fauna, and the environment—the organic fibers we all share—are not unlike the inner workings of man-made machines. Furthermore, nature itself shows the effects of human intervention. From genetically engineered fruits and vegetables to cloned animals, the natural world around us has also been manipulated. The message of interconnectivity and commonality over difference pervades Sime's oeuvre.

For this exhibition featuring twenty-eight tableaus of varying scales drawn from private and institutional collections throughout North America, the artist created two new works, *Tightrope: Silent 1* and *Tightrope: Silent 2* (both 2019; pls. 28, 29), to debut at the Wellin Museum. Both consist solely of computer keys: *Silent 1* is a grid of horizontal and vertical rows, while *Silent 2* is arranged along diagonals. Reminiscent of earlier allover abstractions included in the exhibition, such as *Tightrope: Hands and Feet* (2009–14; pl. 10) and *Tightrope: Behind the Beauty* (2017; pl. 16), these new examples are even more pared down. In the computer keys' resemblance to tesserae, *Silent 1* and *Silent 2* are evocative of ancient Roman mosaics, which were used primarily as floor coverings, echoing Sime's process of composing his works on the ground. Their simplicity casts the silence indicated in their titles as a kind of open and thoughtful space, which, however, like the keys themselves, is loaded with signs. In Sime's words, "Sometimes, thoughts are expressed through noise, and other times, through silence. The keyboard is not loud, but it is full of symbols."

Another recent body of work within the "Tightrope" series, represented by three works in the exhibition, *Tightrope: Noiseless 2*, *Tightrope: Noiseless 12*, and *Tightrope: Noiseless 23* (all 2019; pls. 25–27), also invites us to reconsider the power of silence. In the press release for Sime's 2019 exhibition at James Cohan in New York, the artist noted that "noise is often associated with unpleasant sounds. Noise can . . . seem to create words, or words can be part of noise. Words channel our thinking along familiar paths toward realistic images. The absence of noise allows our minds to create unfamiliar and abstract images. . . . The works in 'Noiseless' aim to reflect the unfamiliar and abstract images created in the mind in the absence of noise."

In addition to the two new tableaus, Sime, with the assistance of Hamilton College students, created a site-specific sculpture at the Wellin for display on the museum's Selch Terrace. Titled *Flowers & Roots* (pl. 1), the work is inspired by the Saunders peony, a variety of flower developed at Hamilton College in the mid-twentieth century by chemistry professor Arthur Percy Saunders.

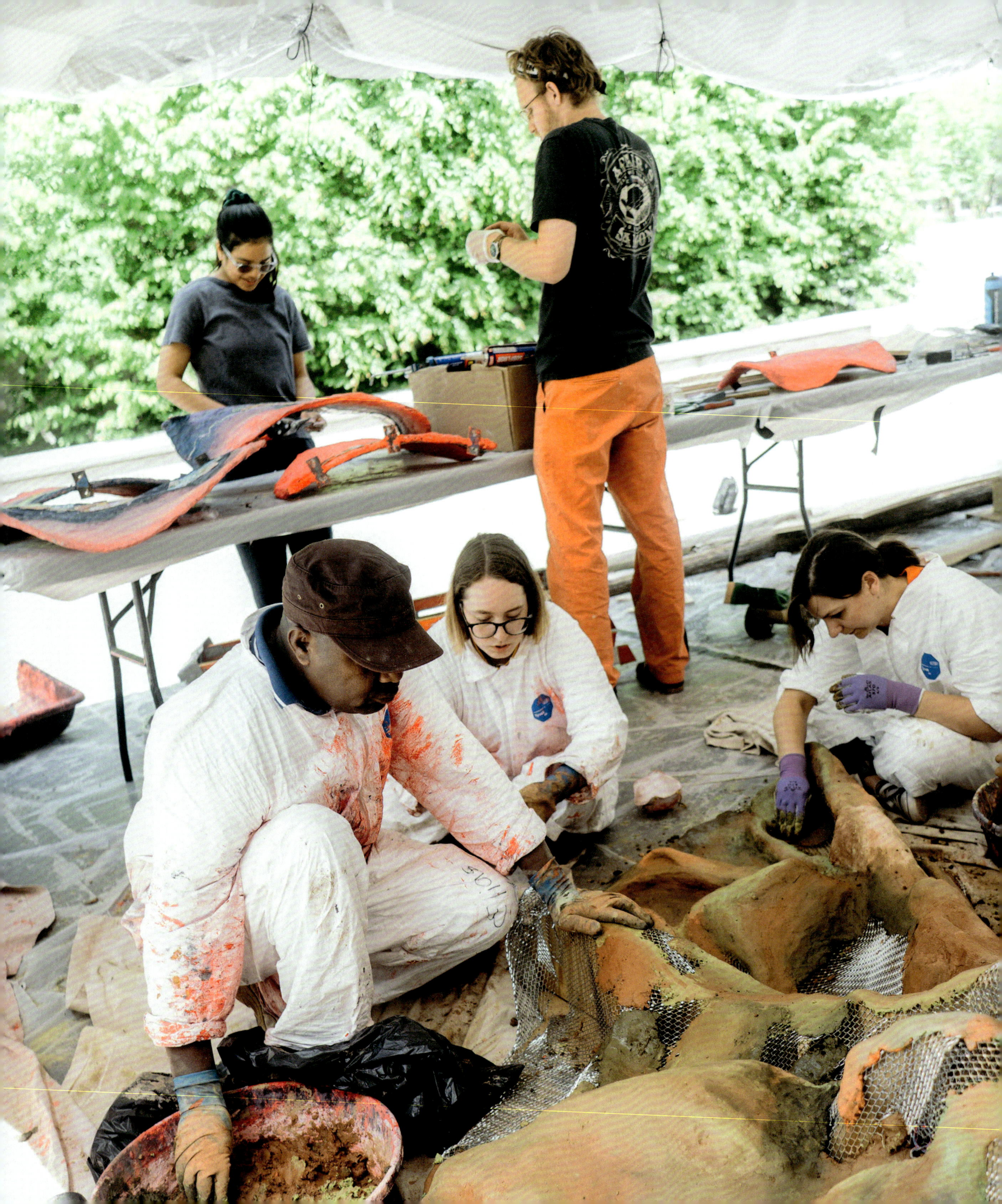

With its twisted and complicated root structure exposed and scaled to over nine feet in height, *Flowers & Roots* allows visitors to pass through it via an archway under the flower's contoured stem. By composing the sculpture of manufactured components—repurposed computer parts, electrical wire, bronze sheeting, and custom-dyed fiber-cement composite made with recycled newsprint—Sime highlights the scientific approach taken by Saunders to engineer and manipulate the flower. According to the project statement written by Assegued,

> *Flowers & Roots* is about duality. Just like the flower, our face, the most visible part of our body, is soft and beautiful. We exert much of our energy protecting and decorating it. We reflect our behaviors through chosen words and facial expressions. Similar to the roots, our twisted and complicated secrets are hidden deep in our subconscious. Flowers and their roots are inseparable and interdependent. Using the peony as an example, Elias is exemplifying the miraculous and sophisticated communication system of roots, including alarming one another about danger and the quick emergency response to heal. The sculpture's circular entrance is about the continuity and strength that come through dependency and collaboration. The fragile and fragrant beautiful flower, with its life-giving pollens, is supported by its twisted and complicated roots hidden underground, with their secret communication techniques. *Flowers & Roots* is about the balance between the overt and the covert.

Similar to the expansive, 63-foot-long site-specific tableau Sime created for Facebook's Menlo Park, California, headquarters in 2018 (fig. 12), which was inspired by the redwood trees of Northern California, *Flowers & Roots* was again sparked by Sime's interest in local flora. During his first site visit to the Wellin in June 2018, many varieties of the Saunders peony were in full bloom in Hamilton's Root Glen. Professor Saunders cultivated the flower in a range of colors, patterns, and shapes, and when they are in season, Hamilton College displays more than seventy cultivars on campus, evincing the astonishing diversity he was able to achieve through his decades of experimentation and singular focus. The artist's decision to respond to such a specific aspect of Hamilton's history, to both honor and remark upon it, emphasizes the wealth of individuality all ecosystems have to offer and the similarities between the creative processes of artists and scientists.

In his 1975 autobiographical work *Roland Barthes by Roland Barthes*, the French philosopher and semiotician mused, "Trees are alphabets," pointing both to the indexical quality of nature, replete with information, and to the fact that trees speak their own language, with its own rules and hidden mysteries. Like Barthes, Sime uncovers and problematizes the complexities of the natural and manufactured worlds. He reveals the fluidity between conditions we typically consider to be in opposition to one another. His work instantiates this philosophy, using man-made materials to evoke natural phenomena so that we can begin to see them as in flux, in dialogue, and perhaps, even, in harmony.

Tracy L. Adler is Johnson-Pote Director of the Ruth and Elmer Wellin Museum of Art and curator of Elias Sime: Tightrope.

Elias Sime collaborating with Hamilton College students on *Flowers & Roots*

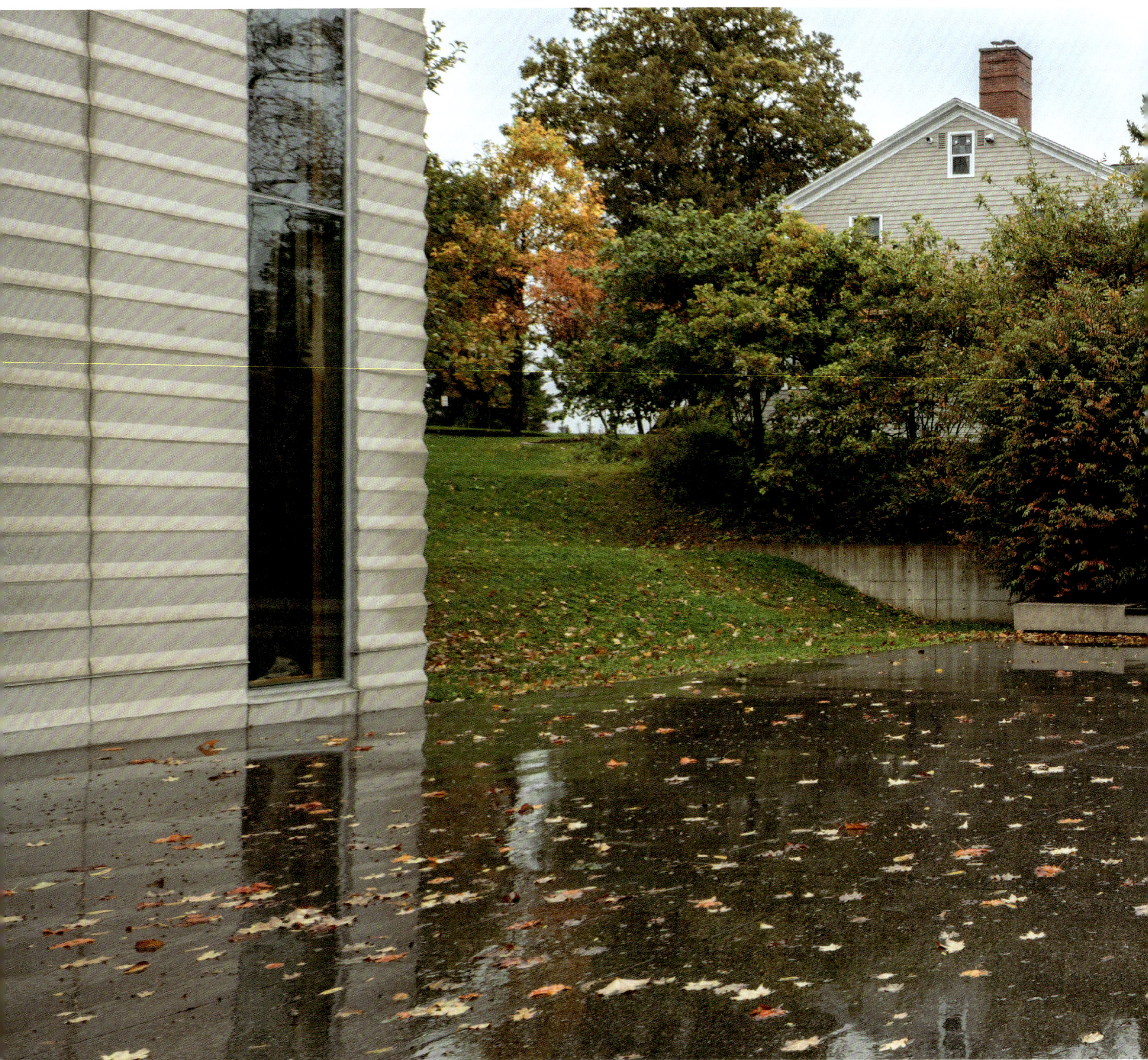

PLATE 1

Flowers & Roots

2019 | Reclaimed electronic components, insulated wire, bronze sheeting, and custom-dyed fiber-cement composite
9 ft. 3 in. × 17 ft. 5 in. × 12 ft. 10 in. (282 × 530.9 × 391.2 cm)
Produced by the Ruth and Elmer Wellin Museum of Art at Hamilton College, Clinton, NY; supported by the Daniel W. Dietrich '64 Fund for Innovation in the Arts

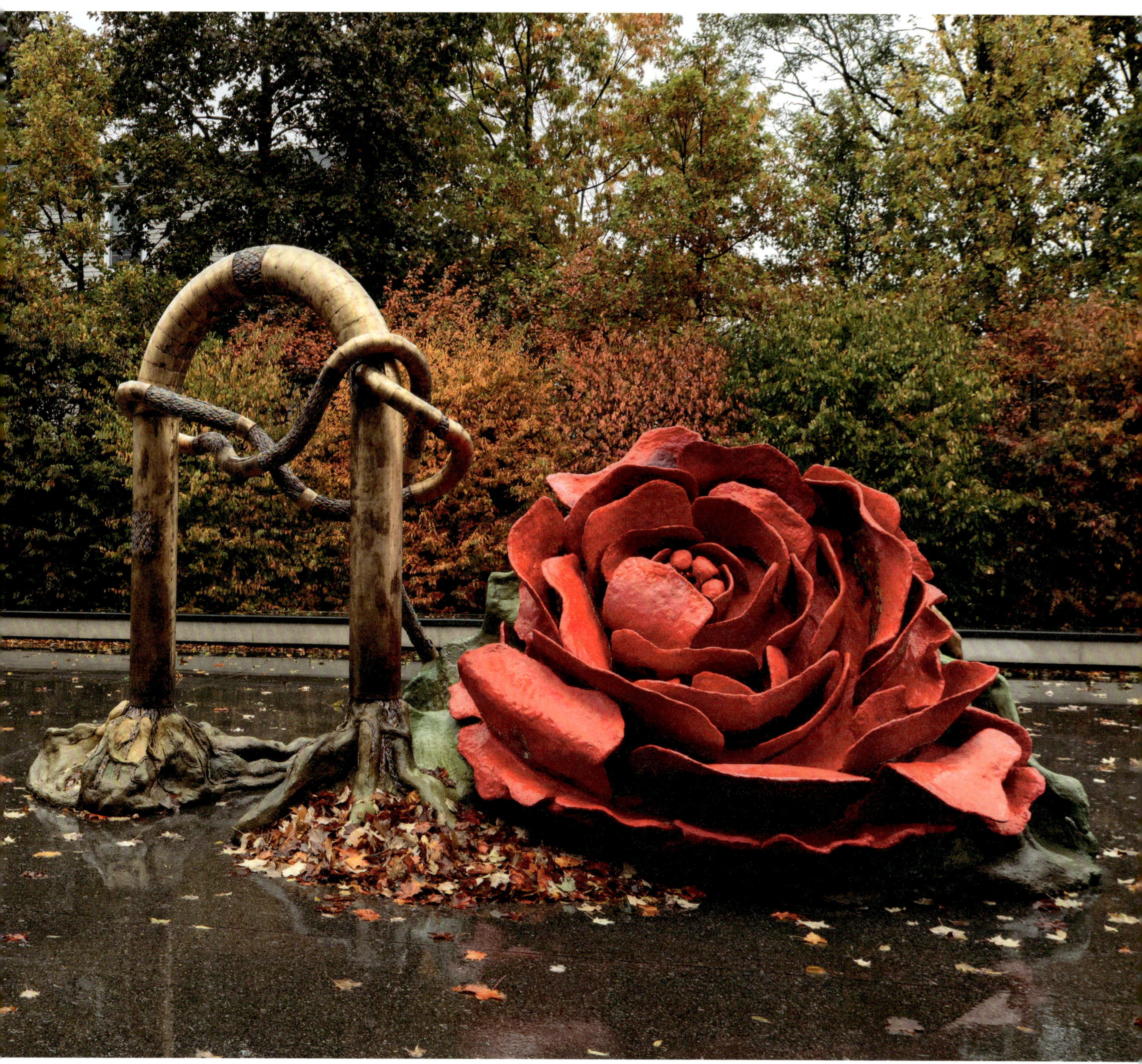

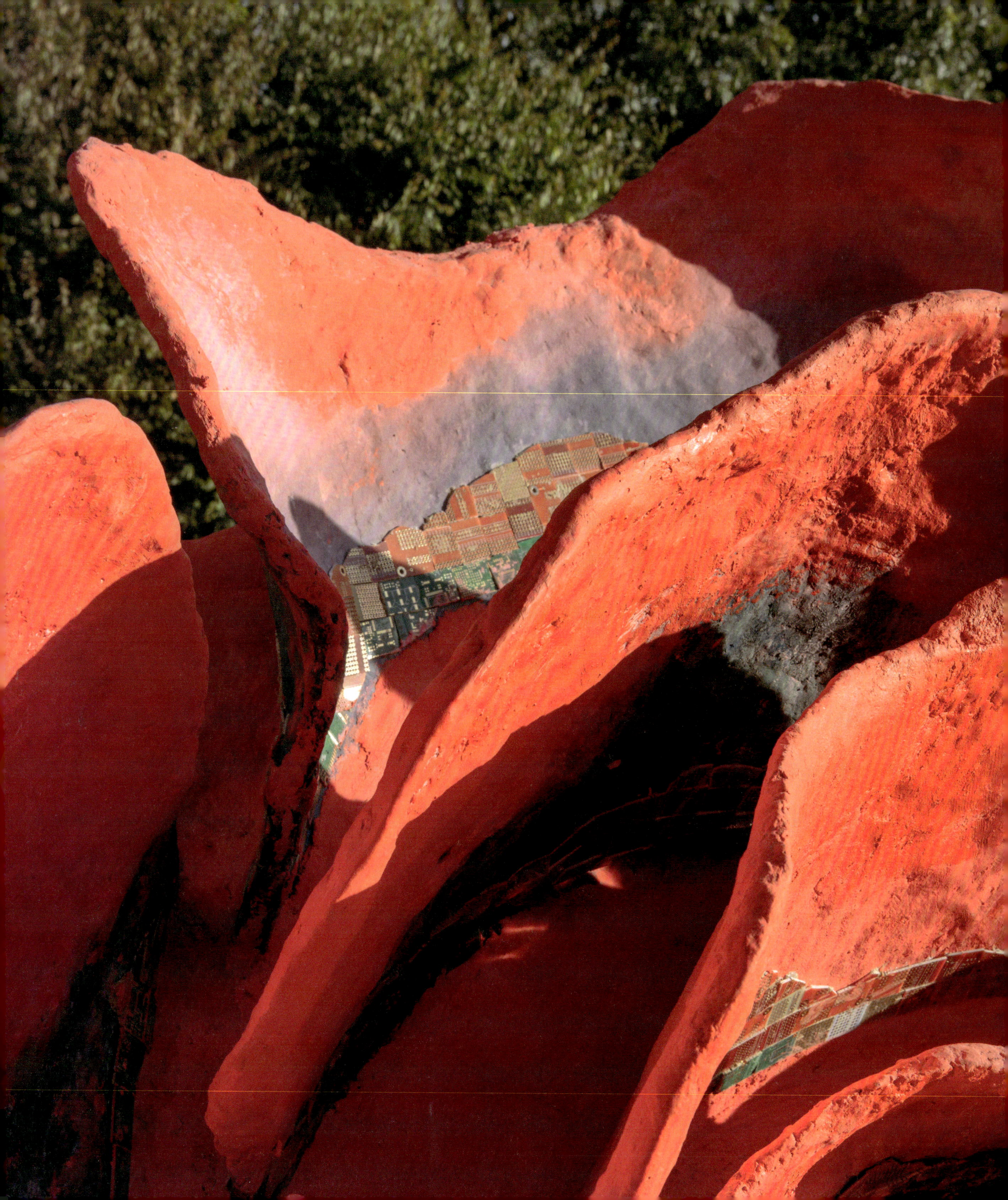

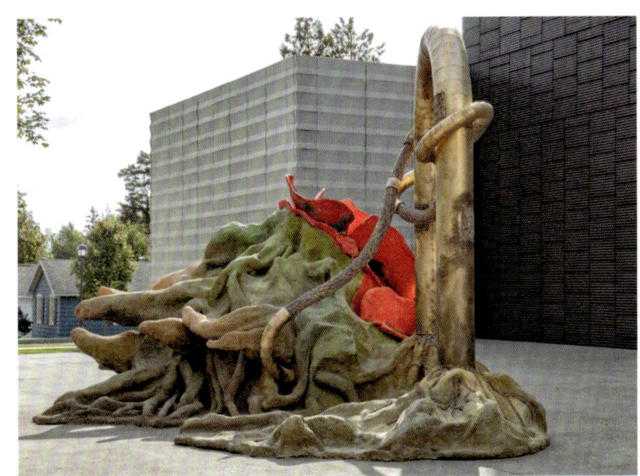
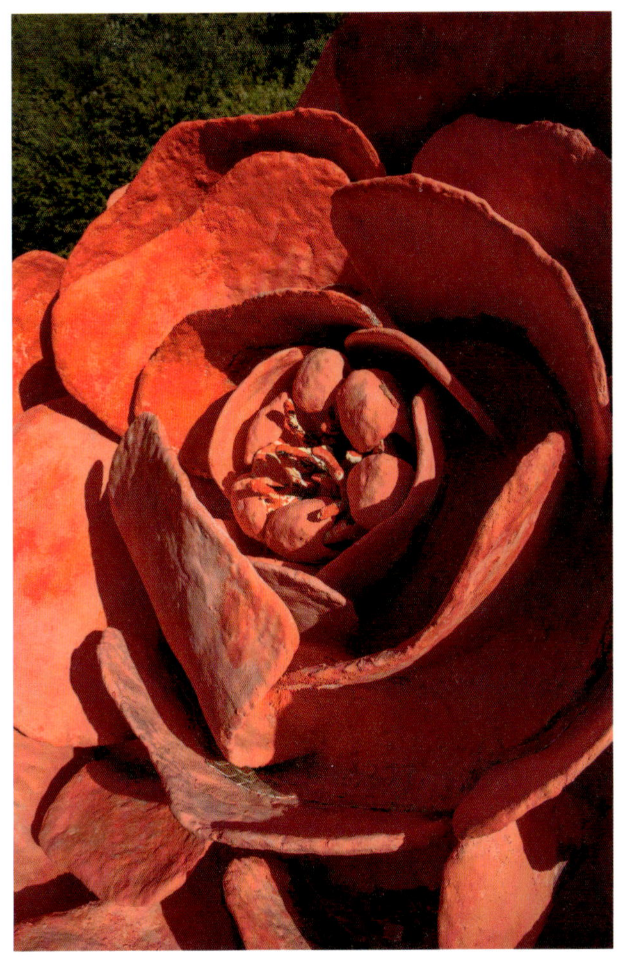
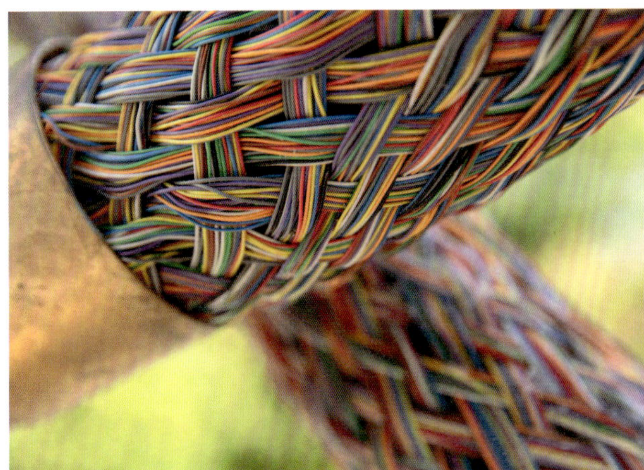
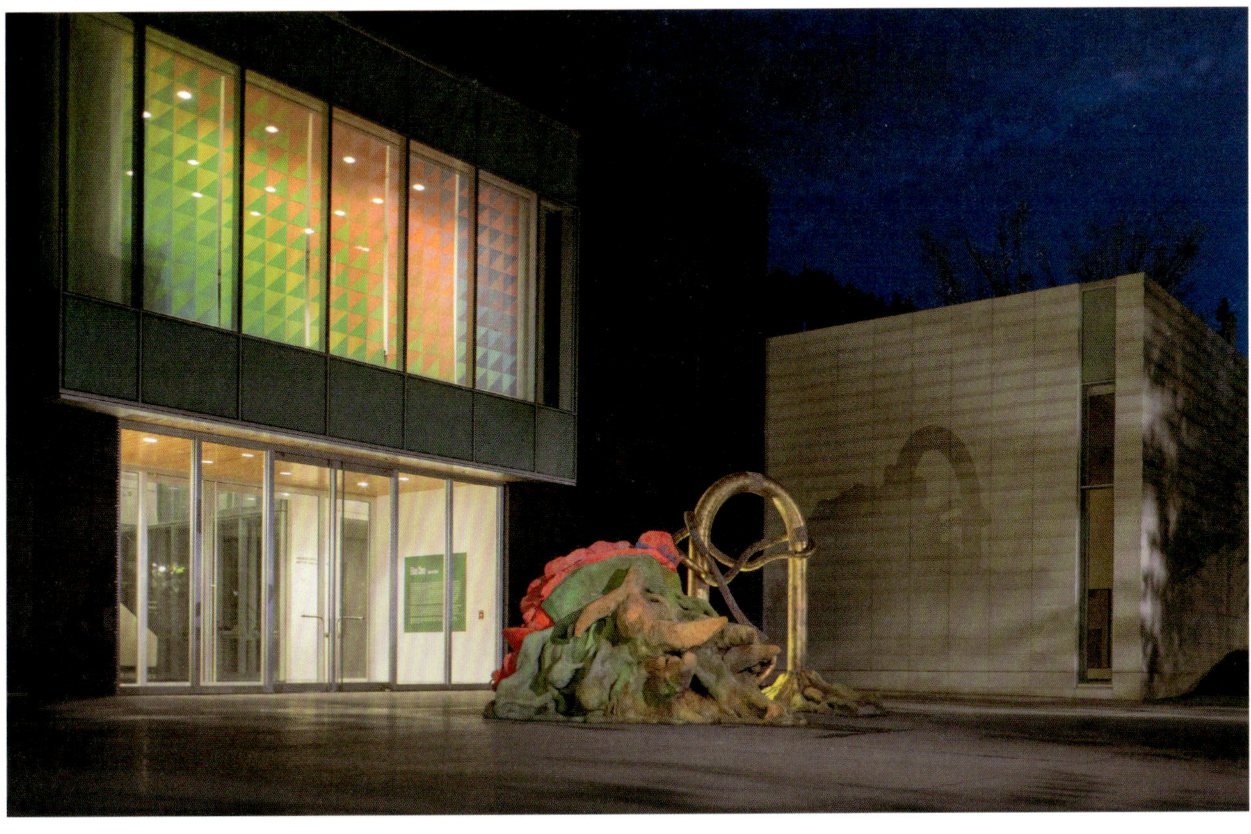

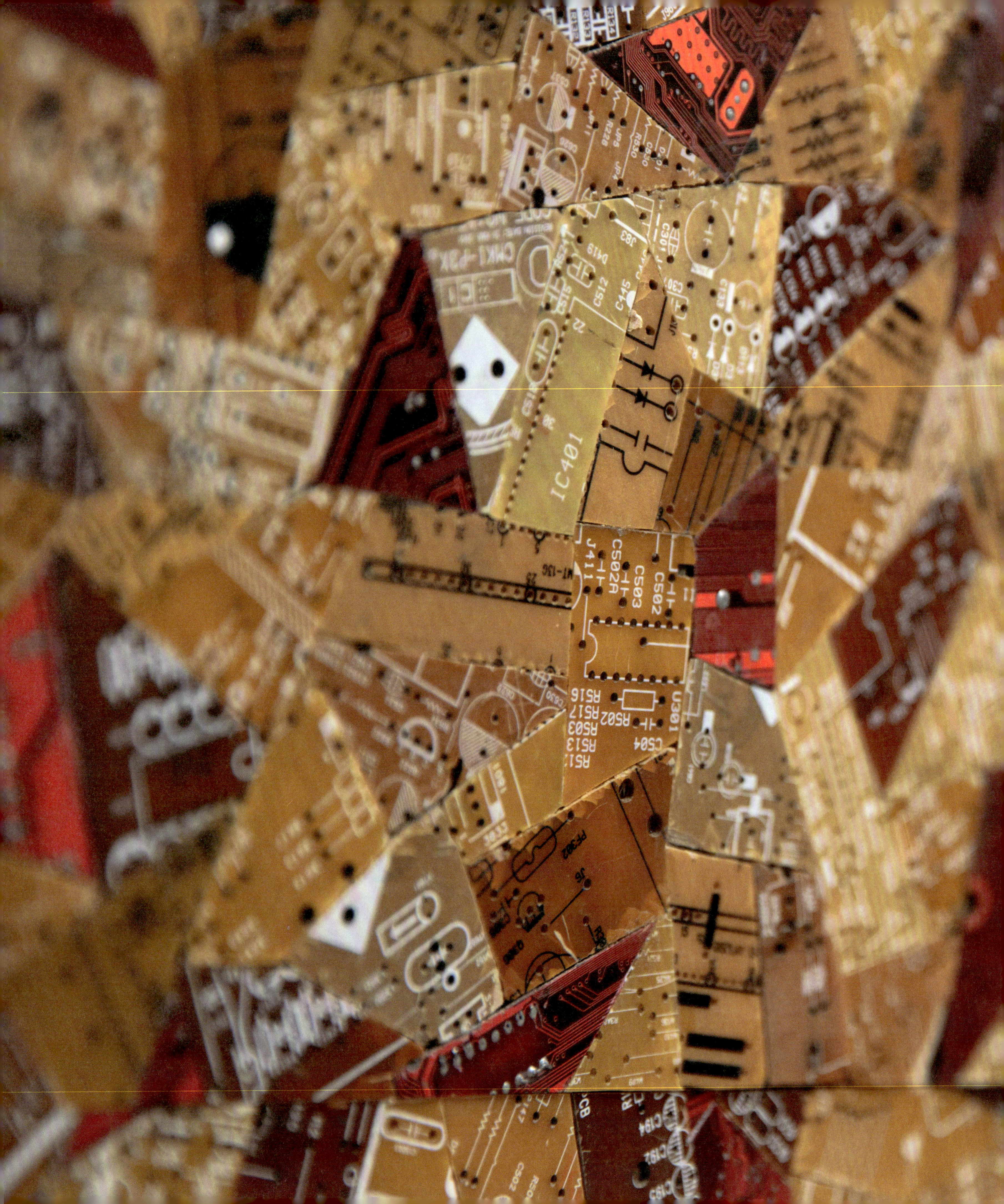

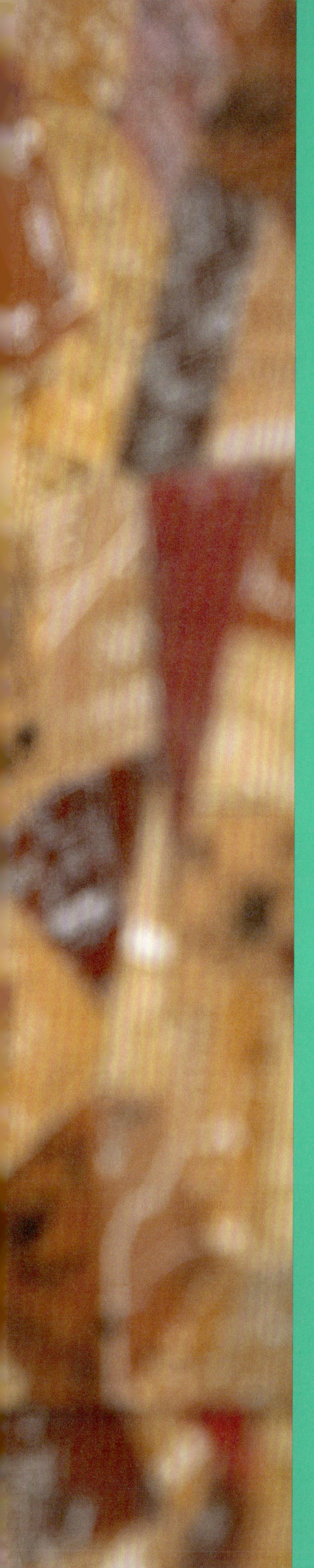

ART, LIFE, AND EMOTION

ELIAS SIME'S AFFECTIVE OBJECTS

UGOCHUKWU-SMOOTH C. NZEWI

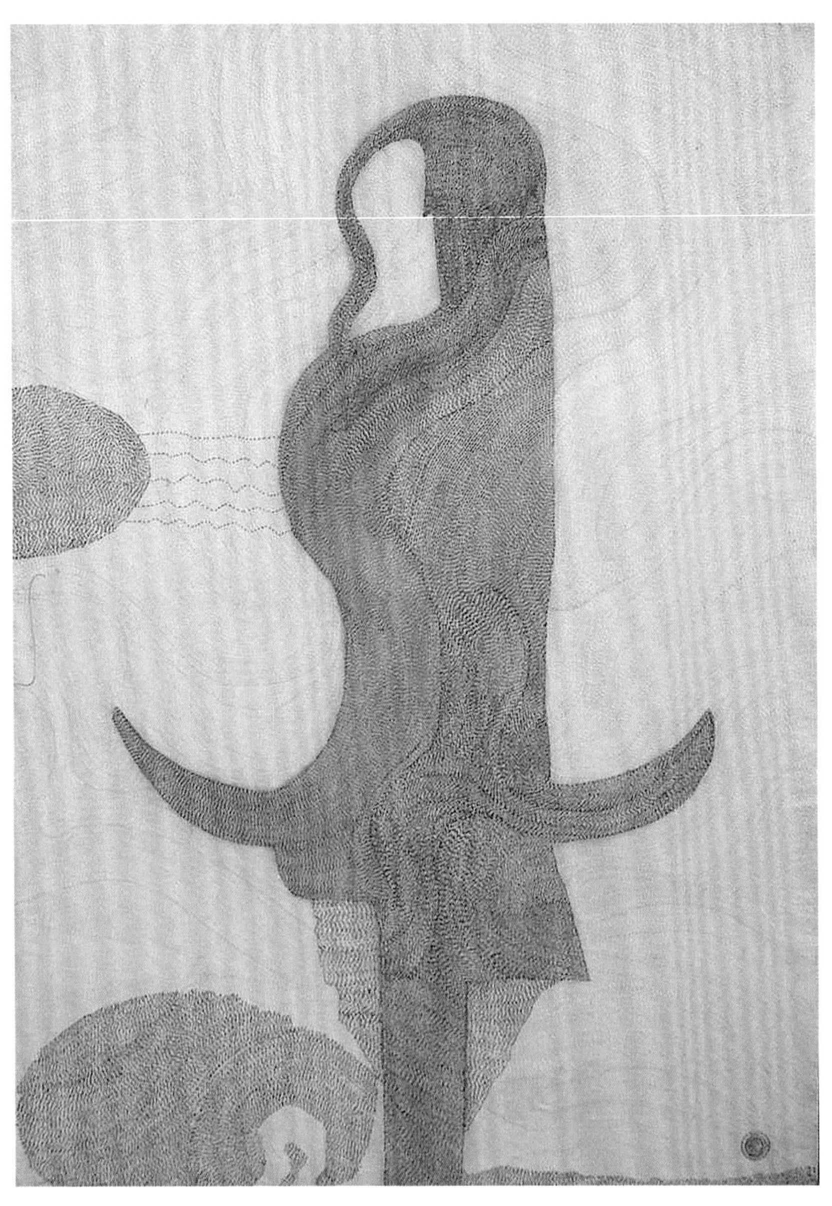

In 2008, the Studio Museum in Harlem, New York, presented *Flow*, an exhibition of works by twenty emerging artists under the age of forty born either in Africa or to African parents. The focus of the exhibition, as conceived by curator Christine Y. Kim, was the role of global flows—of people, capital, resources, and cultures—on artistic consciousness. Elias Sime's works in the exhibition included *Mewled* (literally, "giving birth"; 2006), a field of green and white yarn that, when densely stitched onto canvas, formed a startling abstract relief (fig. 1). The work laid bare the artist's exacting art-making process, described at the time by *New York Times* critic Holland Cotter as "evidence of material richness . . . where crafts traditions and modernist abstraction meet."[1] Sime had manipulated the yarn as if it were paint, a strategy he has applied more recently to less malleable materials, such as discarded electronic components. The Studio Museum exhibition enhanced Sime's visibility on the global stage in the wake of his participation in Senegal's Dak'Art biennial in 2004 and the New Crowned Hope Festival in Vienna in 2006. Moreover, *Flow* presented Sime and the others featured in the show as a group of worldly artists whose work operated in several registers and appealed to multiple audiences in both local and international arenas.

Sime speaks from a specific context—namely, Addis Ababa, his hometown and the capital of Ethiopia. He has also addressed or been inspired by other places in Ethiopia, such as the town of Bonga—the subject of some of his earlier work—and by numerous countries around the world that he has visited. But his art transcends boundaries. This is because of his urgent desire to express human narratives through spent or salvaged materials that once had active social lives, such as buttons, yarn, old clothes, bottle caps, and computer motherboards. He transforms these objects—now defunct, as far as their original purposes are concerned—into audacious, transcendental images. The sheer material force and visual intensity of Sime's art invite comparison to such qualities in the work of the Mexican artist Gabriel Orozco and the Ghanaian-born El Anatsui, both of whom also transmute detritus into captivating forms.

Yet the visceral and enduring impression Sime's art makes on viewers does not necessarily arise from the commanding vigor of his compositions, something he happens to share with Orozco and Anatsui. Instead, he seeks to bring to the fore the traces of human emotion that are embedded in his chosen media, as well as the underlying narratives conveyed by those materials. On offer in his work are narratives of the materials' previous lives—as global commodities traversing public, personal, and intimate spaces; caught up in networks of cultural and economic

Fig. 1 Elias Sime, *Mewled*, 2006. Yarn on canvas, signed with bottle cap, 59 × 42 ⅛ in. (150 × 107 cm). Courtesy of the artist and James Cohan, New York

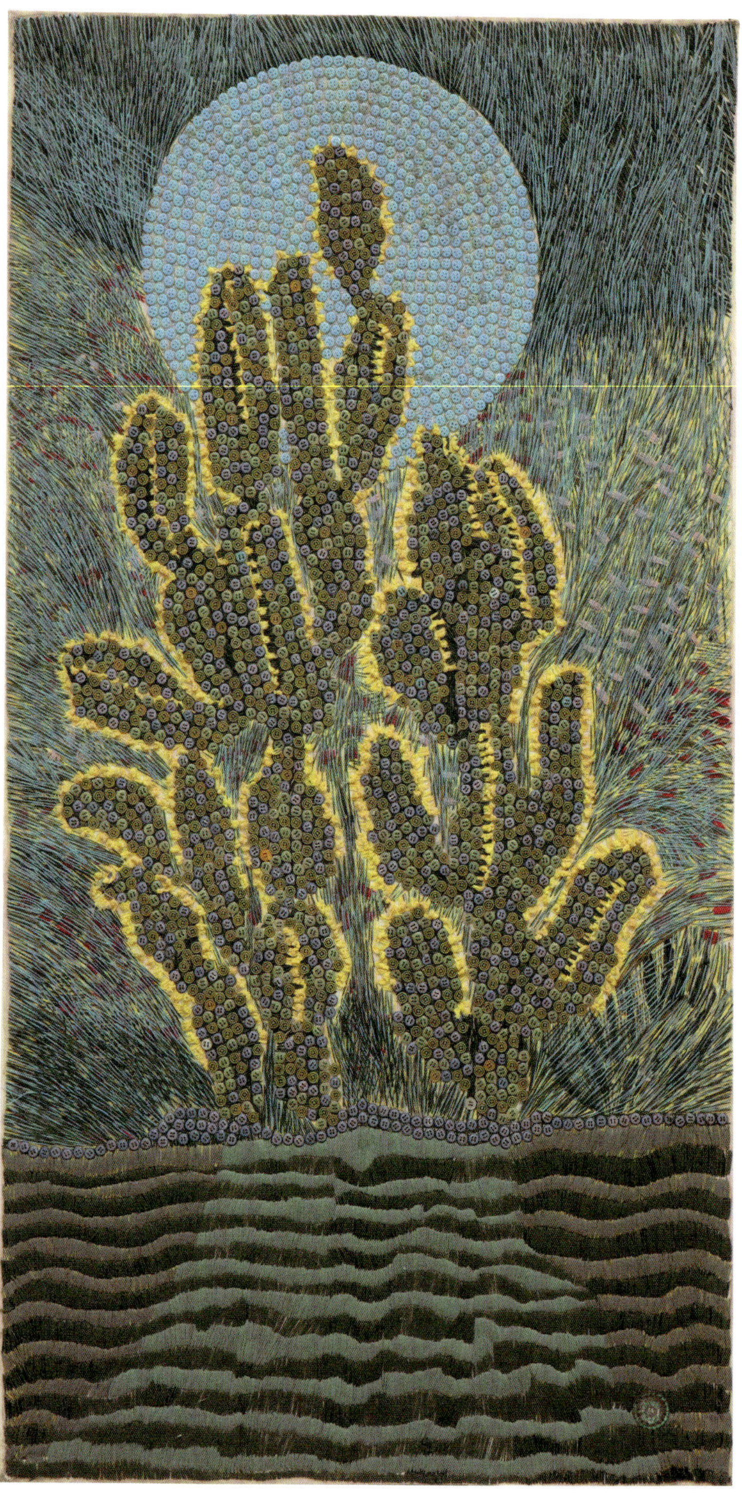

PLATE 2

Cactus 2

2003–4 | Yarn and buttons on canvas, signed with bottle cap | 56 ¼ × 29 ⅛ in. (142.3 × 73.7 cm)
Collection of Beth Rudin DeWoody

exchange; subject to mobility across geographies; and inscribed in genealogies of industrial and technological advancement. For this reason, viewers of Sime's works—be they at Zoma Museum or the Goethe-Institut in Addis Ababa; Grimm Gallery in Amsterdam; Israel Museum in Jerusalem; James Cohan gallery in New York; or Santa Monica Museum of Art in California—respond instinctively. Sime's genius is the imaginative capacity he extends to his audience to rise above the beauty of the composition and seek further spatial and temporal reaches. It is the complexity and richness of ideas, histories, and formal language pervading his work that make him such a compelling artist.

SIME AND (ART) HISTORY

Art historian Peri M. Klemm has suggested that Sime "utilizes found objects to illustrate the rich urban landscapes and stark poverty of Ethiopia's vibrant capital city Addis Ababa."[2] Klemm's observation is true to the extent that Sime sources his materials from his environment and that they reflect the social milieu of his immediate surroundings. The Cherqos (Kirkos) neighborhood, where the artist grew up, was once known for its bustling market and its railroad station, Lehegar, neither of which remains in operation today. The neighborhood and its landmarks served as the initial impetus for Sime's art. Yet his choice of materials and interest in Addis Ababa as a leitmotif have less to do with illustrating the contrasting realities of wealth and poverty, a feature of any city around the world, than with revealing "character and history" through his manipulation of those affective materials.[3] For example, in making *Cactus 2* (2003–4; pl. 2), the artist was drawn to tactile materials that tell all kinds of stories. As Sime explained to this author, "I have done a lot of work using clothes buttons. When you wake up in the morning, you open your button or button up, and you do that with care. It is an expression of love. It puts you in contact with your body. . . . [Buttons] tell the stories of the persons who used them; the human traces they hold are expressions of love."[4]

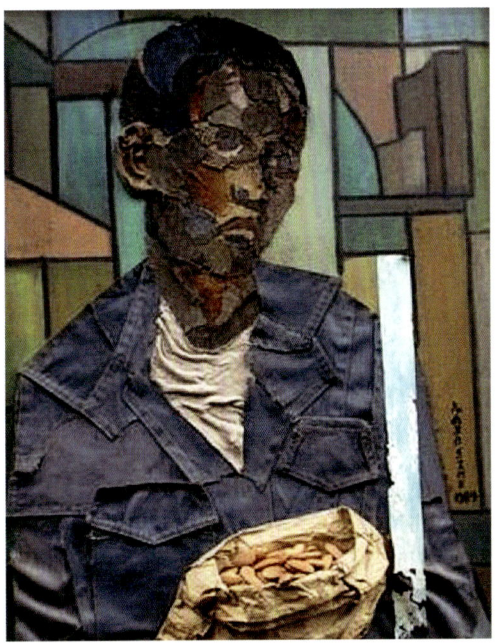

Fig. 2 Elias Sime, *Ocholoni Shach*, 1991. Oil on canvas with repurposed clothing, paper, and nuts, 21 ⅝ × 13 ¾ in. (55 × 35 cm). Courtesy of the artist and James Cohan, New York

Such an emphasis on story, character, and history goes all the way back to the beginning of Sime's career, when he was still hewing to the Socialist Realist conventions imposed by his education, though sometimes in combination with unconventional materials. *Ocholoni Shach* (1991; fig. 2), an important work of his early period and one of his few collage paintings, narrates the existential conditions in Ethiopia at that time in a deeply moving way. It depicts a boy or young man (*ocholoni shach* means "peanut seller") whose forlorn expression extends far beyond the picture's surface. The figure's head, and especially his ear, appear in relief, achieved via an elaborate patchwork of fabric. The rest of the body is garbed in the state-sanctioned navy blue clothing worn by government officials during Ethiopia's Derg period and in a somewhat grubby white shirt that covers his chest region. Colored planes evoking a stained-glass window fill in the background behind the figure. An open bag of actual nuts rests against his torso in the foreground. The peanut seller's grave visage tells of the struggle for survival at a dire moment in the country's recent history.

Sime graduated in graphic art from the School of Fine Arts and Design in 1990, on the cusp of a monumental change in Ethiopia's political life and a seismic shift in global politics. Sime's time in art school, beginning in 1986, had coincided with the waning years of Mengistu Haile Mariam's government, the long-standing and brutal military junta known as the Derg, which transformed into the ruling Workers' Party of Ethiopia in 1987. In these years, the soon-to-be-defunct Soviet Union, dealing with intense economic challenges and its own internal political wrangling, began to withdraw its support for Haile Mariam (known to Ethiopians by his first name, Mengistu, as are most public figures in Ethiopia). By May 1991, the Ethiopian military campaign in Eritrea collapsed, ending a war for political independence waged by the latter over the previous thirty years (Eritrea's official independence came in 1993). Haile Mariam fled Ethiopia, defeated by a coalition of left-wing rebel groups, the Ethiopian People's Revolutionary Democratic Front (EPRDF), that by June 1991 had morphed into a transitional government. On the global stage, the Soviet Union finally dissolved in December 1991, and the Cold War formally ended. It was during this period of political uncertainty, both national and international, that Sime began his professional career. His works of the period, such as *Ocholoni Shach*, capture that atmosphere. Knowing this back story situates *Ocholoni Shach* as a historical work through which to understand late twentieth-century Ethiopia and the contending global forces that contributed to this moment of despair. In addition, it helps to highlight the double register of local and global that defines Sime's work and has been there since the outset of his career.

After hijacking the people's revolution that deposed Emperor Haile Selassie in 1974, the Haile Mariam regime had refashioned the School of Fine Arts' curriculum to convey the Socialist mandate. Modernist sensibilities drawing upon the traditions of the Ethiopian Orthodox Tewahedo Church[5] and other indigenous art forms, as well as on international styles such as abstraction, were largely replaced with Soviet-style Socialist Realism.[6] The Derg government considered pre-revolution art to be elitist and nonobjective. Conversely, Socialist Realism was favored for presenting the rhythms of the everyday in recognizable forms that were readily understood by the broad public and could easily convey government propaganda. Left with no choice, Sime and his fellow students produced art that amplified the state's political agenda.[7] Sime's remarkable experimental spirit and exploration of diverse materials (including animal bones and skins in addition to the aforementioned yarn, buttons, cloth, rusted cans, and bottle tops) stand in sharp contrast to the conservatism of his training. This is not accidental. As the artist explained in an interview, he was never comfortable with the academic instruction he received, although such

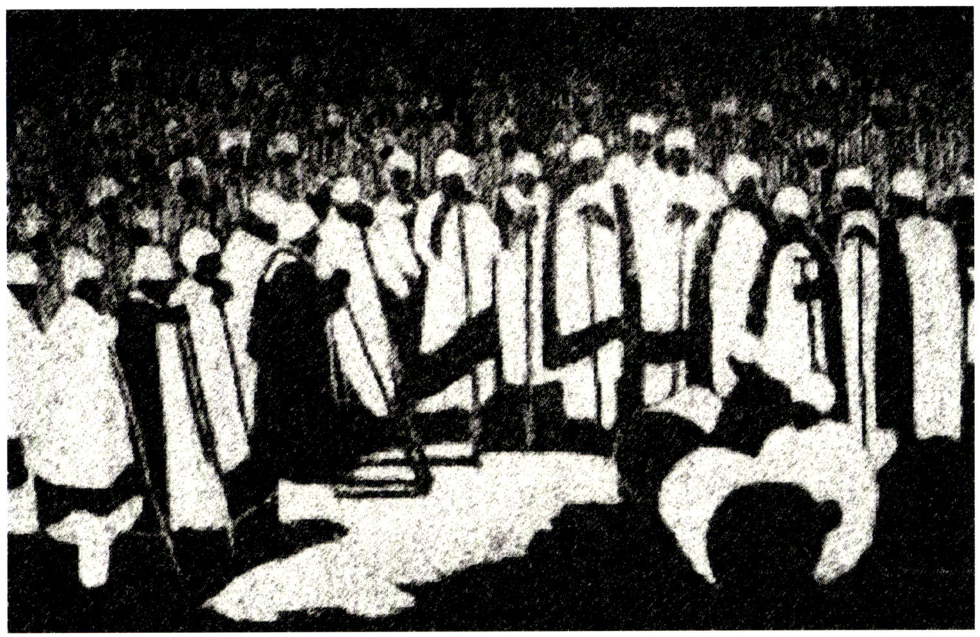

Fig. 3 Elias Sime, *Seatat*, 1989. Woodcut, 11 ⅞ × 23 ⅝ in. (30 × 60 cm). Courtesy of the artist and James Cohan, New York

early works as *Seatat* (fig. 3), a woodcut that depicts the titular ceremony in which Orthodox clergymen, shown wearing the traditional *bernos* and *gabi*, pray all night long (the Church was still very much part of the Ethiopian consciousness under the Derg despite the introduction of Socialism and Communism); *Godana* (literally, "the street"), an oil painting and collage portraying homeless people's makeshift shelters around Addis Ababa; and *Ocholoni Shach* did reflect the dominant aesthetic of their time.[8]

If the works of Sime's early period fell in line with institutionally prescribed Socialist Realism,[9] the direction of his practice from 1997 on suggests the radical tenor of Ethiopian modernism. Although his adoption of a range of unconventional materials happened around the same time, as curator and anthropologist (and the artist's close collaborator) Meskerem Assegued has observed,[10] the shift can arguably be viewed as a broader, and supremely inventive, way of building upon Ethiopia's rich secular and religious art and craft traditions and making the outcome his unequivocal artistic signature. In fact, in the mid-1990s, Sime made a conscious decision to abandon his commercially driven practice and took an eight-year monastic hiatus to develop his ideas and deepen his practice at great personal cost, relying largely on the goodwill of his father.[11] Wavering between variations on abstraction and representation, responding to ideas and visual strategies at the cutting edge of international contemporary art, and inspired by his immediate environment, Sime began exhibiting work in 2004 that indirectly echoed the iconoclastic efforts of artists such as Gebre Kristos Desta and Alexander (Skunder) Boghossian, whose aesthetic sensibilities had played a huge role in defining the contours of the modern in Ethiopian art since the mid-twentieth century.

Desta (1932–1981), the quintessential pre-revolution Ethiopian modernist, produced works such as the masterly *Golgotha* (1963; fig. 4), which reflects the influence of the Orthodox Church (his father was a priest and painter of illuminated manuscripts) and his exposure to German Expressionism, gained from his study at the fine arts academy in Cologne from 1957 to 1960. Within a grid of black, white, and bluish-gray brushstrokes of varied thicknesses, Desta inserted the redemptive narrative of the biblical Golgotha: the schematic red outline of the crucified Christ demonstrates the artist's original approach to abstract form. Although even at the height of his renown, in the 1960s and 1970s, local critics had trouble reconciling Desta's irrepressible abstraction with Ethiopian image-making traditions, his art was, by and large, "embedded in an Ethiopian cultural context."[12] For example, his eye-catching colors mirrored the disorderly ambience of the country's urban settings. Desta acknowledged "customary referents in his work," albeit grudgingly, stating that the Orthodox Church, too, incorporated foreign elements (such as Byzantine styles) and that with just such a synthesis, he believed he could "achieve something in the most modern way."[13]

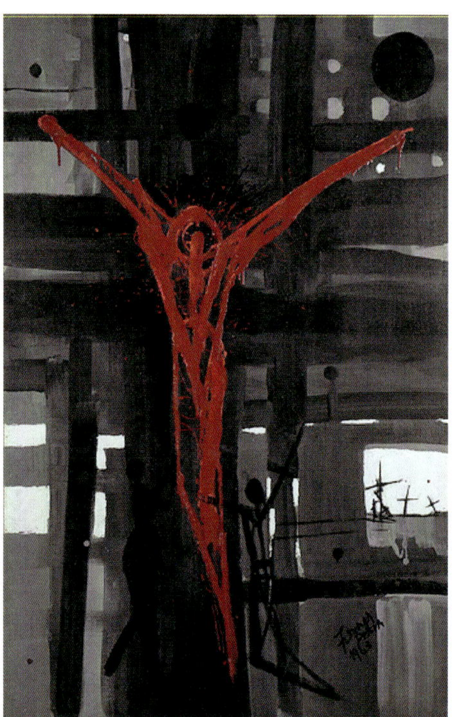

Widely celebrated in Ethiopia and abroad as a visionary modernist, Skunder Boghossian (1937–2003) drew eclectically from Ethiopian and Coptic traditions and from both African and foreign sources. Many have suggested that his powerful works *Night Flight of Dread and Delight* (1964) and *Blue Composition* (ca. 1966–68; fig. 5) were inspired by the phantasmal creatures in Nigerian writer Amos Tutuola's surrealist novels,[14] or perhaps by the uncanny world of evil spirits in Ethiopian folklore. Both paintings have a mystical cadence. In the monochromatic *Blue Composition*, at the lower right, we can see letters in Ge'ez, the liturgical script used in Orthodox illuminated scrolls.[15] Boghossian was known to tell his students at the School of Fine Arts that an artist

Fig. 4 Gebre Kristos Desta, *Golgotha*, 1963. Oil on panel, 72 × 48 in. (183 × 122 cm). Modern Art Museum–Gebre Kristos Desta Center, Addis Ababa University

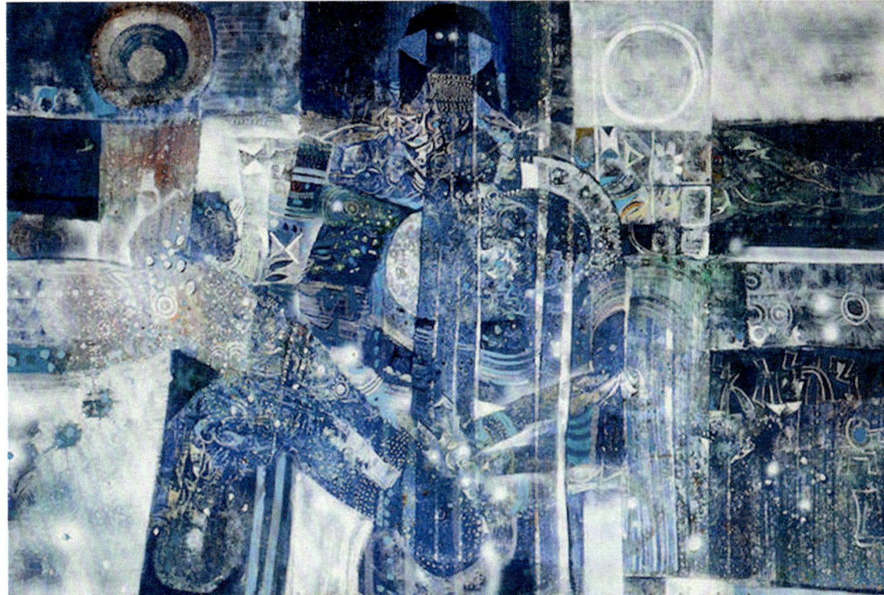

Fig. 5 Alexander (Skunder) Boghossian, *Blue Composition*, ca. 1966–68. Acrylic, gouache, and airbrush on panel, 47 × 72 ½ in. (119.4 × 184.2 cm). Private collection

must have an identity,[16] while Desta contended that artists should be malleable.[17] Both descriptions apply to Sime, who developed a unique vocabulary that draws upon his Ethiopian context. At the same time, he has transcended local identity in fashioning an original artistic voice with an international timbre.

If we are to consider the trajectory of Ethiopian modernist and contemporary art, Sime is a peerless and groundbreaking figure. Yet unlike his illustrious predecessors Desta and Boghossian and others who followed them, such as Zerihun Yetmgeta (born 1941; fig. 15), a notable modernist who explores Ethiopian Coptic icons and manuscripts and African mask forms in his mixed-media paintings on animal skin and bamboo, and Eshetu Tiruneh (born 1952), whose expansive Socialist Realist paintings captured the social landscape of Ethiopia during the Derg period, Sime has yet to attract notable disciples. Desta and Boghossian each had a profound impact on the Ethiopian art scene as professors in the 1960s and early 1970s and helped to shape the artistic consciousness of generations of artists, including Yetmgeta, who was a student of both artists.[18] Yetmgeta and Tiruneh themselves were very influential as professors at the School of Fine Arts during the late 1980s, when Sime was a student; he took classes with both of them, particularly Yetmgeta, who taught two-dimensional art and graphics.[19] Because Sime has not worked in a formal academic environment, it stands to reason that he has not had the opportunity to influence students directly. His numerous studio assistants over the years have mostly lacked formal training and, as such, may not have been interested in pursuing an independent art practice.[20] Also, Sime's arduous methods may not be particularly attractive to any potential acolyte.

As in the works of Desta and Boghossian, expressive lines and iridescent colors are consistently present in Sime's oeuvre. They appear as intricate spirals, bold geometric forms, or supple undulations in works such as *Fertility* (2005) and the stitched-yarn-on-canvas series "What Is Love?" (2007–8; figs. 6–8). With the exception of *What Is Love? 1*, these works were included in the Metropolitan Museum of Art's 2008 exhibition *The Essential Art of African Textiles: Design without End*, curated by Alisa LaGamma and Christine Giuntini, which explored the enduring influence of African textiles on the work of contemporary artists.[21] In an interview with LaGamma, Sime stated that "weaving and embroidery are an integral part of Ethiopian culture . . . traditionally . . . done by men. I grew up in the midst of this tradition. Consequently, I am inspired by the intricate nature of creating with Ethiopian fibers, but at the same time, I am a contemporary artist engaged in expressing my reactions to my environment. I use a variety of different colored yarn in my work. I find this material perfect for expressing my ideas and my identity."[22]

Sime's capacity to orchestrate sublime and lustrous waves of color with carefully selected yarns sewn by hand onto stretched canvas in the aforementioned works, as well as in *Gorée Island* (2004; fig. 25) and *Ants and Ceramicists 11* (2009–14; pl. 3), defies the imagination. The tableaus in his more recent "Tightrope" series—the major focus of the present survey—build naturally on the yarn works, displaying similarly resplendent colors and complex patterns. However, the hand-stitched yarns have been replaced by braided electrical wires fastened to the panels with nails. It is from his female studio assistants that Sime learned many local braiding techniques, incorporating two to as many as twenty-four strands. The works in "Tightrope" oscillate from pure abstraction, where Sime appears to be interested only in what colors can do (pl. 16); to semi-abstraction, in which he creates grid-like structures or disrupts the consistency of the surface (pls. 8, 19); to representational compositions that dazzle and confound (pls. 9, 19). In some of the "Tightrope" works, he seems to have been most interested in purity of form and composition, and the material force was secondary. In others, he may have been more interested in how the medium yielded to his dictates, his control. In still others, he allowed his medium to control his direction. Always, he flows with the tide, with his medium as a muse, leading him deep into the recesses of his imagination.

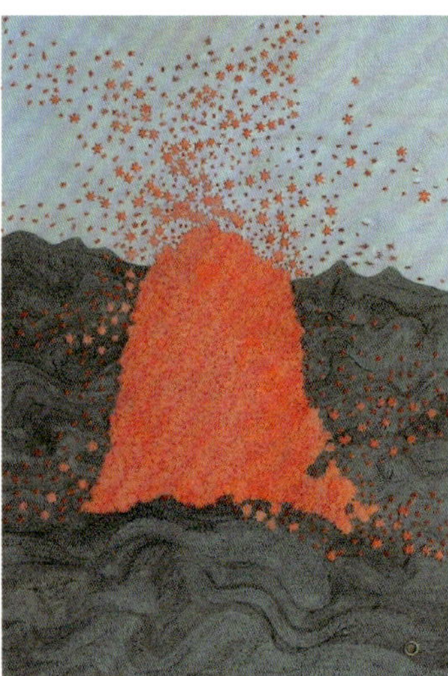

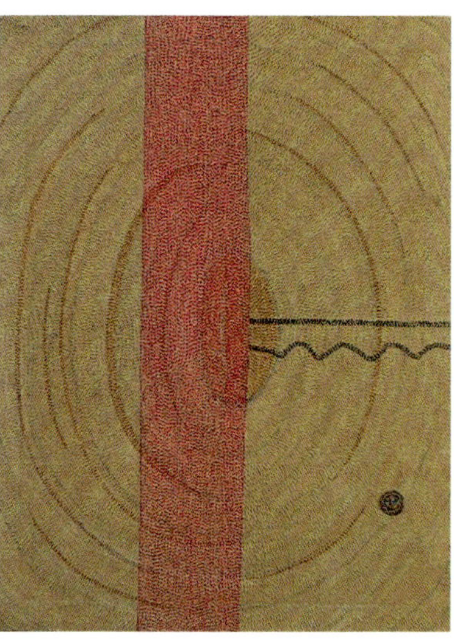

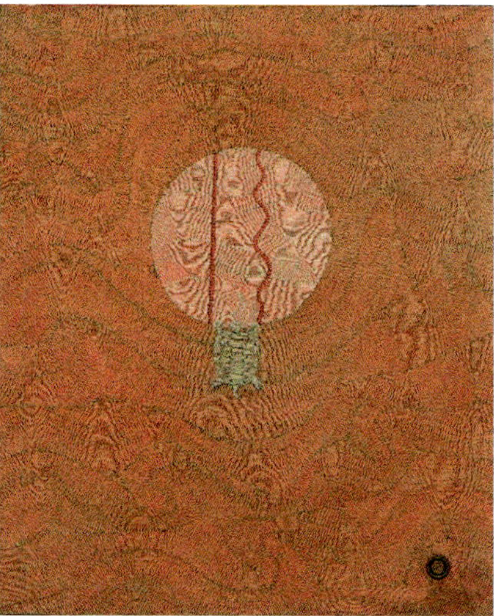

Fig. 6 Elias Sime, *What Is Love? 1*, 2007–8. Yarn on canvas, signed with bottle cap, 74 × 52 in. (188 × 132 cm)

Fig. 7 Elias Sime, *What Is Love? 5*, 2008. Yarn on canvas, signed with bottle cap, 38 ¼ × 29 ½ in. (97 × 75 cm)

Fig. 8 Elias Sime, *What Is Love? 6*, 2008. Yarn on canvas, signed with bottle cap, 38 × 32 ½ in. (96.5 × 82.5 cm)

All courtesy of the artist and James Cohan, New York

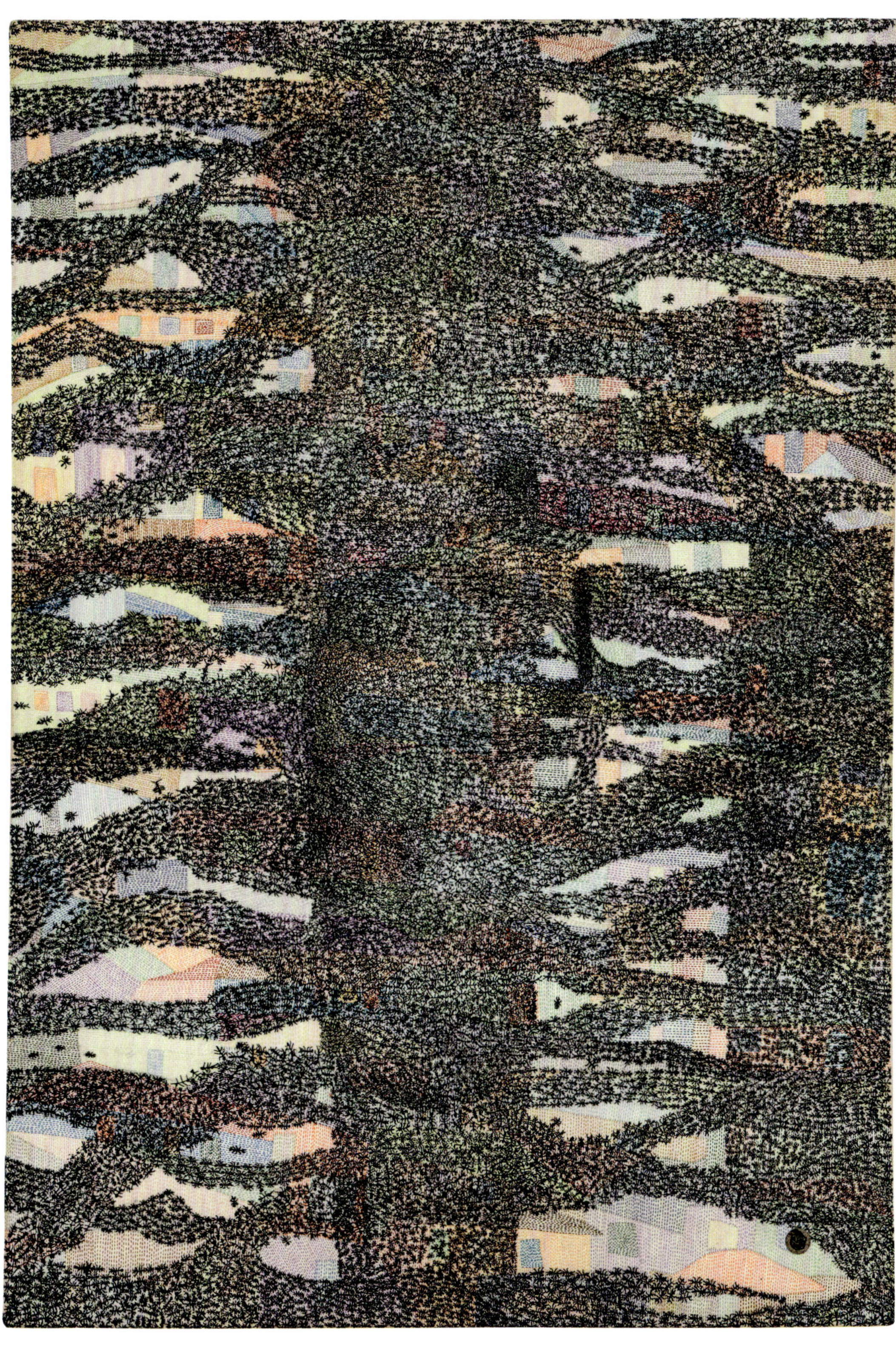

PLATE 3

Ants and Ceramicists II

2009–14 | Yarn on canvas, signed with bottle cap | 73 ⅜ × 51 ⅝ in. (186.4 × 131.1 cm)
Collection of Erica Tennenbaum and Alex Friedman, New York

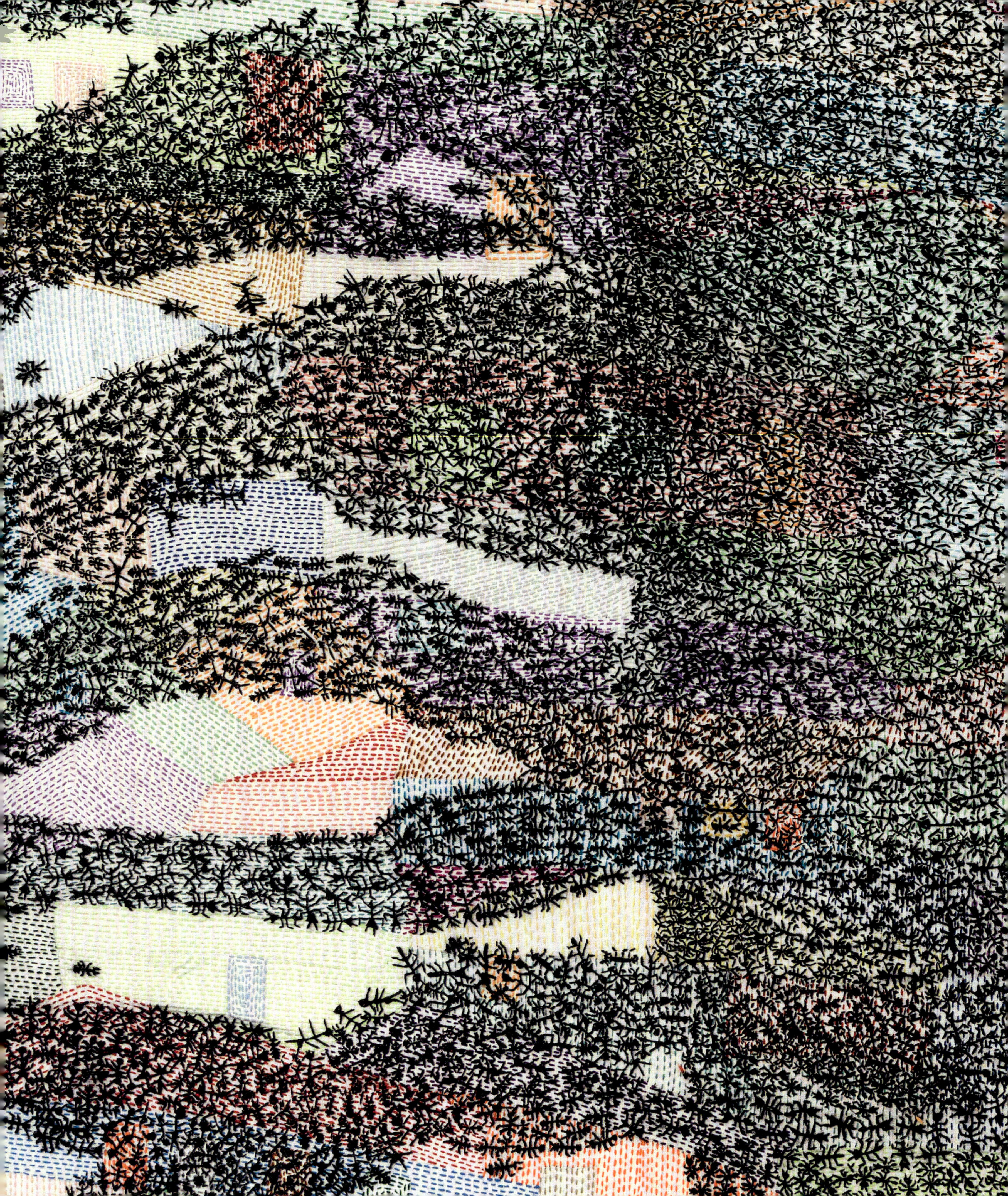

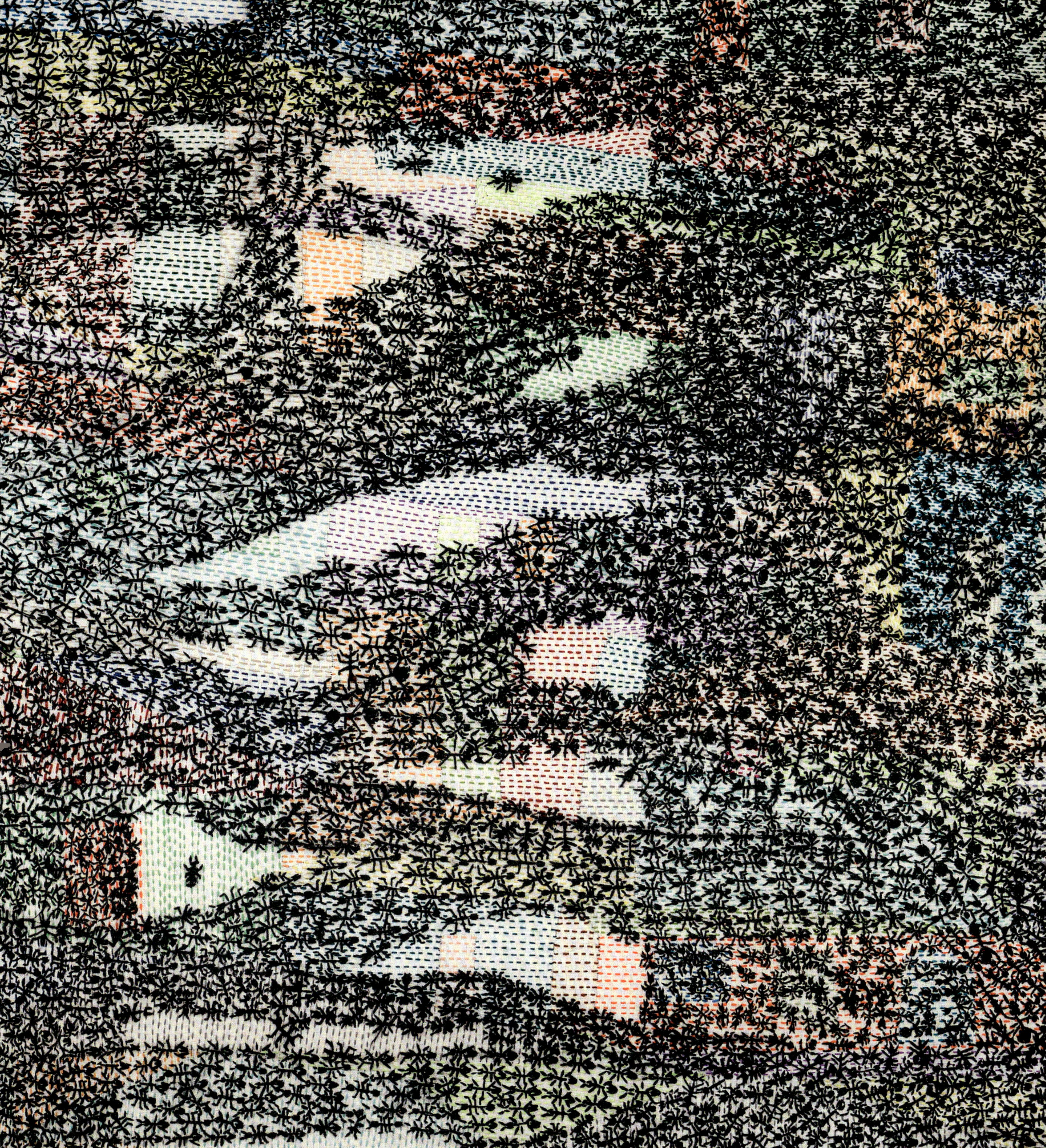

AFFECTIVE OBJECTS: "TIGHTROPE"

Sime's foray in the "Tightrope" series into cast-away motherboards, electrical wires, and components of the ubiquitous cheap mobile phones found throughout Africa is informed by a consideration of the profound impact technology has had in shaping human consciousness and our relationship with the environment. It took the artist over fifteen years to amass the electronic components with which he created the first works in the series. The phones alone were collected from places as distant as the United States, France, and China as well as in Ethiopia. Debuting in 2013 at four different venues in Addis Ababa—the British Council, Goethe-Institut, Istituto Italiano di Cultura, and Alliance Éthio-Française—"Tightrope" marks a milestone in Sime's practice. It amplifies his fetish for experimental rigor without compromising the interest he has shown from the outset in social issues of both existential and ontological dimensions, as seen in *Ocholoni Shach* and *Godana*. More significant is that in addition to exploring the quotidian grind of the urban environment, Sime seeks out aesthetic form in various configurations (topographical, aerial, and structural) of the modern city.

According to Sime, "Tightrope" initially referred to the precarious balance, or tension, a city must navigate in the face of rapid urban development.[23] He has since expanded the idea to capture the incalculable role of technology in ordering modern life. This impact is not limited to infrastructure changes in Addis Ababa or to the power of technology to dictate living conditions in Africa but

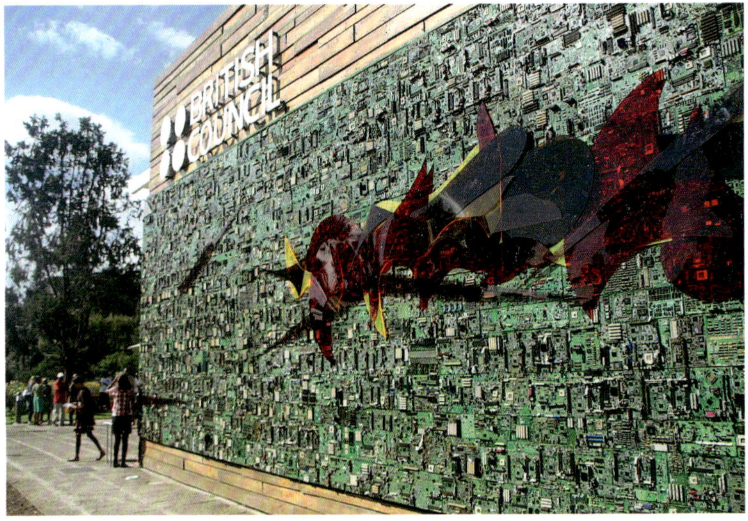

Fig. 9 Elias Sime, *Tightrope 1*, 2013. Reclaimed electronic components and plastic on panel, 12 ft. 5 ⅝ in. × 45 ft. 11 ⅛ in. (380 × 1400 cm). Installation view, British Council, Addis Ababa

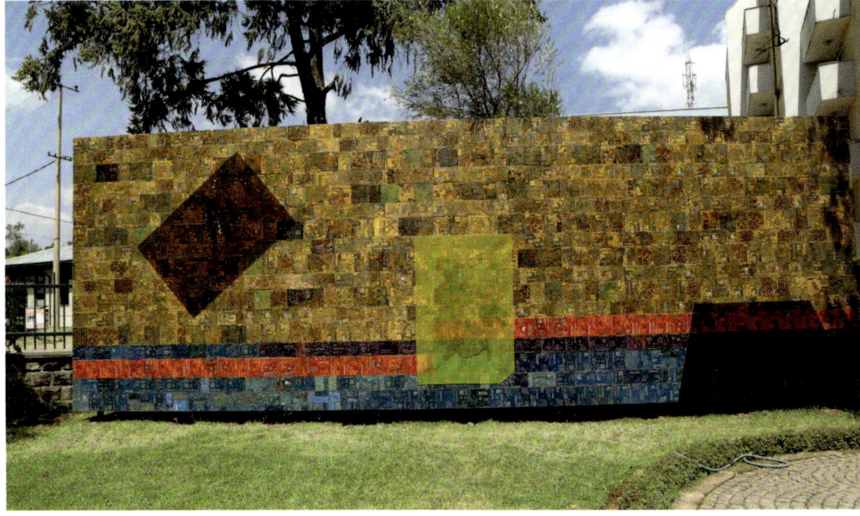

Fig. 10 Elias Sime, *Tightrope 4*, 2013. Reclaimed electronic components on panel, 11 ft. 7 ⅜ in. × 34 ft. 1 ½ in. (354 × 1040 cm). Installation view, Goethe-Institut, Addis Ababa

extends to technology's dominion across the span of human life on earth. This is a crucial point to bear in mind. Although his materials are gathered mostly in Addis Ababa in the current moment, they capture technological advancements made over the entire course of the twentieth century and into the twenty-first, around the world. Close examination of the different electronic components he has employed since the beginning of the series reveals the history of their manufacture—the big picture of a massive technological shift and the depth of human connectivity.

In the inaugural 2013 "Tightrope" exhibition curated by Meskerem Assegued, numbering about thirty-six wall pieces and one floor installation, Sime presented a stunning kaleidoscope of the city, pulsating with energy and bristling with a network of roads, overlapping bridges, high-rises, water courses, and fallow and green areas. While it could be argued that the motherboard, the principal material in the initial corpus of "Tightrope," easily lends itself to the spatial and structural layout of the city, it is clear that Sime pushed the boundaries of his medium in *Tightrope 1* (fig. 9), his mural on the façade of the British Council building, and *Tightrope 4* (fig. 10), his freestanding installation on the grounds of the Goethe-Institut, as well as in the wall pieces shown at the Istituto Italiano di Cultura and Alliance Éthio-Française. In a review of the exhibition, art historian Kate Cowcher observed that each piece "revealed an intense selectivity, an obsessive ordering of the component parts. Just as when they had powered a machine, they functioned here in an ordered collaboration. Arranged by color, or shape, or size, Elias had sifted thousands of tiny pieces, giving each of them a precise position in his overall composition."[24]

During a public conversation at the opening of the exhibition, when a member of the audience asked Sime where he had obtained his materials, he said that he had "purchased moribund electrical parts by the truckload from a guy in the Merkato, Addis's enormous trading hub."[25] The relationship between Sime and the tradespeople of the Merkato, one of the largest open-air markets in Africa, is well established. There is a deeper and more compelling significance, however, to such markets beyond the daily commercial transactions that occur in them. Haggling is a key *social* act that establishes trust between the seller and the buyer. Emotions are exchanged between the two parties, as well as money and goods. Emotion is also transferred between the buyer and the goods. Part of haggling is touching the objects on offer, feeling them, and identifying the ones that meet the buyer's criteria. The materials Sime works with bear witness to this social spirit. One can imagine that, when Sime is working with found or reclaimed materials, he relives such scenarios—that he imagines the human traces and emotions invested in material objects.

Africa is a thriving market for secondhand goods, very much including electronics. Imported secondhand goods carry with them the experiences they have undergone before their arrival at the market. In some instances, imported secondhand goods used by Sime would also have changed hands several times locally. Exhausted of any remaining commercial value but imbued with deep emotional traces, these objects end up in garbage dumps to be salvaged. Their lifespans are renewed once more. When they are collected by Sime, they are reinvested with value, or status, as art materials and ultimately gain new life as works of art.

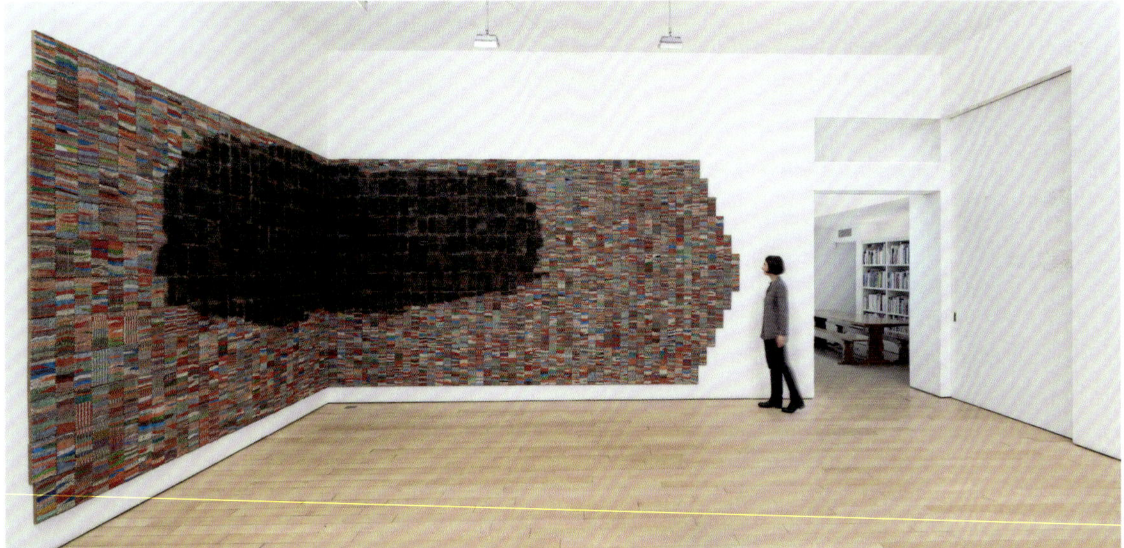

It is worth reiterating the importance of the human stories and memories invested in Sime's artistic media. His work stimulates a deep emotional response regardless of where it is shown. During an interview with this author, Meskerem Assegued recalled a particular incident involving a woman who was moved to tears upon encountering the artist's work during the opening of *Elias Sime: Eye of the Needle, Eye of the Heart*, presented at the Santa Monica Museum of Art in 2009.[26] Yet it is necessary to ask to what extent it may be the artist's industry and his manipulation of materials—the sheer assemblage and intricate, time-consuming piecing together of objects—that produces an *affect*. Admittedly, Sime's work has a seductive appeal and a rhythmic cadence. To make *Tightrope: I Burned It* (2019; fig. 11), for example, he braided a copious amount of electrical wire, nailed it into intricate patterns on sheets of particleboard, assembled the sheets into an ambitious composition, and charred a large section in the middle. The resulting visual poetry tugs at the emotions.

In 2018, Sime undertook a large-scale commission for Facebook's headquarters in Menlo Park, California (fig. 12). Comprising electrical wires, circuit boards, computer keyboard keys, buttons, and other components, the installation, 63 feet long and almost 15 feet tall, is a vast field of color and form. Its placement on a wall recalls *Tightrope 1* in Addis Ababa, which evoked networks and grids. Conversely, the untitled Facebook installation, stratified into four horizontal expanses of varied coloration and intensity, suggests an underwater-scape. In making it, however, Sime was largely inspired by the redwood trees of Northern California, and his intention was to depict two large trees lying opposite each other horizontally, with their roots connecting in the center. The top part of the work is composed mostly of small rubber domes from the insides of computer keyboards, while the remaining sections were created with electrical wires, electronic components, and so on. Sime carved into the underlying plywood and then applied accretions of assorted material to create the interweaving, slug-shaped grooves. This is an approach he has

Fig. 11 Elias Sime, *Tightrope: I Burned It*, 2019. Reclaimed electronic components and insulated wire on panel, 8 ft. 8 in. × 26 ft. 8 in. (264.2 × 812.8 cm). Courtesy of the artist and James Cohan, New York

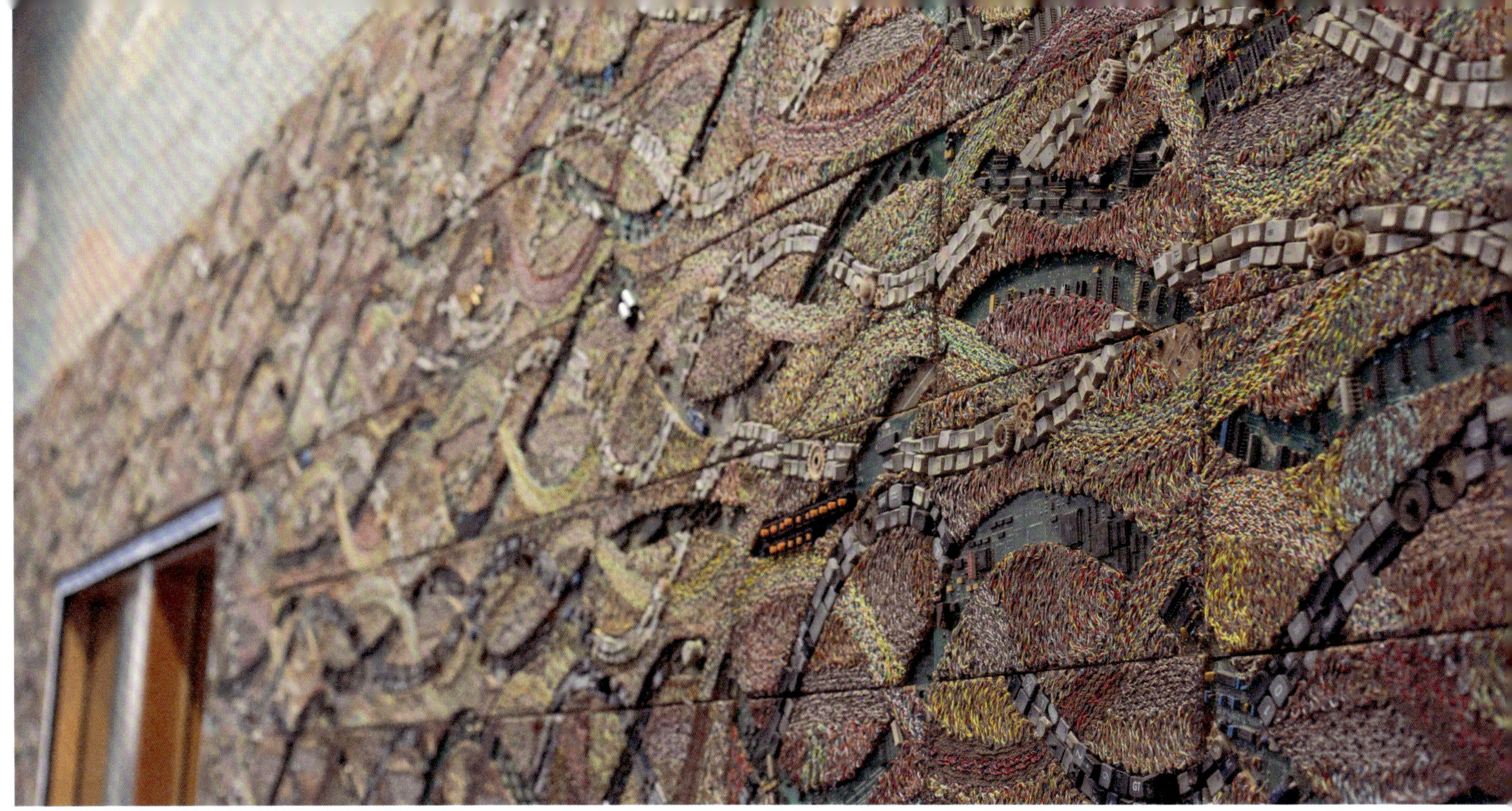

previously used in his architectural work—as in the buildings of Zoma Contemporary Art Center, which predated his and Assegued's Zoma Museum (fig. 13)—but has also begun to apply in the more recent "Tightrope" works. As the slug shapes weave in and out of one another in flamboyant resonance, they remain suggestive of squids or other underwater life-forms. Sime's aesthetic is typically reiterative in that he returns to stock techniques (some invented by him and others borrowed from Ethiopian traditions) again and again, applying them in ways that keep them fresh and original. Toward the middle of the Facebook mural, the stratified horizontal layers collapse into a cascade that stretches from top to bottom. Here, it appears as if the suggested underwater life-forms are emptying out into a rivulet or being swept up into a powerful waterspout. In another view, the work may be seen to evoke the structure of the Earth; according to Sime, the stratum with the trees represents the topsoil or Earth's crust, while the lower portion, which is predominantly brown in color, represents the deeper underground. Sime's creativity is in full effect here—the sculptural and the painterly, the abstract and the representational, all merging into a tour de force.

Fig. 12 Elias Sime, *Untitled* (detail), 2018. Reclaimed electronic components and insulated wire on panel, 14 ft. 9 in. × 63 ft. 6 in. (449.6 × 1935.5 cm). Installation view, Facebook, Inc., Menlo Park, CA

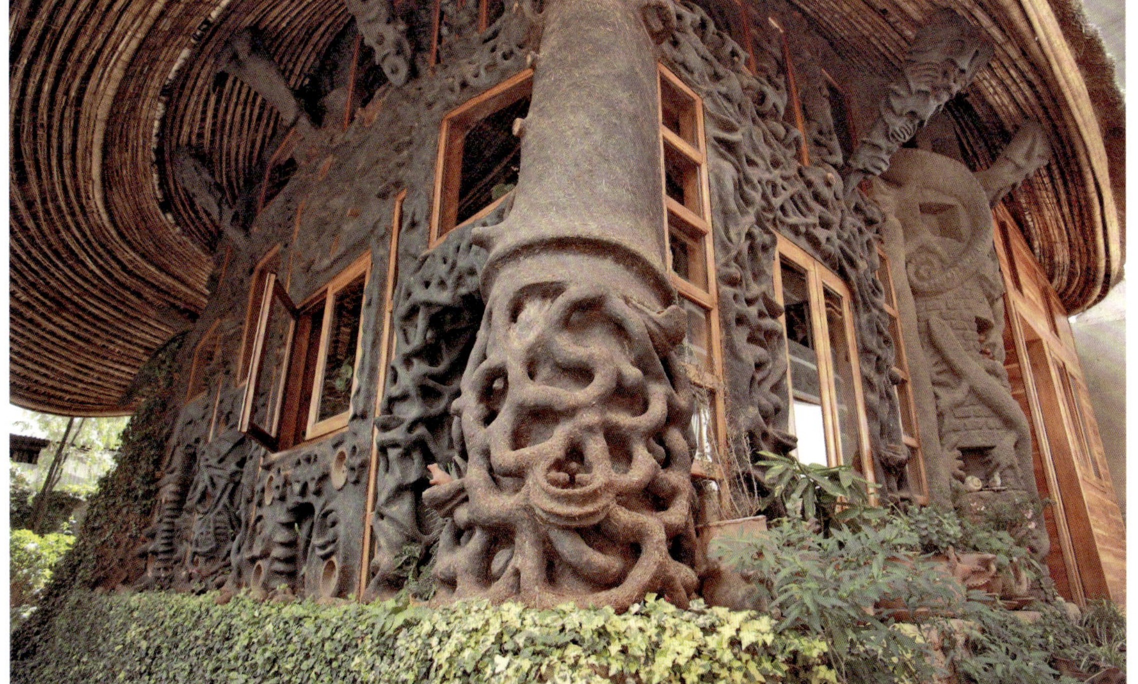

Fig. 13 Zoma Contemporary Art Center, Addis Ababa

A GRIOT OF THE WORLD

Sime's practice is located at the intersection of the local and the global. The artist operates with a spacious creative license, addressing the experiences of his immediate environment while mirroring and transcending Ethiopia's rich artistic traditions, cultural heritage, and history to come into his own as an image and object maker. Sime insists that his work speaks not of Ethiopia or of Africa per se but of human experience. With "Tightrope," especially, he makes a persuasive argument that his work must be approached as a humanist inquiry, not reductively. If the Studio Museum's *Flow* exhibition, mentioned at the beginning of this essay, announced Sime as an international contemporary artist, *Elias Sime: Eye of the Needle, Eye of the Heart*, the 2009 Santa Monica Museum exhibition, affirmed his reputation. The exhibition, which traveled to the North Dakota Museum of Art, Grand Forks, featured a broad range of work in a variety of media and at different scales (fig. 14). It included more than sixty sculptures, about forty paintings, seven mixed-media "thrones," and five wall reliefs, created with buttons, yarn, plastic, threadbare fabric, discarded bottle caps, wood, mud, straw, stuffed goat hides, metal, and more—thus demonstrating the breadth of his practice and span of his career over the previous two decades. The current exhibition confirms how Sime's unique artistic voice has acquired further sophistication since 2009. It places his more recent production in dialogue with earlier work and engages audiences in multiple North American locations, from the northeastern United States to the Midwest to Toronto, Canada—mapping yet another part of the road Sime has traveled to global renown.

Ugochukwu-Smooth C. Nzewi is Steven and Lisa Tananbaum Curator in the Department of Painting and Sculpture at the Museum of Modern Art, New York.

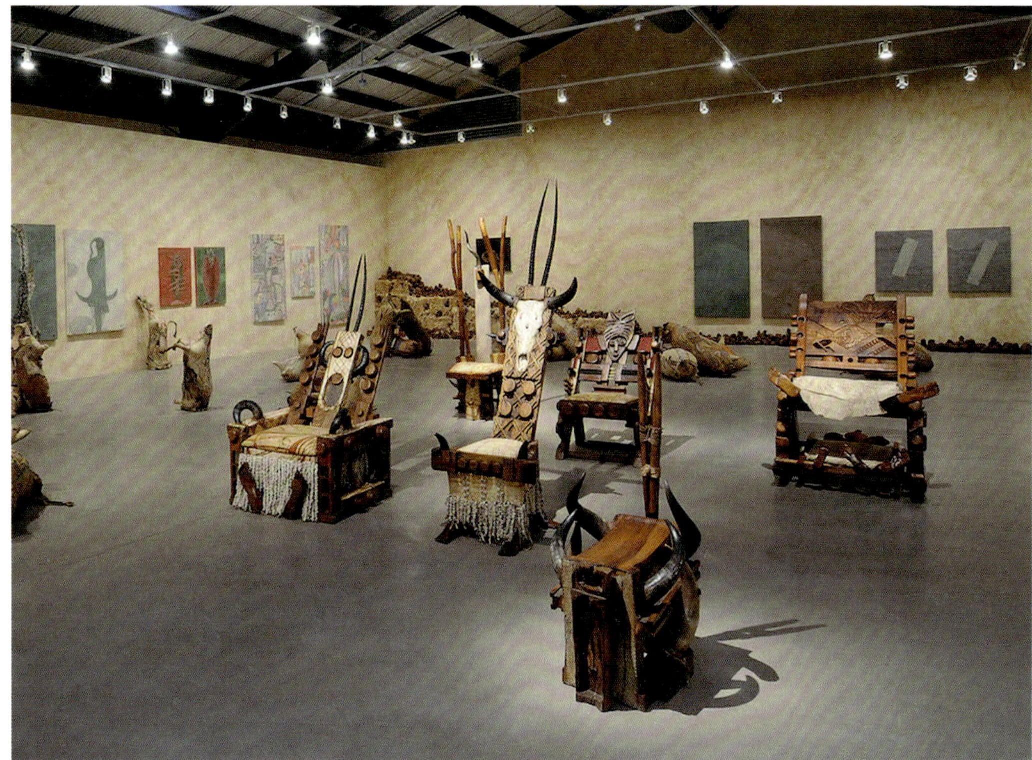

Fig. 14 Installation view of *Elias Sime: Eye of the Needle, Eye of the Heart*, Santa Monica Museum of Art, CA (January 24–April 18, 2009)

1. Holland Cotter, "Out of Africa, Whatever Africa May Be," *New York Times*, April 4, 2008, https://www.nytimes.com/2008/04/04/arts/design/04flow.html.

2. Peri M. Klemm, "Reviewed Work: *Elias Sime: Eye of the Needle, Eye of the Heart*," *African Arts* 43, no. 1 (2010): 84.

3. Meskerem Assegued, with Sheba Brown, eds., *Tightrope*, exh. brochure (Addis Ababa: Zoma Contemporary Art Center, 2013), https://www.jamescohan.com/attachment/en/599f12405a4091c6048b4568/News/599f13385a4091c6048b7a92.

4. Elias Sime and Meskerem Assegued, in conversation with the author, James Cohan gallery, New York, May 25, 2018.

5. Although currently independent of each other, the Ethiopian Orthodox Tewahedo Church and the Coptic Orthodox Church of Alexandria are interlinked. From the twelfth century, the *abuna* (archbishop) of the Ethiopian Orthodox Church was typically an Egyptian Coptic monk; in 1950, a native Ethiopian was appointed for the first time. An autonomous Ethiopian patriarchate was established in 1959, but the honorary primacy of the Coptic patriarch is still recognized today.

6. Salah M. Hassan and Achamyeleh Debela, "Addis Connections: The Making of the Modern Ethiopian Art Movement," in Clémentine Deliss, ed., *Seven Stories about Modern Art in Africa*, exh. cat. (London: Whitechapel Art Gallery, 1995), 139.

7. According to Meskerem Assegued, students were "required to produce signs and banners with slogans such as *Ethiopia Tikdem!* (Forward Ethiopia!); *Abyotawi Enat Ager Woyem Mot!* (Revolution in our Motherland or Death!); *Arengwade Zemecha Byeaktachaw!* (Green Revolution in Every Direction!); *Ke-Guad Likemember Mengestu Hailelmariam* [*sic*] *gar wedefit!* (Move Forward with Comrade Chairman Mengistu Hailemariam!) and *Marxism Leninism Memeriachen new!* (Marxism and Leninism are our Principles!)." See Meskerem Assegued, "A Retrospective Observation of Elias Sime," *African Identities* 6, no. 4 (November 2008): 480.

8. Sime wanted to drop out of art school because he felt it stifled his creativity but was convinced to stay by his father, whom he deeply respected. *Seatat* was part of his graduation project. Elias Sime and Meskerem Assegued, interview by the author and Karen E. Milbourne, Addis Ababa, February 25, 2019.

9. See Assegued, "Retrospective Observation," 479–82.

10. Ibid.

11. Sime and Assegued, interview by the author and Milbourne, February 25, 2019.

12. Elizabeth W. Giorgis, *Modernist Art in Ethiopia* (Athens: Ohio University Press, 2019), 126–27.

13. Ibid.

14. See, for example, Okwui Enwezor, Katy Siegel, and Ulrich Wilmens, eds., *Postwar: Art between the Pacific and Atlantic, 1945–1965*, exh. cat. (Munich: Haus der Kunst, 2016).

15. *Blue Composition* was acquired by a private collector in the late 1960s, soon after it was painted. It remained out of circulation until recently, when it came to public attention on May 3, 2019, during Bonhams' contemporary African art auctions in New York.

16. Alle School of Fine Arts and Design professor Tadesse Mesfin, interview by the author and Karen E. Milbourne, Addis Ababa, February 28, 2019.

17. Ibid.

18. See Rebecca Martin Nagy, *Continuity and Change: Three Generations of Ethiopian Artists*, exh. cat. (Gainesville, FL: Samuel P. Harn Museum of Art, 2007), 74–75; Raymond Silverman, "Zerihun Yetmgeta: Portfolios," *African Arts* 30, no. 1 (1997): 52–57.

19. Yetmgeta, whose long career as a professor at the School of Fine Arts and Design began in 1978, considers Desta to be Ethiopia's greatest artist and a major influence on his own work. Yetmgeta shared a studio with Boghossian in the mid-1960s. Tiruneh, who studied at the School of Fine Arts and subsequently at the fine arts academy in Moscow, eventually left his teaching position at the former in frustration and established a private art school in Addis Ababa called the Enlightenment Art Academy.

20. Sime recruits his assistants from the neighborhoods where his many studios—or, rather, the spaces where he works (he does not have conventional studios), including his personal home and that of Meskerem Assegued, his close collaborator—are located. Sime and Assegued, interview by the author and Milbourne, February 25, 2019.

21. The three works by Sime included in the show were *hors catalogue*.

22. Elias Sime, quoted in wall text prepared by Alisa LaGamma for the 2008–9 exhibition *The Essential Art of African Textiles: Design without End* at the Metropolitan Museum of Art, New York

23. Sime and Assegued, conversation with the author, May 25, 2018.

24. Kate Cowcher, "Tightrope: Elias Sime—Review (British Council, Goethe Institute, Italian Cultural Institute and Alliance Éthio-Française, Addis Ababa, Ethiopia, October 19–December 31, 2013)," *African Arts* 47, no. 4 (2014): 89.

25. Ibid.

26. The Santa Monica Museum of Art closed in May 2015 and reopened in 2017 in downtown Los Angeles as the Institute of Contemporary Art, Los Angeles (ICA LA).

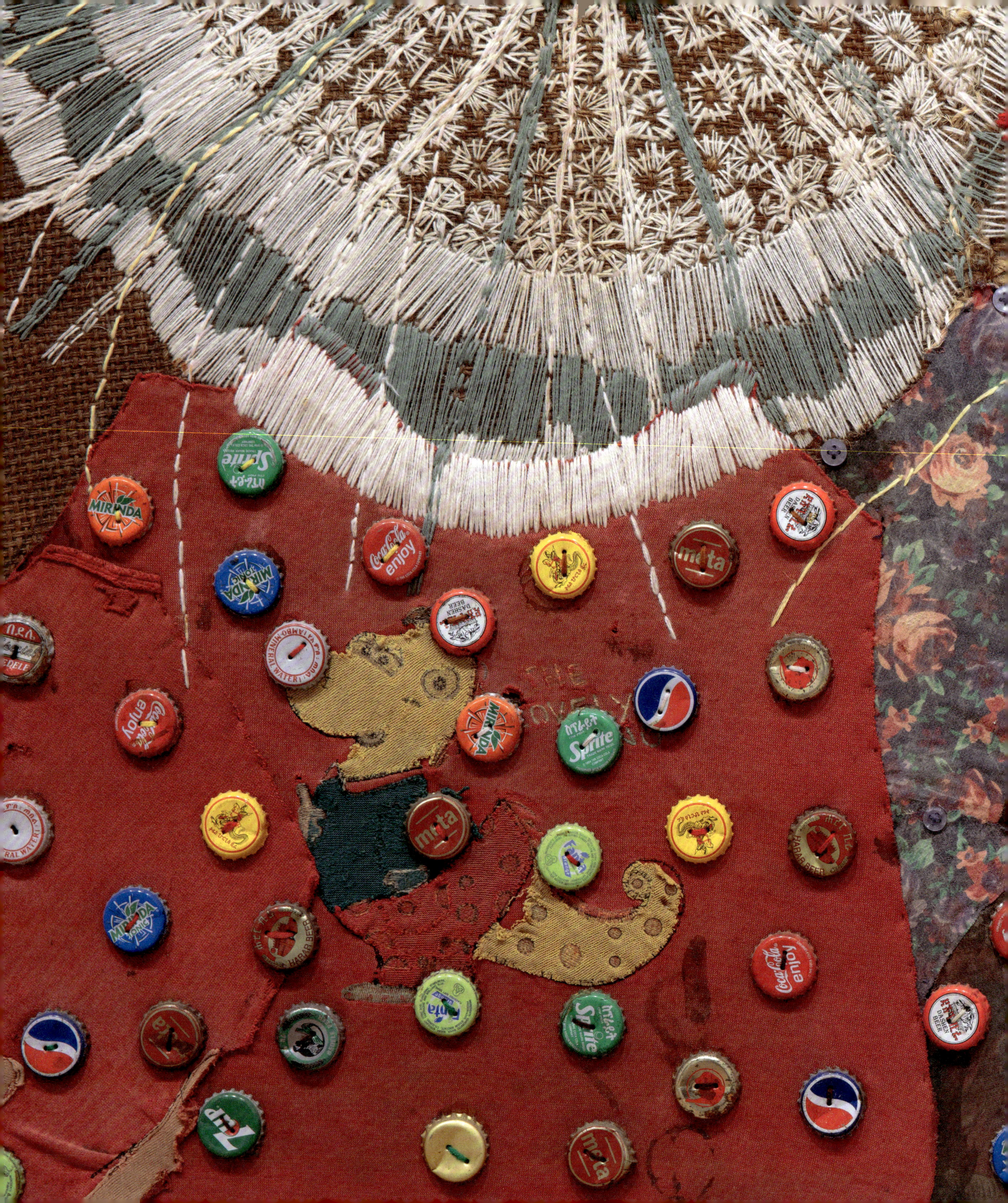

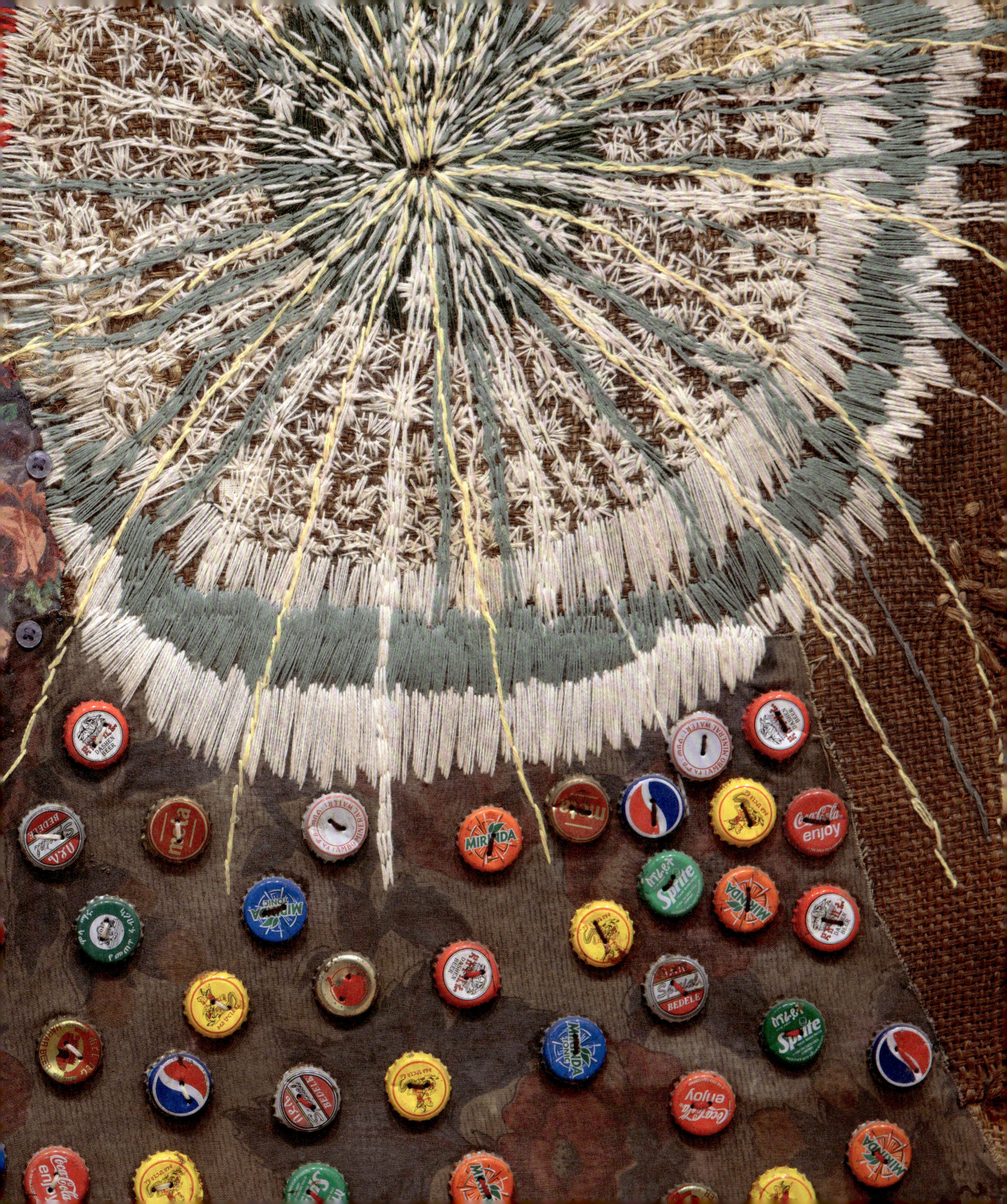
MIRINDA
Coca-Cola
enjoy
Sprite
Sprite
BEDELE

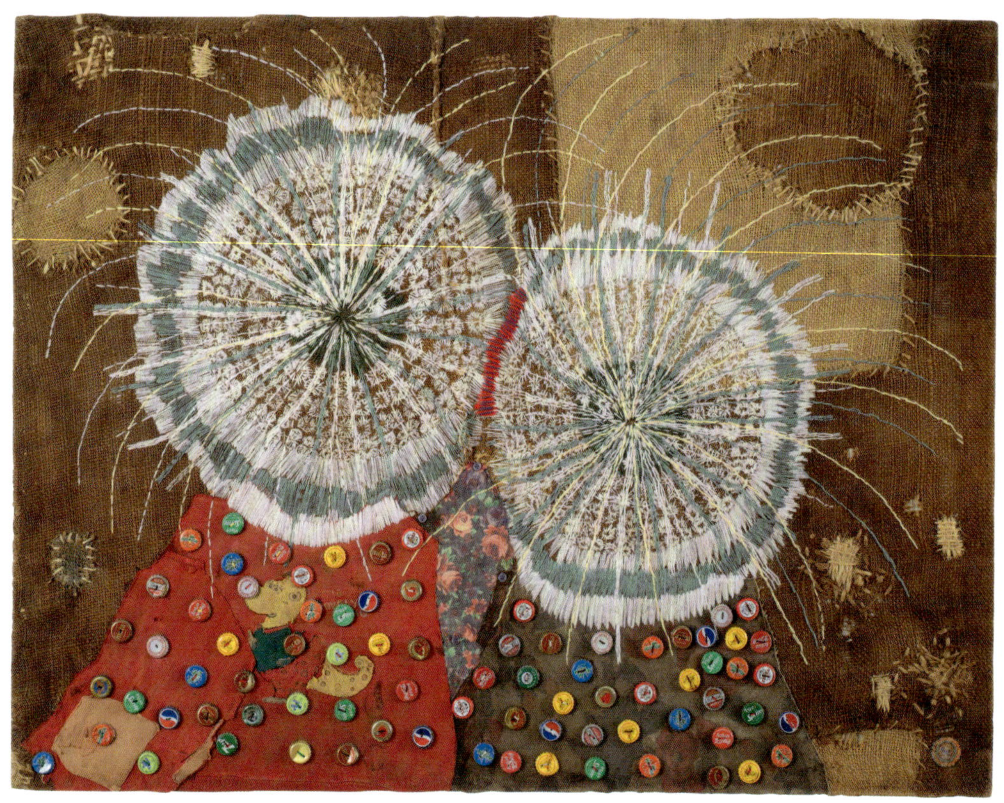

PLATE 4

Aremoch

2004 | Yarn, bottle caps, and fabric on burlap, mounted on canvas, signed with bottle cap | 35 ⅝ × 51 ½ in. (90.5 × 130.8 cm)
Collection of Tony and Sandra Tamer

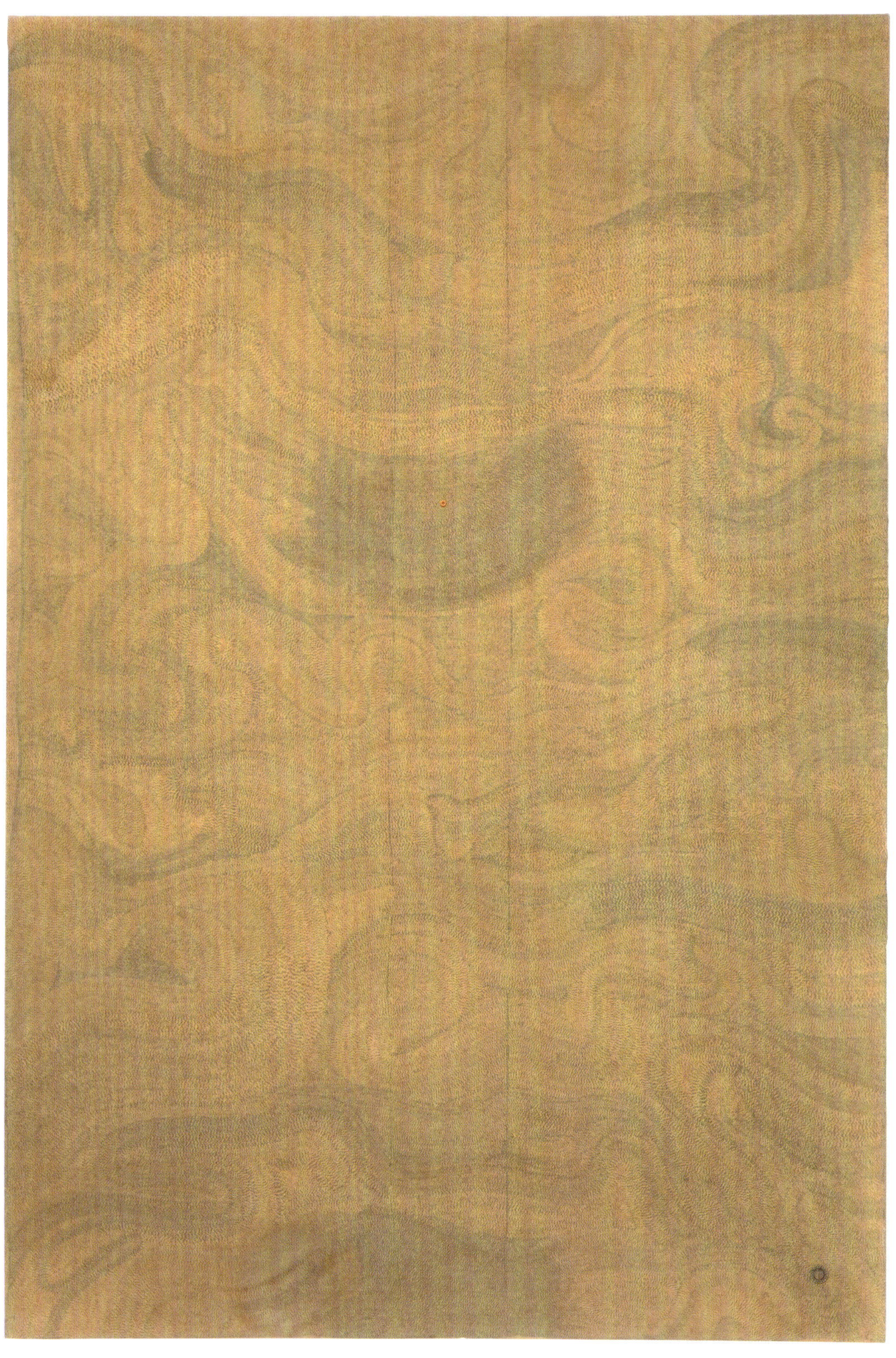

PLATE 5

Splash of a Pebble in Muddy Water

2006 | Yarn on canvas, signed with bottle cap | 9 ft. ½ in. × 74 ½ in. (275.6 × 189.2 cm)
Collection of Bill and Christy Gautreaux, Kansas City, MO

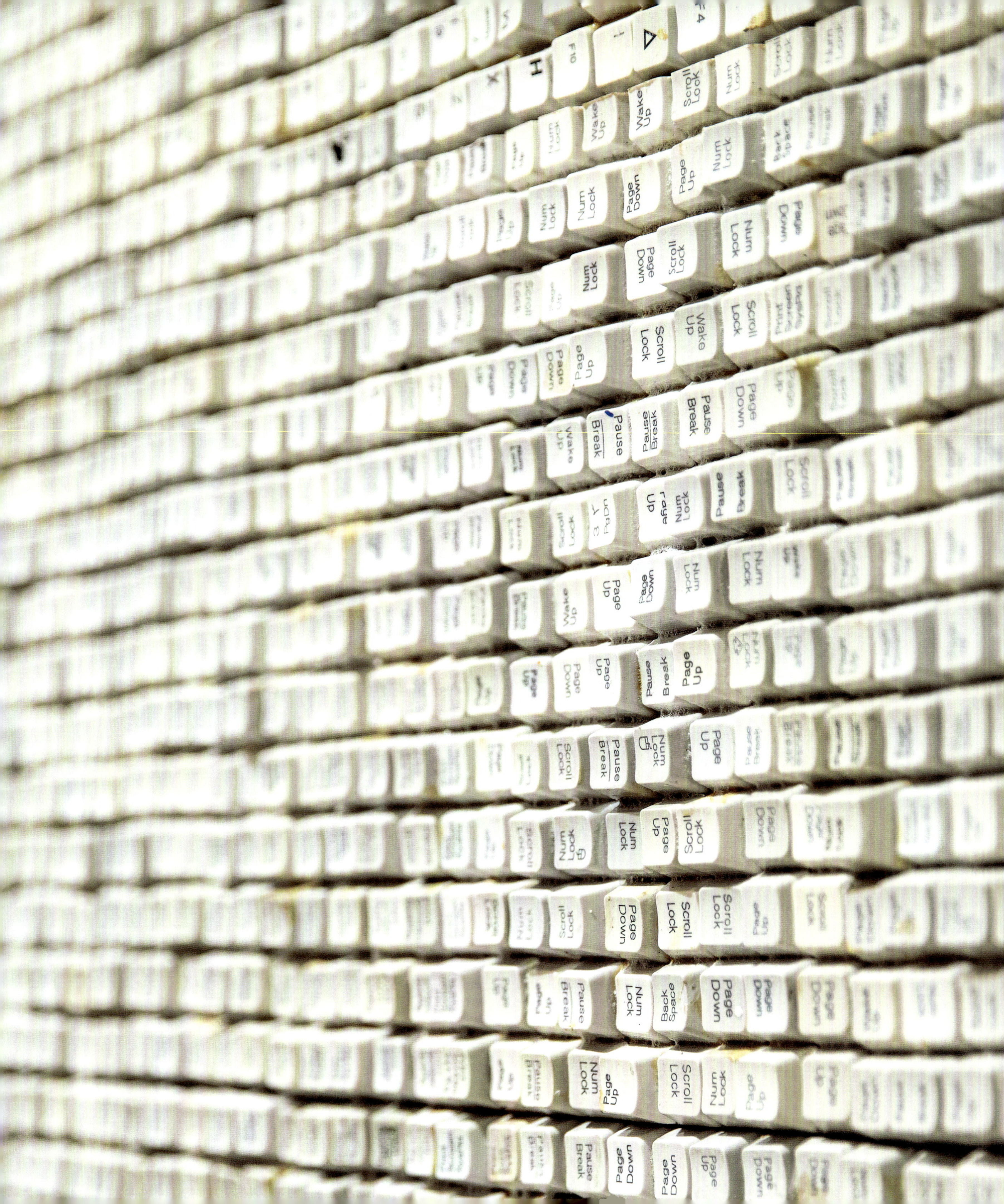

PERSONAL TOUCH

VITAL MATERIALISM IN THE WORK OF ELIAS SIME

KAREN E. MILBOURNE

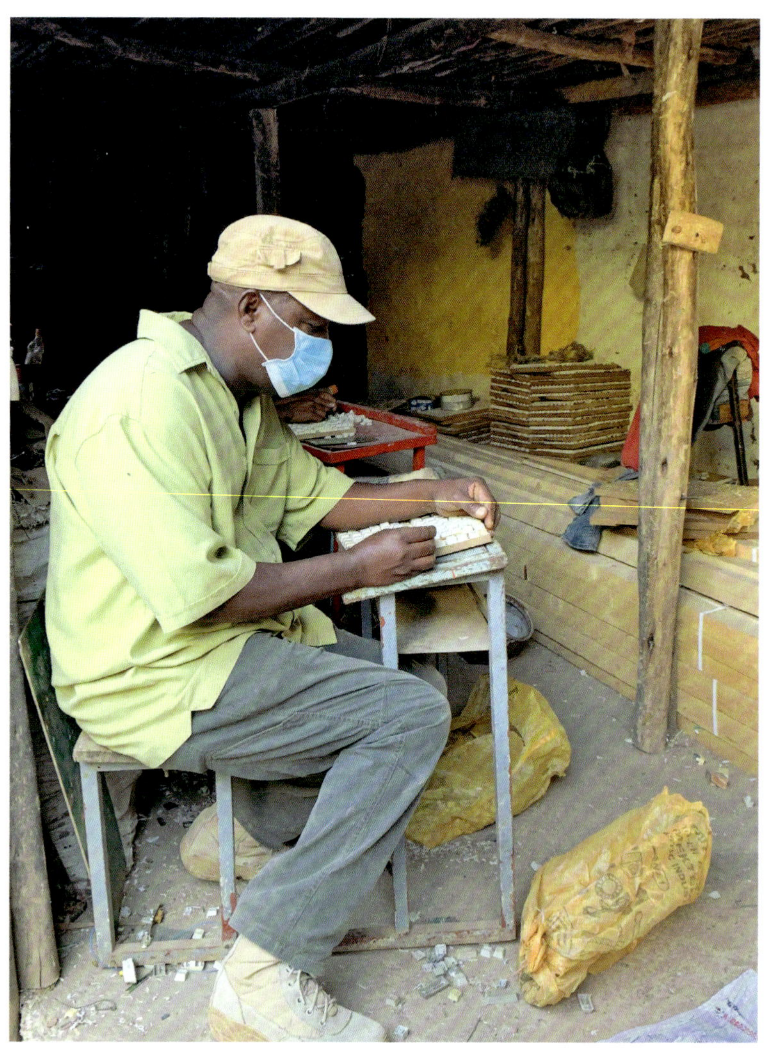
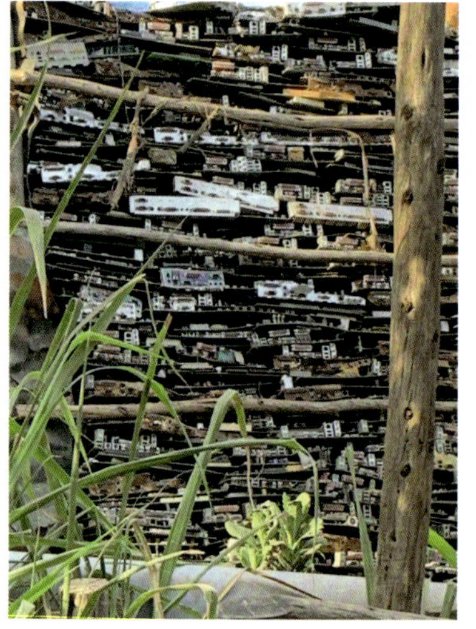
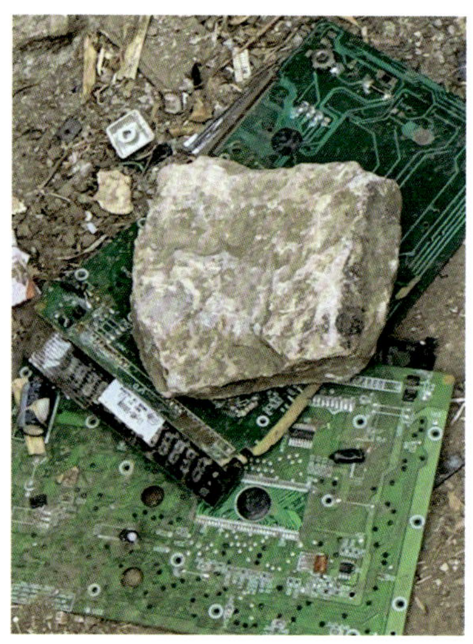
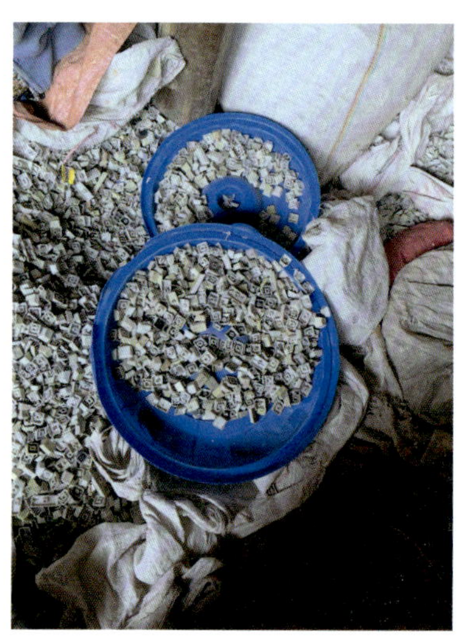
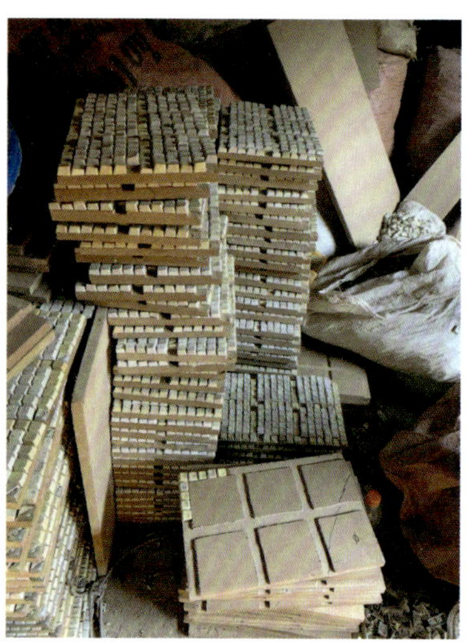
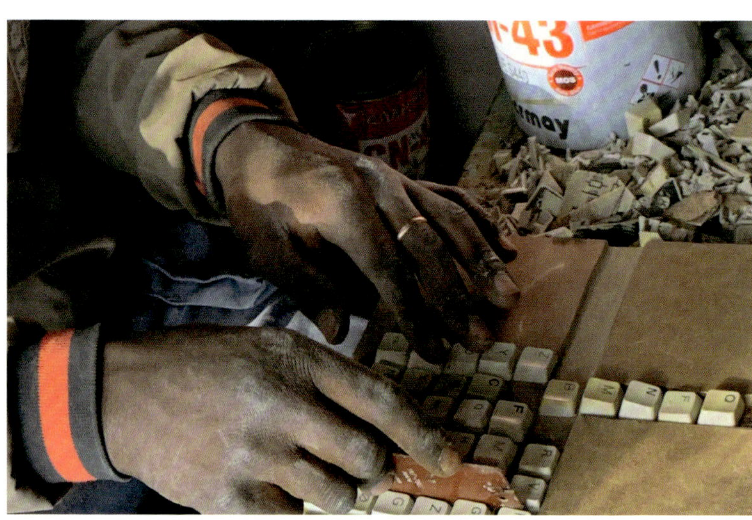
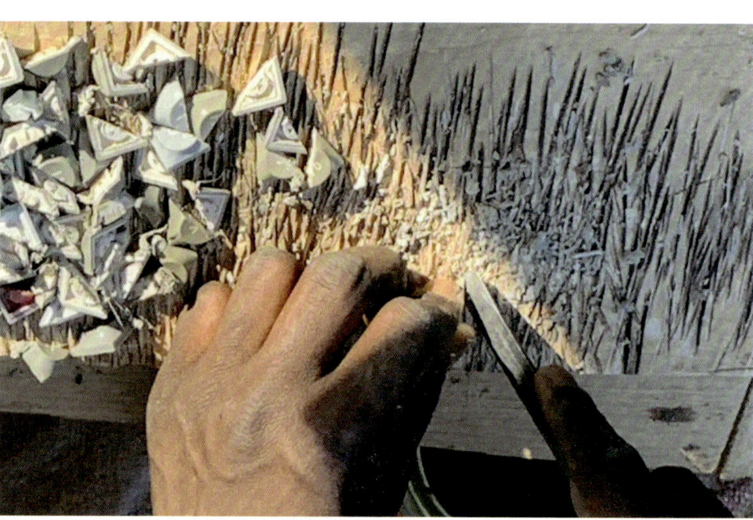

"Global connections are everywhere."

—**Anna Lowenhaupt Tsing**

On a warm and breezy late afternoon in February 2019, Ugochukwu-Smooth C. Nzewi and I sat chatting with Elias Sime and his intellectual partner and collaborator, Meskerem Assegued, in one of Sime's studios—this one tucked at the periphery of the pair's recently opened Zoma Museum in Addis Ababa, Ethiopia. Sime has multiple studios, which shift in scale, number, and location—although, to be honest, Sime has never had what might be conceived as a formal studio. As Assegued jokingly shared, "My house is also a studio. Actually, I have to squeeze to park my car because [Sime's] artwork has taken over my entire compound. And then his studio, which is next door to my house, at his place, that's filled up with a bunch of stuff. So, anywhere he can work and do his art, anywhere he has space, becomes his studio."[1]

One look around Sime's workplace reveals the combined force of this soft-spoken artist's collecting impulses, work ethic, aesthetic vision, and detailed attention to the lived power of things (see opposite). Along the back wall of this particular space stands a towering stack of electronic components, awaiting future dissection. Mechanical debris is ground into the soil surrounding the studio, evidence of long hours of intense activity. The artist says, "I don't like the materials to move from where they are. I don't want to clean them up. I want to find them exactly where I put them yesterday, I want to repeat the mood." In the rafters, on the floor, and on most every remaining surface are sacks of materials awaiting use in future projects and stacks of the cut-wood tiles the artist uses as backing when he reconfigures the materials into wall-engaged artworks. On the day we were there, Sime and his team were cutting apart computer keyboards and attaching the keys to wood tiles in preparation for an installation to commemorate the opening of Zoma Museum, a technique akin to that used in *Tightrope: Silent 1* and *Tightrope: Silent 2* (both 2019; pls. 28, 29).[2] Of these components and the host of other materials the artist has employed over his three-decade career, Sime says, "I transform things I find into art. I prefer things that have touched or been in contact with people."[3]

THE VITALITY OF THINGS

Buttons, flip-flops, mud, plastic bags, roof linings, thread, wire, and motherboards intersect, interweave, and are ultimately transformed in Sime's hands. For more than twenty-five years, the artist has harnessed what political theorist Jane Bennet describes as "vibrant matter." Bennet offers a way of looking at the nonhuman components of our world—be they plastic cups, globs of fat, or jolts of electricity—as "bona fide agents rather than as instrumentalities, techniques of power, recalcitrant objects, or social constructs."[4] She describes a "thing-power" that "draws attention to an efficacy of objects in excess of the human meanings, designs, or purposes they express or serve."[5] Seen as "vibrant matter," Sime's buttons, bags, computer bits, and other collectibles are not passive. Instead, the ideas promoted by Bennet and other advocates of a "new materialism" allow for a more intertwined understanding of human and nonhuman elements, one that echoes Sime's approach, as opposed to other rubrics of environmental consciousness that create hierarchies between humans and their things.

Like Bennet, Sime recognizes the intersecting forces of human and nonhuman entities, and he brings this awareness of vital materiality to his works, resulting in compositions that are at once aesthetically delightful and intellectually complex. He picks up discarded things—not to clean up or because he does not have access to paint or other materials, but because the things have been touched, and because "when he touches them with his fingers they become alive emotionally, connecting him to the stories" of those who have touched them before and of the things themselves.[6] He has even gone so far as to assert that he works "with used materials not because of shortage of money to buy paint and brushes. It is because I believe that painting limits my creativity and quest for new ideas."[7] Indeed, when I asked Sime if he would use electrical wire still on its original spool, not yet used in a home or mechanical device, to compose a work, he simply replied, "You won't find anything that hasn't been touched." Someone mined the copper, worked the machines to spin it into wire, processed its plastic coating, and even loaded the truck that carried it to a store. New and old, *everything* carries fingerprints. To return to the words of the artist,

> The only thing I think about when I pick the cellular phone motherboard, for instance, is the excitement of the person who owned it the first time they got it, the hope they felt about the future, the eagerness to use it. That for me is what love is all about, to realize that we are all connected and that human contact, that touch, is created in every object we take for granted.[8]

For Sime, the encounter with and subsequent relationship to each material is a love affair. Love is, in fact, the term the artist uses most often in describing how he selects materials, works with each thing, and thinks about his process: "I collect all kinds of different material. Sometimes, I just get into it completely and it's hard to get out of it for a while." When asked why this is the case, he replies, "When you pick it up and move it, you have to love it. . . . Don't even try to work with it if you don't love it. Otherwise, you will be tired of it."

Sime's attraction to the "social life of things"—to borrow an oft-cited turn of phrase from anthropologist Arjun Appadurai[9]—began during his childhood in Addis Ababa in what was considered a tough neighborhood, Cherqos, with an open-air market at its center.[10] As Sime has described,

> Growing up in Cherqos, in the middle of the open market, was very influential for my artistic development. When the merchants leave the market at the end of the day, they leave their trash all over the ground. For me, this was the most exciting part of the day. I collected anything I found interesting and made art with it.[11]

As Assegued has written elsewhere of Sime's practice, "Everything, from the materials he selects to the ways he applies them, is done with a purpose."[12] Early in his career, the connection between the materials Sime selected and the subjects of his compositions was direct—when depicting an impoverished boy selling peanuts, he worked with the tattered remnants of workers' garments and even incorporated actual nuts into the portrait (fig. 2). In recent years, Sime's works have varied between the abstract and the pictorial, and while the materials the artist uses remain potent—like "actors" affecting the world around them[13]—their associations are more expansive. Interlooping wires and circuit boards might speak to specific locations, like California's redwood forests or Senegal's Gorée Island; to particular techniques, such as West African strip weaving; or to cellular structures or the vastness of cosmic realms (pl. 18).

Even during his student days, Sime experimented with diverse materials. In preparing for his graduate project in graphic art at what is now the Alle School of Fine Arts and Design at Addis Ababa University, he submitted a composition depicting Ethiopian Orthodox Tewahedo clergy in their raiments, which he had collaged from patches of black and white textiles of the type worn by priests. These were the final days of the Derg regime, however, during which Soviet-influenced Socialist Realism in support of the government was de rigueur.[14] While the faculty rejected Sime's submission in favor of a more traditional woodblock print of the scene (fig. 3), the artist's love affair with local materials and formal experimentation was well under way.

Sime speaks of his art-school years with frustration—it was challenging to make art while navigating the politics of a controlling Communist regime, irrespective of one's unconventional approach to media—but he does share certain affinities with some of his teachers of that time, such as Zerihun Yetmgeta (born 1941; fig. 15). Both artists have explored wood carving,

Fig. 15 Zerihun Yetmgeta, *Wax and Gold*, 1991. Mixed media on animal skin and bamboo, 38 ⅛ × 25 ½ in. (96.8 x 64.8 cm). Eli and Edyth Broad Art Museum, Michigan State University, East Lansing, MSU purchase

used goatskins, and incorporated the structures of weaving into their works, and they share a preference for mixed-media combinations that "knead," "stretch" and test the "elasticity" of the "expanding fields" of painting and sculpture.[15] Whereas Yetmgeta directly appropriates the signs and styles of medicine scrolls and Ethiopian Orthodox art forms into his practice, Sime has embraced the *gestures* found in the expression of faith. His work is rarely likened to that of his compatriots—in part, perhaps, because of his departure from the references to Amharic script and Orthodox arts more characteristically found in works by Yetmgeta, Gebre Kristos Desta (1932–1981; fig. 4), Alexander (Skunder) Boghossian (1937–2003; fig. 5), and Wosene Kosrof (born 1950)—but the undulating patterns of his woven wires and yarn stitches are reminiscent of ritual rhythms found across Ethiopia, including the rocking movement of a priest's staff as he calls out a prayer (fig. 16). Sociologist Abebe Zegeye has aptly described Sime's subversions as possessing a "phenomenal particularity."[16] The artist brings to each of his works an experiential, qualitative character informed by his travels within his homeland, frequently in Assegued's company, in his quest to understand the materials and processes that shape Ethiopia's diverse and distinctive landscapes and cultures.

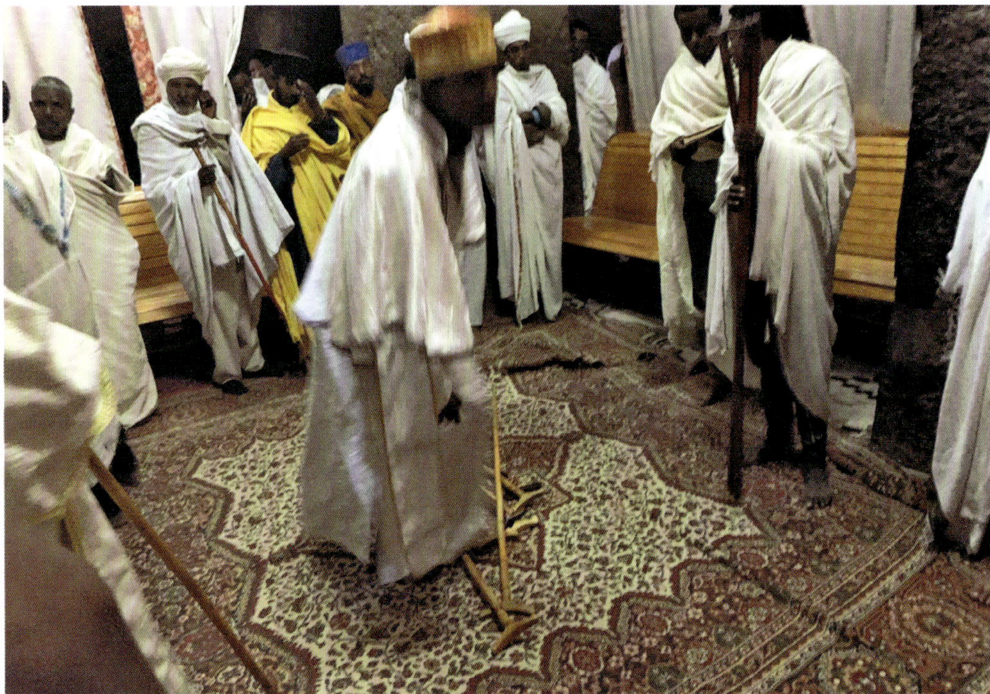

Fig. 16 Ethiopian Orthodox priest calling out a prayer at Beta Medhane Alem (Church of the Redeemer), Lalibela, Ethiopia, March 2019

MATERIAL AND EXPERIENTIAL CONNECTIONS

The vitality of Sime's materials is matched by the performative, experiential nature of his manipulation of them, and yet gesture and movement remain underrecognized facets of his practice. According to the artist, he does not *give* life to the materials in his works; he *joins* them on their journey through life. As he describes it, "I don't philosophize and think about whether I give the materials life or not. But, the moment I start playing with it is when [my life with it] begins. This is what makes me happy, the moment I start working with it." His interactions with his materials are immersive and ongoing and extend to the manner in which he carries out research and pursues new techniques. Sime's travels with Assegued to understand and document the architectural and ritual heritage of the Gurage and other communities within Ethiopia have also resulted in accumulated knowledge that informs not just the artist's materials, ideas, and techniques but the very ways in which his projects are realized.

In 2005, having participated in the previous year's Dak'Art biennial of contemporary African art in Dakar, Senegal, Sime shocked friends and colleagues alike with a live performance at the School of Fine Arts and Design in Addis Ababa that illustrates just how fundamental performance and lived experience are to his practice. For a week, he mixed mud and straw—the key ingredients in so much Ethiopian architecture—in the middle of the gallery floor. For the exhibition's closing, Sime arrived wearing a suit jacket, a necktie, and formal shoes (fig. 17). He walked into the middle of the pile of mud and straw, churned it with his feet, sat down, and began to speak patiently about the differences between mud, straw, and the mixture of the two, especially regarding the strength of this last material, which can endure for over a century when formed into the walls of a home. He continued to explain that while his clothing ultimately came from the same source, a blazer or tie has no bearing on one's humanity and cannot contain the qualities we all share as humans. To conclude, he removed his shoes and walked out barefoot, his feet tracking mud across the floor.[17]

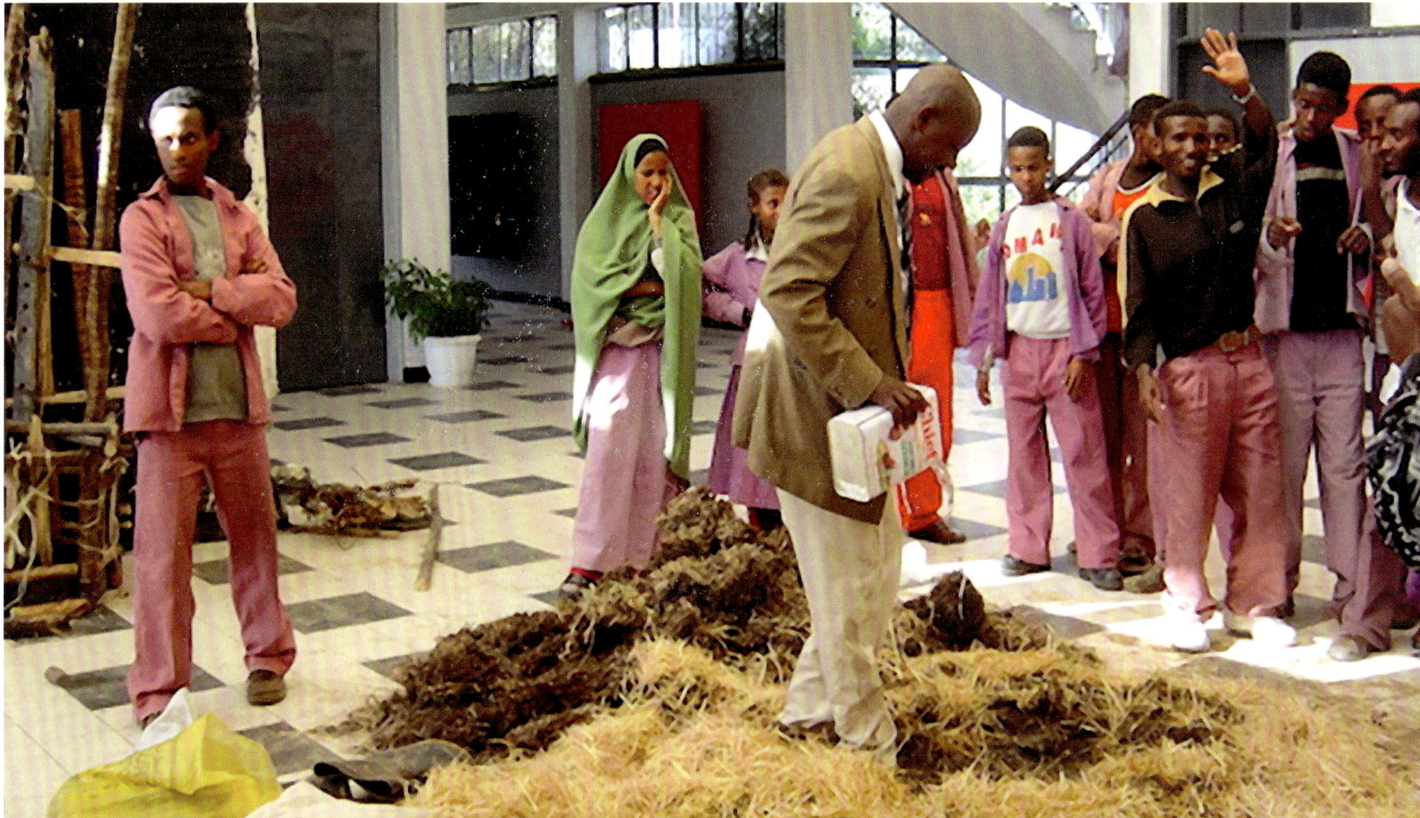

Fig. 17 Elias Sime performing during the exhibition *Addis Ababa Zare*, School of Fine Arts and Design, Addis Ababa University, 2005

Mud and straw remain salient materials for Sime, speaking to the vital materiality of both the Earth and the humans who live in balance with it. Recently, he has used mud and straw to build fantastical "granaries" (*gota*), Zoma Museum's guesthouse complex, and other structures on the museum's campus, including the gallery and dining and educational spaces (fig. 18, 19). He considers the museum and its grounds to be an ongoing work of art; its maintenance, an ongoing performance. Across the surfaces of the many earthen walls Sime has painstakingly built up, unsung creatures—ants, caterpillars, frogs, spiders, turtles—recur as motifs, speaking to resilience, the possibility of transformation, and the beauty of the undervalued. Just as the tortoise, for Sime, is a "symbol of being able to patiently but determinedly get from one place to another," the fabrics, flip-flops, and other materials he uses have undergone similarly patient and determined journeys—journeys that connect us all and inspire him to create anew.[18]

As anthropologist Allen Roberts once noted, "Through animal symbolism human creativity is provoked, thought is organized, and meaning [is] made."[19] Animals—not just any animals, but specific ones—facilitate expression and communication. They can be effective either in visualizing familiar, domestic spaces (with their associated concepts of order and control) or, in contrast, in alluding to the unknown, untamed expanses of the wild. They may also serve as symbols of endurance and community involvement, as in Sime's "Ants and Ceramicists" series (2009–14; pls. 3, 6, 7). For centuries (millennia, actually), animals have helped us to imagine—to borrow from art theorist Hal Foster's definition of "visuality"—"how we see, how we are able, allowed or made to see, and how we see this seeing or the unseen therein."[20] Not only do animals provoke thought, but they also provide a means of expressing and visualizing that thought. Equally potent—not just in their capacity to organize thought and make meaning but in their impact on our lives—are the inorganic materials populating Sime's works and put into action by him.

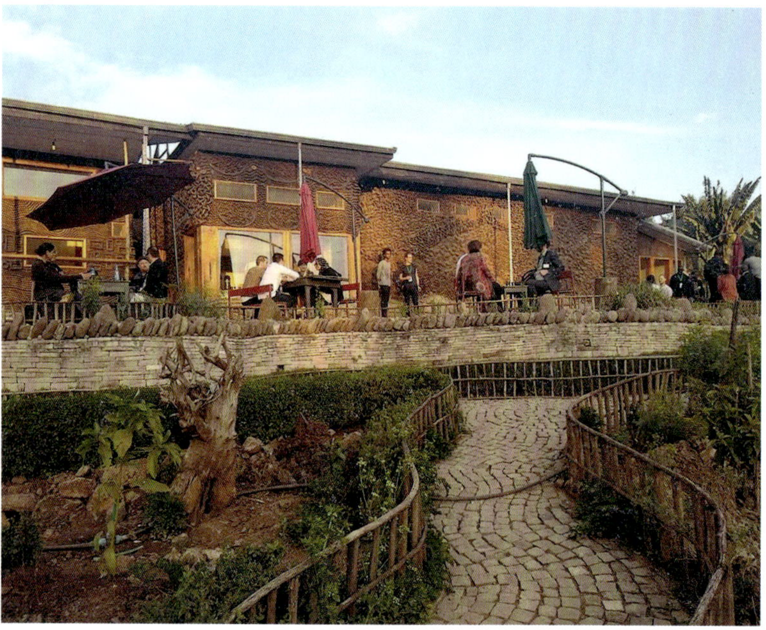

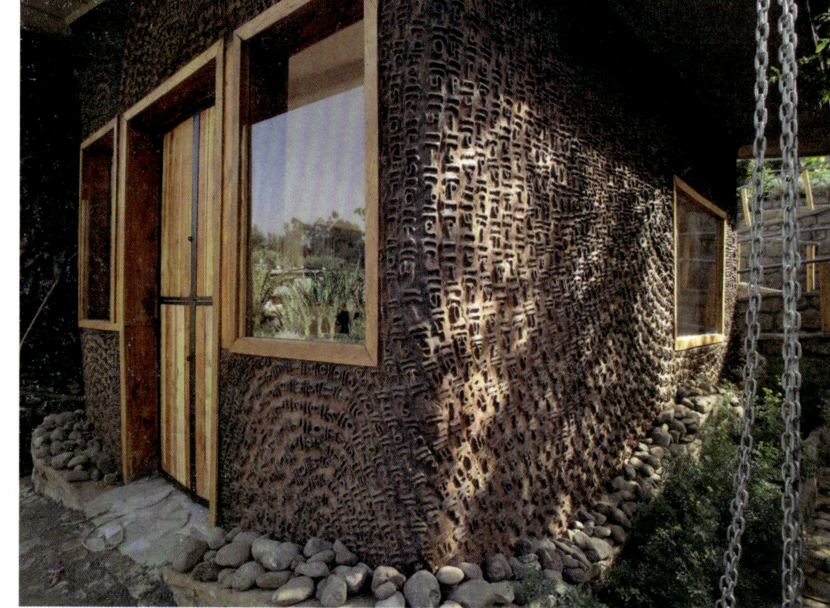

Figs. 18, 19 Zoma Museum, Addis Ababa

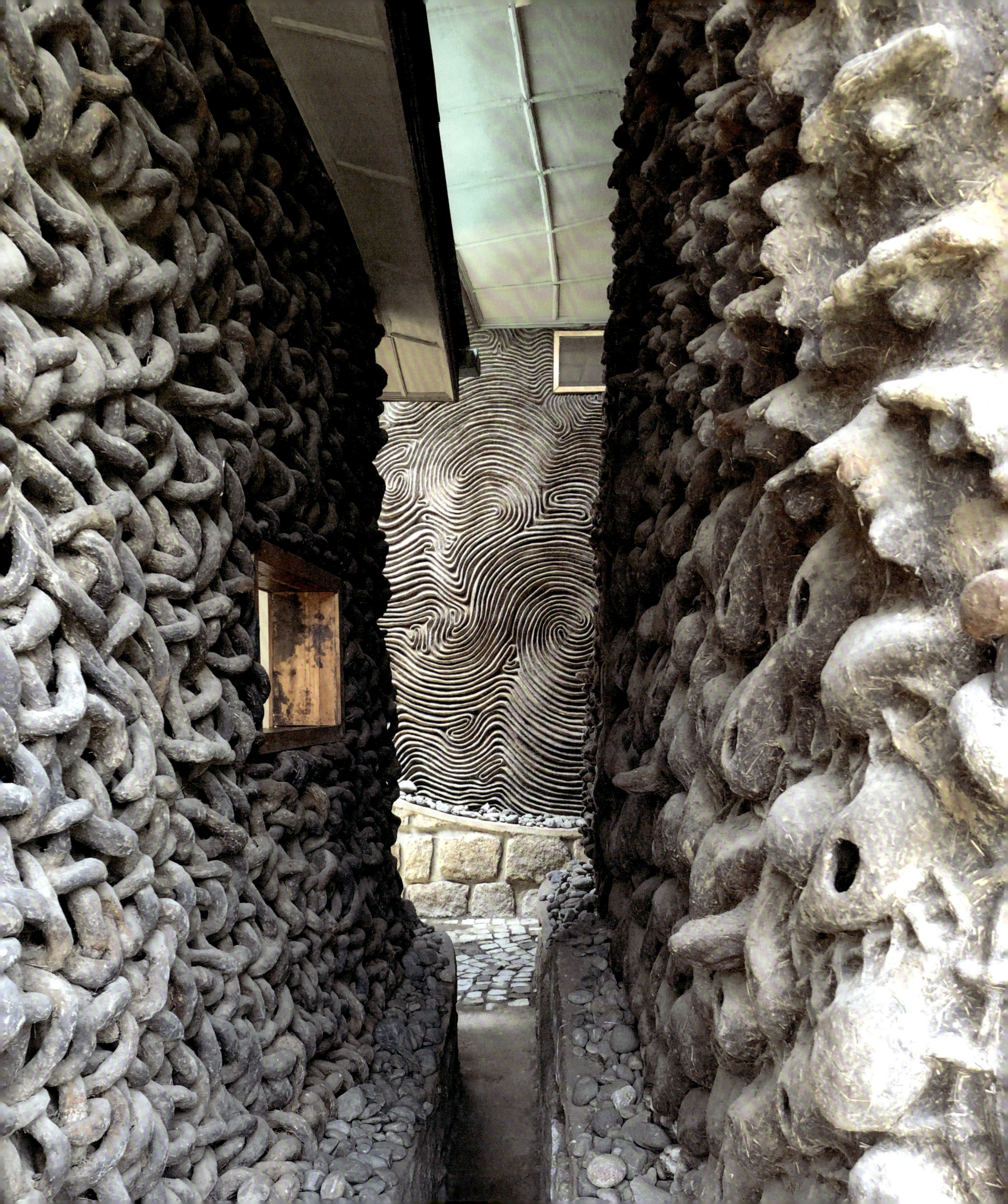

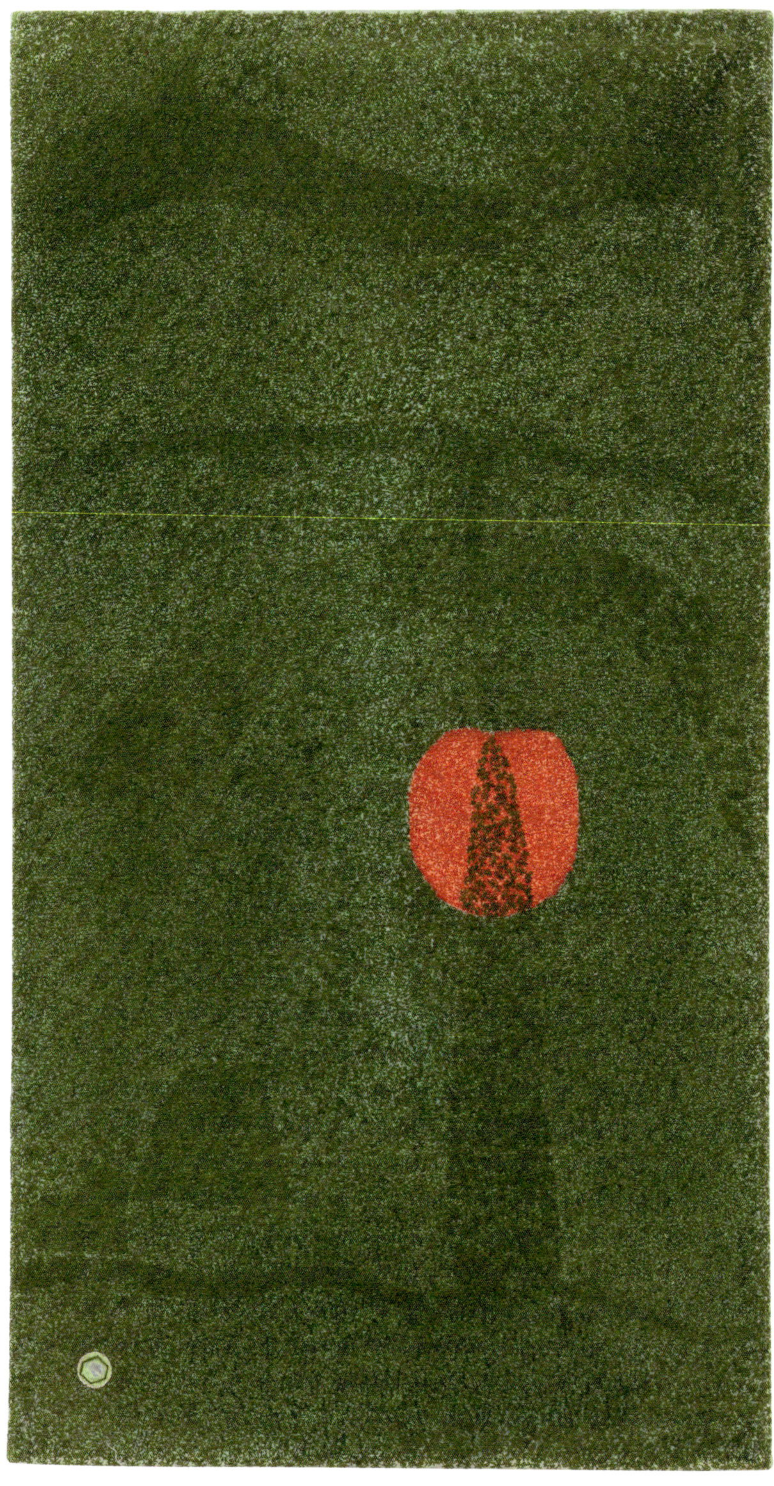

PLATE 6

Ants and Ceramicists 6

2009–14 | Yarn on canvas, signed with bottle cap | 61 × 33 in. (154.9 × 83.8 cm)
Courtesy of the artist and James Cohan, New York

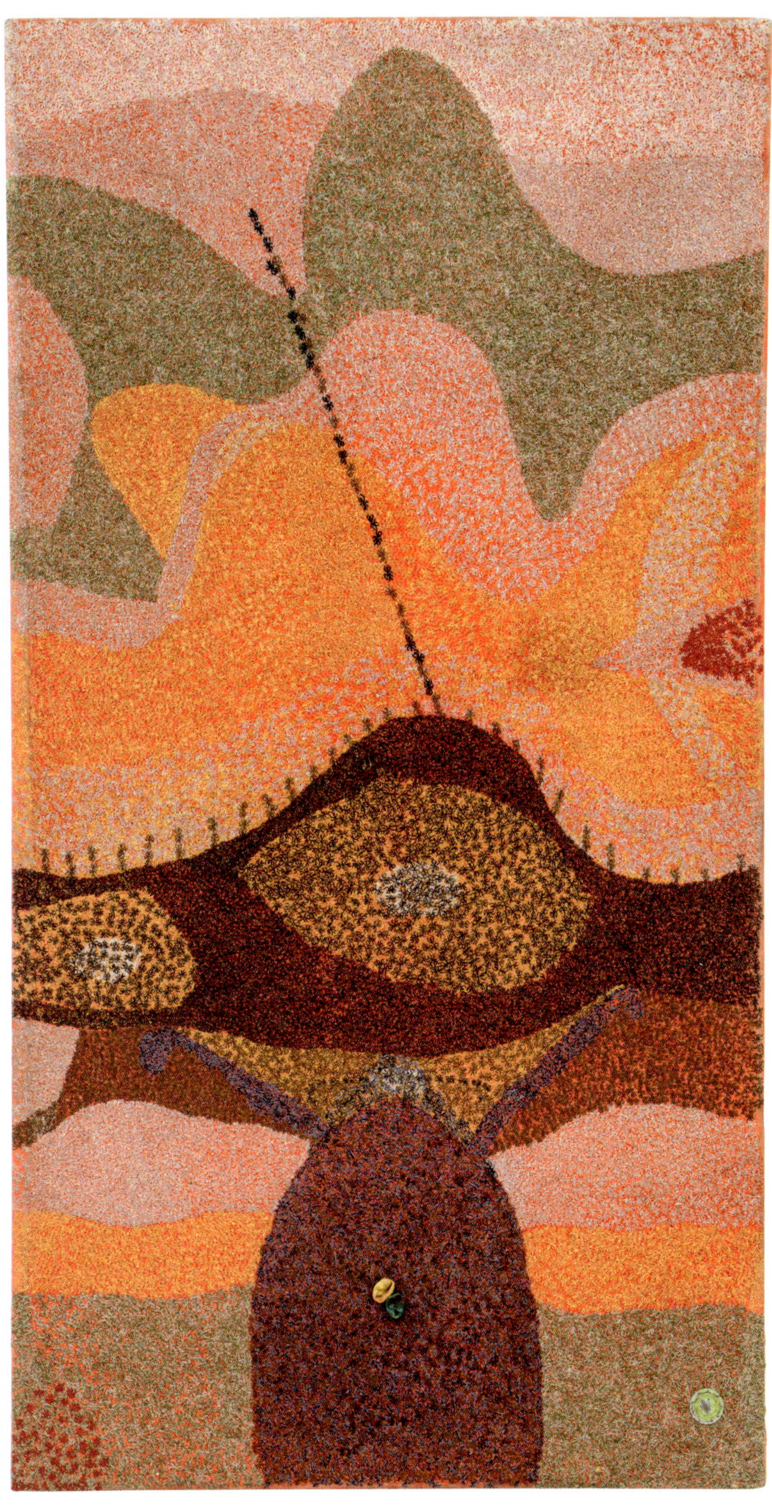

PLATE 7

Ants and Ceramicists 10

2009–14 | Yarn and found objects on canvas, signed with bottle cap | 61 × 33 in. (154.9 × 83.8 cm)
Collection of James Zang, Portugal

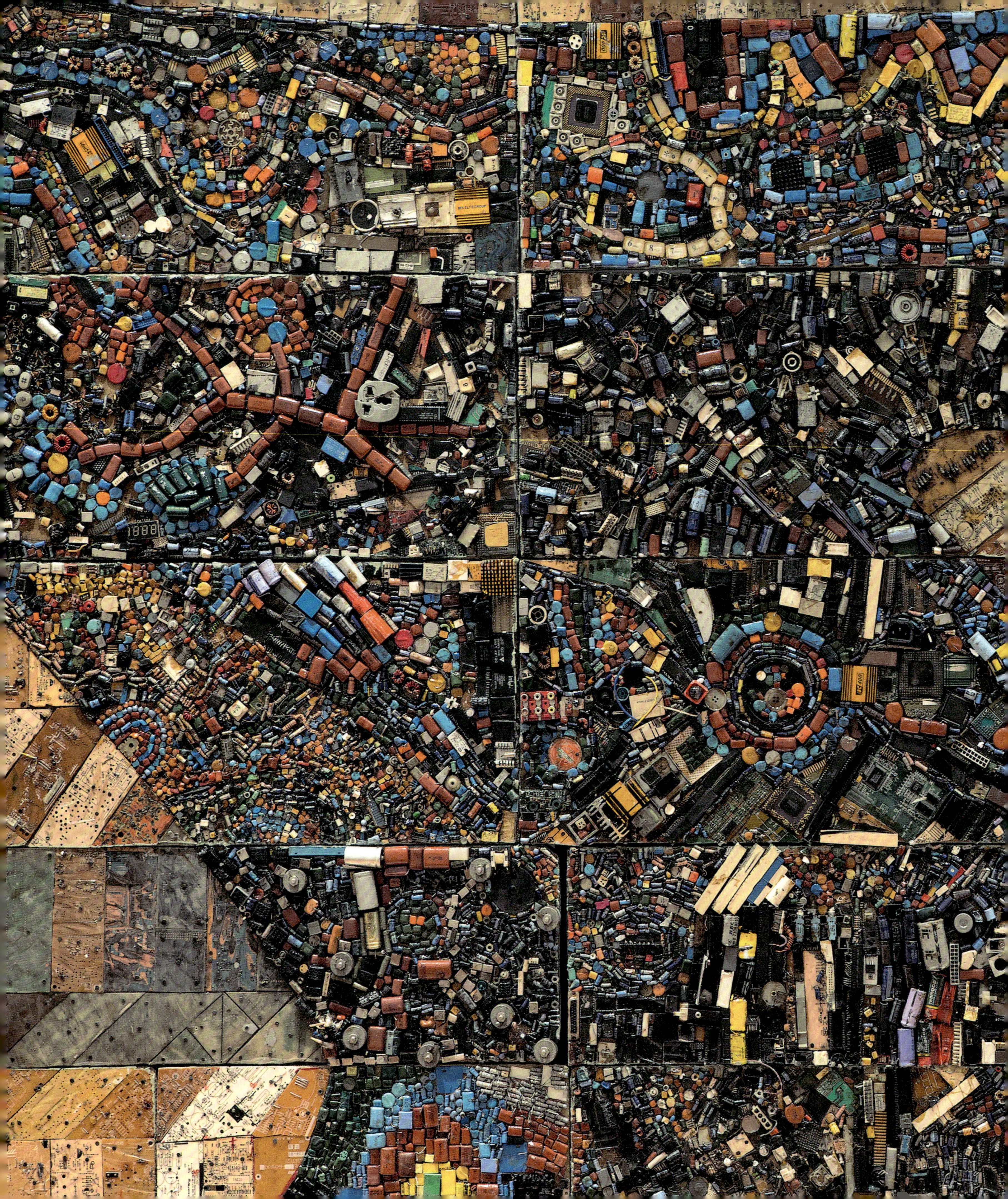

Nearly seven feet high and well over twenty feet long, *Tightrope: Zooming In* (2012; fig. 20) is composed of an untold number of motherboards, some with their chips, ports, and controllers still attached and others shaved clean. Each element provokes consideration of how we are "able, allowed, or made to see" as well as the story of every hand that has touched it and the weight of the desires and changes manifested by all such "vital" things. This technological "stuff" (as literary theorist Maurizia Boscagli has called it)—"unstable, recyclable, made of elements put in place by different networks of power and meaning"[21]—has itself become an "active principle," an "outside or alien power" pushing back on and into our lives.[22] To return to the words of the artist, "Technology is very tactile. It's connected to us. That doesn't mean it's going to be beneficial for us, 100 percent. It actually made us lose a lot of things, too. We have lost that calmness, tranquility and quiet. We have lost sitting down and spending time, touching one another and feeling one another."[23]

Sime lyrically captures this push-and-pull relationship between humans and technological matter in works such as *Tightrope: Zooming In*. Epic in scale, it reads like an aerial view of urban sprawl, seeming to swoop in on and swallow neatly groomed agricultural fields; or, perhaps, the darker areas can be read as a character akin to the mighty Atlas, the ancient Titan who takes the weight of the world onto his shoulders. The work is simultaneously a "chaos of castoffs," as art critic Holland Cotter described it[24]; a ganglion of mythical and terrestrial allusions; and a treatise on the impact of communication technologies on human interactions. Writing about the tableaus in the first "Tightrope" exhibition, art historian Kate Cowcher noted the inclusion of

> stripped-down motherboards from the 1970s, TV circuit boards with their traces indicating the former presence of a tube, a pre-LED lighting system known as Nixi [*sic*] tubes, and the remnants of obsolete manufacturers such as Zilog. Here, 1960s color-coded resistors and early read-only memory appear alongside an Intel i486 processor from 1991, and components marked as being manufactured in Japan, Malaysia, Singapore, Portugal, Brazil, Germany, and Russia.[25]

In this multinational cacophony is a history of global flows, of human aspirations and ambitions made into commodities, and an archive of love, loss, and renewal.

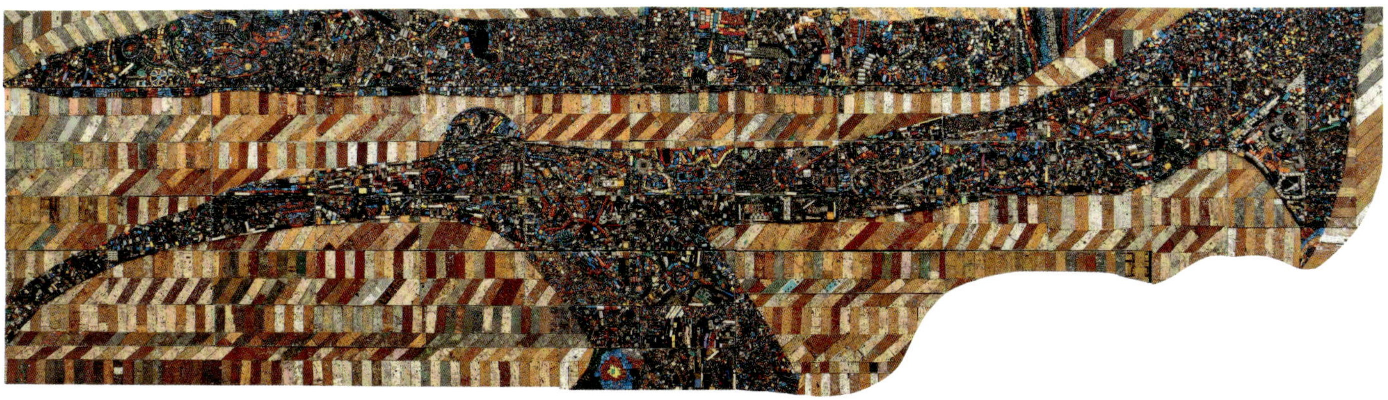

Fig. 20 Elias Sime, *Tightrope: Zooming In*, 2012. Reclaimed electronic components on panel, 83 ½ in. × 26 ft. 1 in. (212.1 × 795 cm). Toledo Museum of Art, Purchased with funds from the Florence Scott Libbey Bequest in Memory of her Father, Maurice A. Scott, 2018

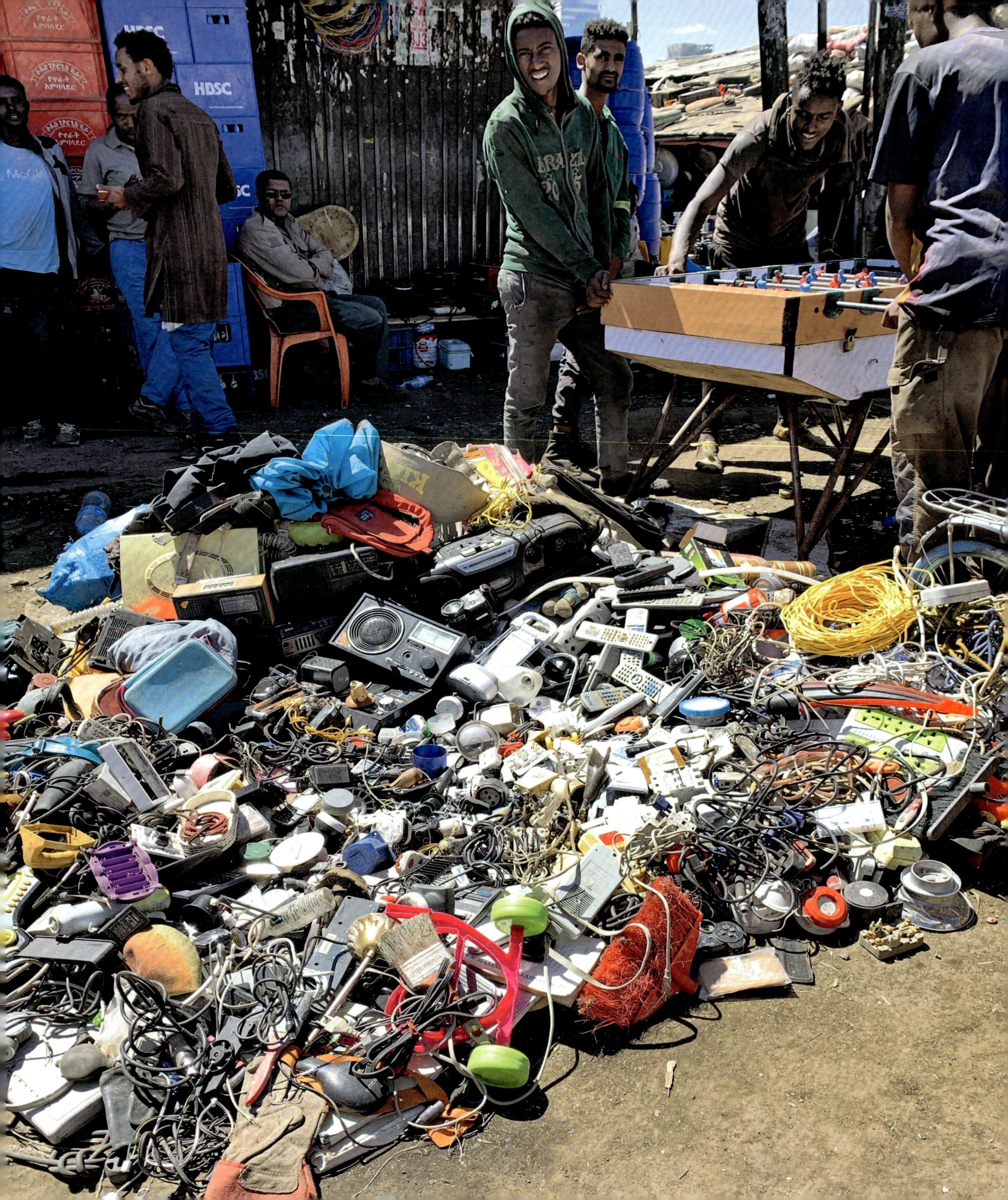
HBSC
HBSC

MOVING MATERIALS

Detritus is universal, but the travels of things—whether through something like the handing down between family members of spare buttons for clothing or the international traffic in e-waste—provide, in the words of anthropologist Anna Lowenhaupt Tsing, a "particular kind of universality" that "can only be charged in the sticky materiality of practical encounters."[26] Many of the circuit boards, wires, nails, and keyboard keys that populate Sime's compositions arrived as waste from distant lands, but not all of them. In addition to booths and shops for fashions and other merchandise, the Merkato, Addis Ababa's sprawling market, is home to multistory buildings housing, on the ground floor, new electronics for sale and, on the floors above, rebuilt equipment and repair services (figs. 21–24). In the vast, open spaces that surround such shops, entrepreneurs find or buy broken electronics and disassemble them so that their parts may be used again.

Sime knows the people from whom he acquires most of his materials. Merchants and laborers in the Merkato are familiar with Sime and, until recently, have sought out and stored materials specifically for the artist. In 2009, Assegued explained,

> One of Elias' unique characteristics is his relationship with his neighbors. When a family has a conflict, he is frequently asked to mediate. The children in the neighborhood look for his approval. They bring their report cards or the prizes they have won to show him. As a reward, he buys them cookies from the little neighborhood kiosk. Until recently, every Sunday, the children would bring piles of old and rusted bottle caps they had collected over the week to his small veranda. There, he would sit and negotiate prices with each of them. All the children would have to report to him what they had done with the money they had earned from their last sale. If they had spent it wisely, on school materials or to help their parents, he would reward them by buying more. Besides teaching the children responsibility—from selecting the right material, to earning and figuring out what to do with the money—this activity was also great fun for the children, their parents, and Elias. He says that watching the children early in the morning, eagerly waiting at his door to show him their collections, was one of the most exciting parts of his art.[27]

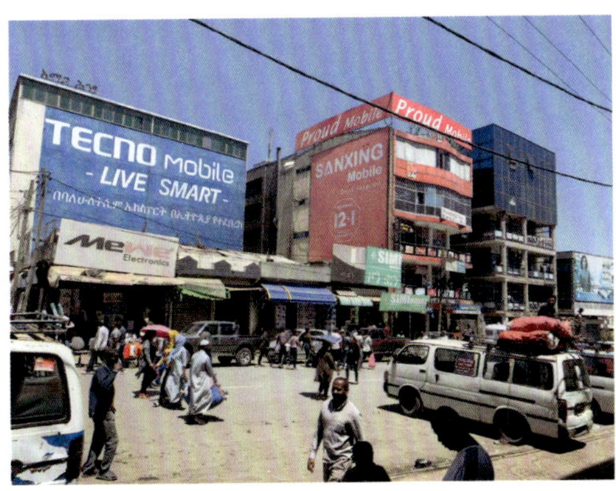

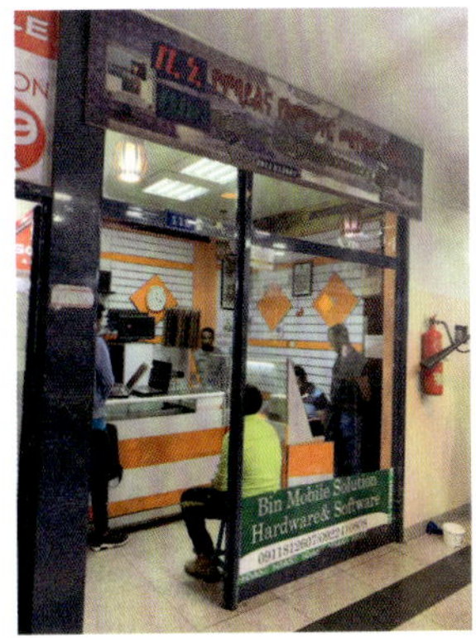

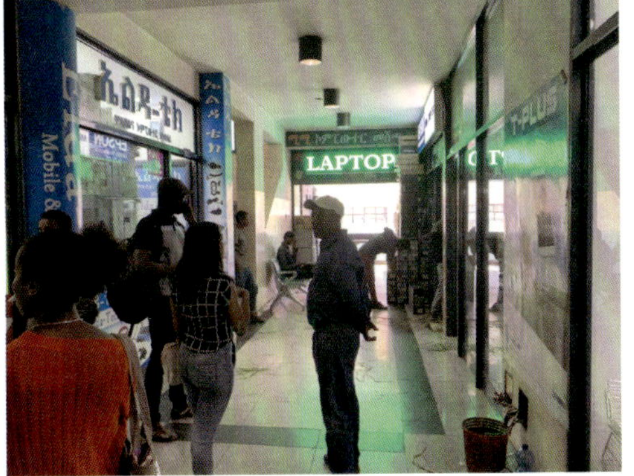

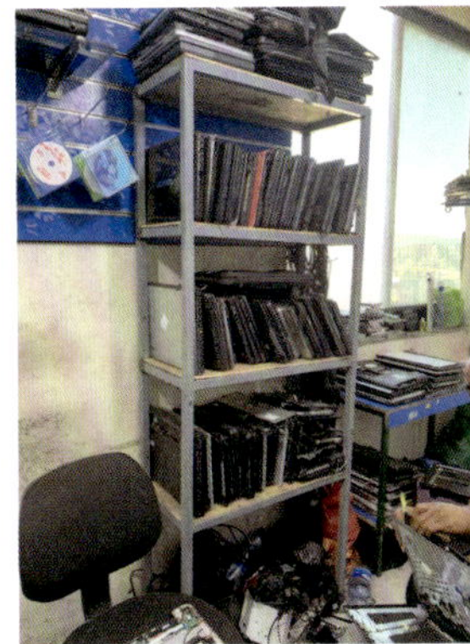

Figs. 21–24 The Merkato, Addis Ababa, February 2019

For the artist, "finding the material" is not just exciting; the process is "itself a part of the art." It is never easy to accumulate enough material for Sime's ambitious projects—he recounts that it took fifteen years to amass sufficient electronic components for his first "Tightrope" exhibition—and it is becoming increasingly difficult as supplies get exhausted or merchants grow wary on account of the attention the artist is receiving. According to Sime, the most challenging aspect of his practice is sourcing the material. Regarding the electrical material, he says that, these days, "It is like gold, you can't really find it"—which causes him some anxiety that he will not be able to complete the seemingly infinite ideas he continues to pour out in notes and sketches but also challenges him and propels his work in new directions. In general, the artist has yet to exhaust the potential he sees in any given material or theme. Of the techniques he has tried to date—stitching yarn, manipulating mud, melting plastic, adhering buttons, nailing wires, gluing keyboard keys—the only one to which he says he would not return is stitching, because it is now too hard on his eyes. The artist moves on because a new material captures his interest or sometimes because, even when the same materials are available, he resists complacency and strives to push himself to see new connections, find new ideas in the materials, and pursue new directions in his work.

In 2019, in one of Sime's most recent efforts, he spent months intricately weaving multicolored electrical wires to evoke the patterns and techniques of West African strip weavers. Assegued recounts that the artist laid the massive composition out one evening, and when she returned the next morning, she found that he had used a blowtorch to burn a large section of it. Even though Sime had already used a blowtorch experimentally in an earlier work featuring reclaimed electrical wire, Assegued was flabbergasted. She asked why he had done it, and he replied that, while the weaving technique was new with this work, he nevertheless did not want to become complacent. It was time to force himself to try something new, to approach his materials anew.[28] Sime titled the work *Tightrope: I Burned It* (fig. 11).

While the artist asserts that he begins every work with a design, his sketches and plans are more like notes. The final compositions emerge as he negotiates color, form, concept, and his own drive to metamorphize in his practice, like the caterpillars and frogs he so admires. He concedes that "of course it [his work] is designed. Of course there is thought. The problem is, how do I manage these and still have it look good." Sometimes the story emerges from a color, and at other times, from a shape, a technique, or a location.

The work to which Sime had taken flames before *Tightrope: I Burned It* was a smaller piece entitled *Tightrope: (11) While Observing . . .* (2018; fig. 26), in which braided green wires undulate around a large scorch mark. The composition recalls a 2004 work, *Gorée Island* (fig. 25), in which a silhouette shaped like a landmass emerges from a field of blue, gray, mauve, and pink yarn embroidered into patterns of swirling fish. Sime named this earlier work after an island just off the coast of Dakar, Senegal, whose history testifies to how human entanglements are suffused with brutality and not just beauty. From the fifteenth to the nineteenth century, Gorée Island was one of the largest centers for the trade in captured and enslaved Africans along the West African

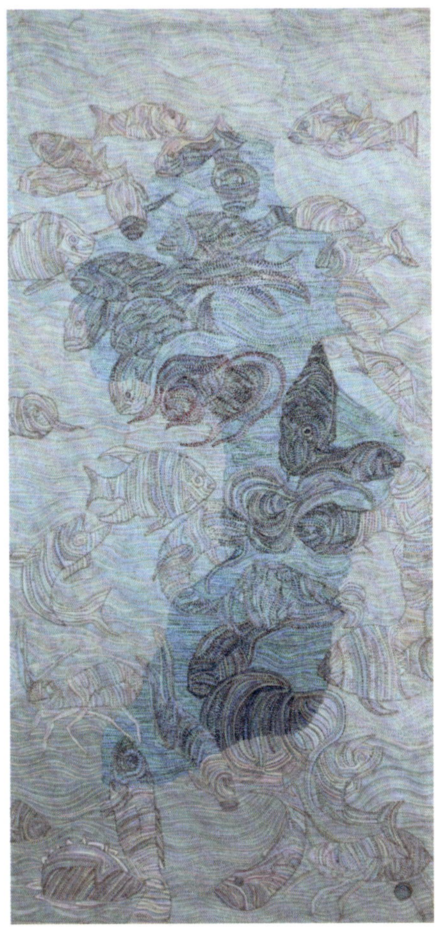

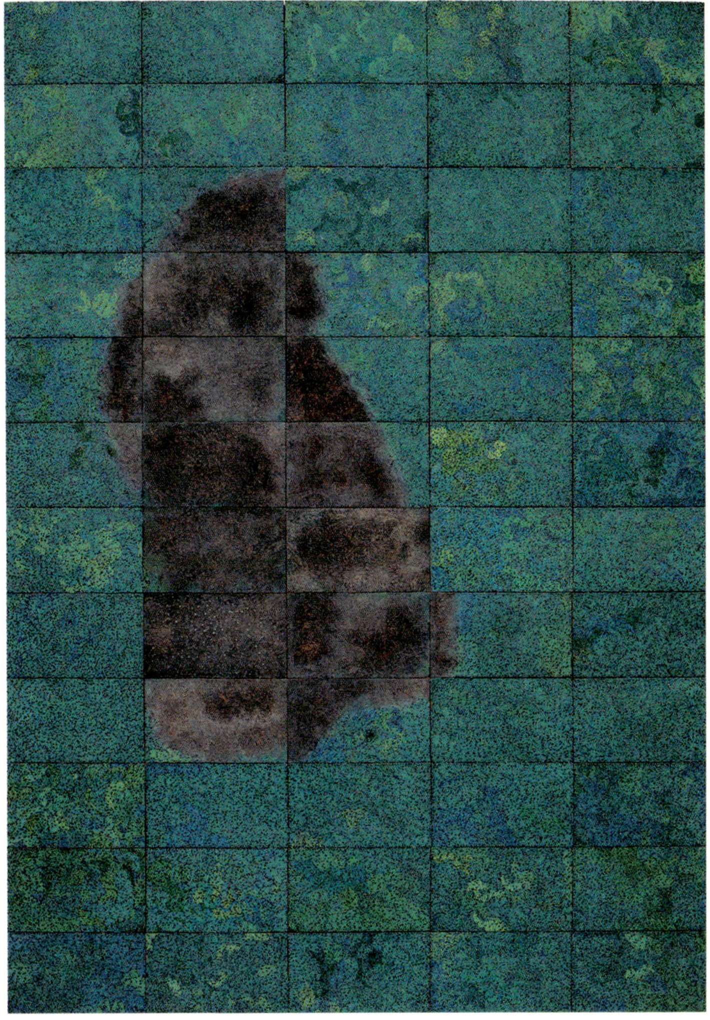

coast.[29] As if to suture the wounds bound up in this history—and to tease out the metaphorical associations between literal thread and human connections across distance and time—Sime sewed. As Assegued has suggested, the artist is "continually mending life" in his selection of materials and techniques.[30] While the 2004 work is not cartographically accurate, its amorphous central form, identified by the title as an island, reveals an additional layer by which to understand the "blobs," splotches, cells, and astral bodies that recur in the artist's work. The isolated dark mark of *Tightrope: (11) While Observing . . .*, when read as an island, seems not just to burn through the layers of insulated wire but also to cut through the web of history.

Fig. 25 Elias Sime, *Gorée Island*, 2004.
Yarn on canvas, 78 11/16 × 39 5/16 in. (199.8 × 99.9 cm).
Collection of Daniel R. Lewis, Miami

Fig. 26 Elias Sime, *Tightrope: (11) While Observing . . .*, 2018.
Reclaimed insulated wire on panel, 108 5/8 × 78 5/8 in. (276 × 200 cm).
Courtesy of the artist and James Cohan, New York

Sime's return to forms and subjects found in his practice fourteen years earlier reveals the process-based nature of his practice and the breadth of his inspirations, some of which likely stem from his passion for reading. Just as he collects cloth and computer parts, he also collects books. His home is filled with volumes of all sorts, especially ones related to the history of materials. And like the multivalent materials he uses, Sime's approach to his practice is to never consider it finished or "done." His ideas and formal explorations also find renewals and returns.

CODA: THE SCALE OF THINGS

Although Sime's freestanding and wall-engaged works both range in size, the artist is clear that he is "not too crazy about making small art." He says, "It stresses me when I do small art. It bothers me. . . . What I like to do is something big, something wide." The larger the work, the greater the capacity for new ideas and connections to emerge. Sime makes room to tackle new formal and technical challenges, to make space for the consideration of important histories both local and global, and to take "seriously the idea that technological and natural materialities [are] themselves actors alongside and within us."[31] For, as political theorists Diana Coole and Samantha Frost remind us,

> As human beings, we inhabit an ineluctably material world. We live our everyday lives surrounded by, immersed in, matter. We are ourselves composed of matter. We experience its restlessness and intransigence even as we reconfigure and consume it. . . . In light of this massive materiality, how could we be anything other than materialist? How could we ignore the power of matter . . . ?[32]

From intricately stitched works like *Gorée Island* to the grandeur of *Tightrope: Zooming In* and current experiments such as *Tightrope: I Burned It*, Sime brings his own personal touch to the bags, buttons, fabrics, flip-flops, motherboards, mud, skins, wires, and yarn he collects. From this "stuff," which countless hands have touched, he unleashes a vital materialism that is uncompromising in its aesthetic, incisive in its intellectual underpinnings, and adroit in its technical realization. In an era in which conceptualism tends to be favored over visual pleasure in the arts, Sime has managed to wed form and content—and in ways that promise to yield more surprises in the future.

Karen E. Milbourne is Senior Curator at the National Museum of African Art, Smithsonian Institution, Washington, DC.

Epigraph: Anna Lowenhaupt Tsing, *Friction: An Ethnography of Global Connection* (Princeton, NJ: Princeton University Press, 2005), 1.

1. Unless indicated otherwise, all quotations are from conversations held between the author, Elias Sime, Meskerem Assegued, and Ugochukwu-Smooth C. Nzewi in Addis Ababa between February 22 and March 3, 2019. This particular conversation took place on February 25. Tremendous thanks go to Elias, Meski, and Smooth for their generosity of time and ideas throughout this busy period. Additional thanks go to the Wellin Museum and the James Cohan gallery—and to their outstanding teams—for their support of this project.

2. All the works in Sime's "Tightrope" series use electronic components to explore the tensions between the connectedness promised by technology and the experience of isolation in an increasingly technological world.

3. Mik Awake, "Ethiopian Enterprise," *Art News* 117, no. 2 (Summer 2018): 74.

4. Jane Bennet, "A Vitalist Stopover on the Way to a New Materialism," in Diana Coole and Samantha Frost, eds., *New Materialisms: Ontology, Agency, and Politics* (Durham, NC, and London: Duke University Press, 2010), 47.

5. Jane Bennet, *Vibrant Matter: A Political Ecology of Things* (Durham, NC, and London: Duke University Press, 2010), 20.

6. Meskerem Assegued, "Green Flame," in *New Crowned Hope: Festival Wien 14.11–13.12.2006* (Vienna: Wiener Festwochen, 2006), 226.

7. Makda Teklemichael, "Artist: Elias Sime," in Christine Y. Kim, ed., *Flow*, exh. cat. (New York: Studio Museum in Harlem, 2004), 98.

8. Mekdes Asefa, "Tightrope," *It! Magazine* (Addis Ababa), January 2014, 11.

9. Arjun Appadurai, *The Social Life of Things: Commodities in Cultural Perspective* (Cambridge: Cambridge University Press, 1988).

10. Transliterations from Amharic to English spell this, and other names, variably. The name of the neighborhood is most commonly rendered "Kirkos," but I have chosen to follow the spelling used by Meskerem Assegued, particularly as it is more phonetic. The Cherqos market is no longer in existence, and Sime now frequents the larger Merkato.

11. Meskerem Assegued, "A Retrospective Observation of Elias Sime," *African Identities* 6, no. 4 (2008): 477.

12. Meskerem Assegued, "Elias Sime: Eye of the Needle, Eye of the Heart," exh. brochure (Santa Monica, CA: Santa Monica Museum of Art, 2009), n.p.

13. Bennet, *Vibrant Matter*, 21.

14. See Ugochukwu-Smooth C. Nzewi's essay in this volume, pp. 44–47, for a brief account of this historical period.

15. Rosalind Krauss, "Sculpture in the Expanded Field," *October*, no. 8 (Spring 1979): 30. Krauss was not, of course, referring to either Sime's or Yetmgeta's specific practices but was discussing sculpture more generally.

16. Abebe Zegeye, "The Seamingly [*sic*] Seamless Subversion of Sime," *East African Literary and Cultural Studies* 3, no. 1 (2017): 53.

17. Assegued, "Retrospective Observation," 489.

18. Ibid., 495. It should be noted that at Zoma, one building (containing the restrooms and the coin museum) is adorned with sculpted plants, not animals. The educational space is decorated with pre-Amharic numerals, and the central structure celebrates the metamorphoses of the butterfly from egg to larva to caterpillar, all arranged in the pattern of an outstretched wing.

19. Allen Roberts, *Animals in African Art: From the Familiar to the Marvelous*, exh. cat. (New York: Museum for African Art; Munich: Prestel, 1995), 16.

20. Hal Foster, *Vision and Visuality* (New York: New Press, 1988), ix.

21. Maurizia Boscagli, *Stuff Theory: Everyday Objects, Radical Materialism* (New York: Bloomsbury, 2014), 5.

22. Bennet, "Vitalist Stopover," 47.

23. Katy Donohugh, "Elias Sime," *Whitewall*, no. 53 (Spring 2019): 90.

24. Holland Cotter, "Elias Sime Recycles Discarded Objects into Abstract Works," *New York Times*, October 1, 2015.

25. Kate Cowcher, "Tightrope: Elias Sime," *African Arts* 47, no. 4 (2014): 88–90. It should be noted that Zilog, Inc., an American manufacturer of 8-bit and 16-bit microcontrollers, remains in operation.

26. Tsing, *Friction*, 1.

27. Assegued, "Sime: Eye of the Needle," 2009.

28. Lunch conversation between the author, James Cohan, Meskerem Assegued, Elias Sime, and Christine Mullen Kreamer, Washington, DC, April 22, 2019.

29. Assegued, "Retrospective Observation," 481.

30. Today, guided tours and a museum offer respectful and poignant examinations of this history, but the island itself is also home to a resilient population, with artists at work surrounded by water, sky, and historic architecture. See https://whc.unesco.org/en/list/26/.

31. Bennet, "Vitalist Stopover," 47.

32. Diana Coole and Samantha Frost, "Introducing the New Materialism," in Coole and Frost, *New Materialisms*, 1.

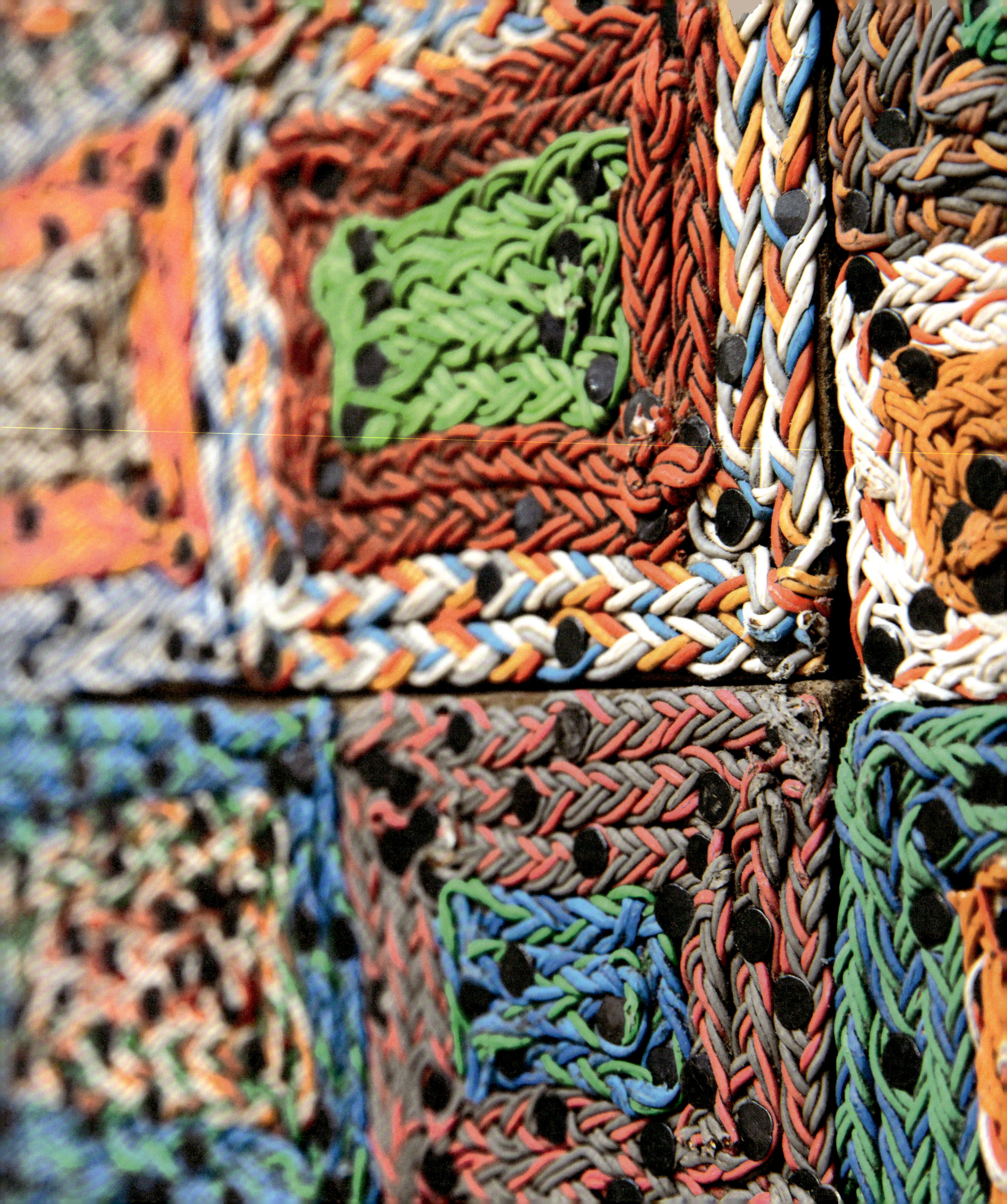

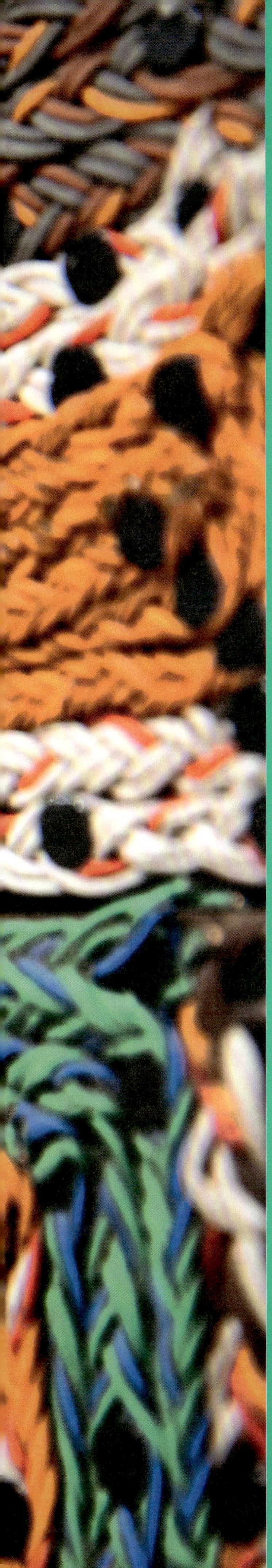

TIGHTROPE

PLATES

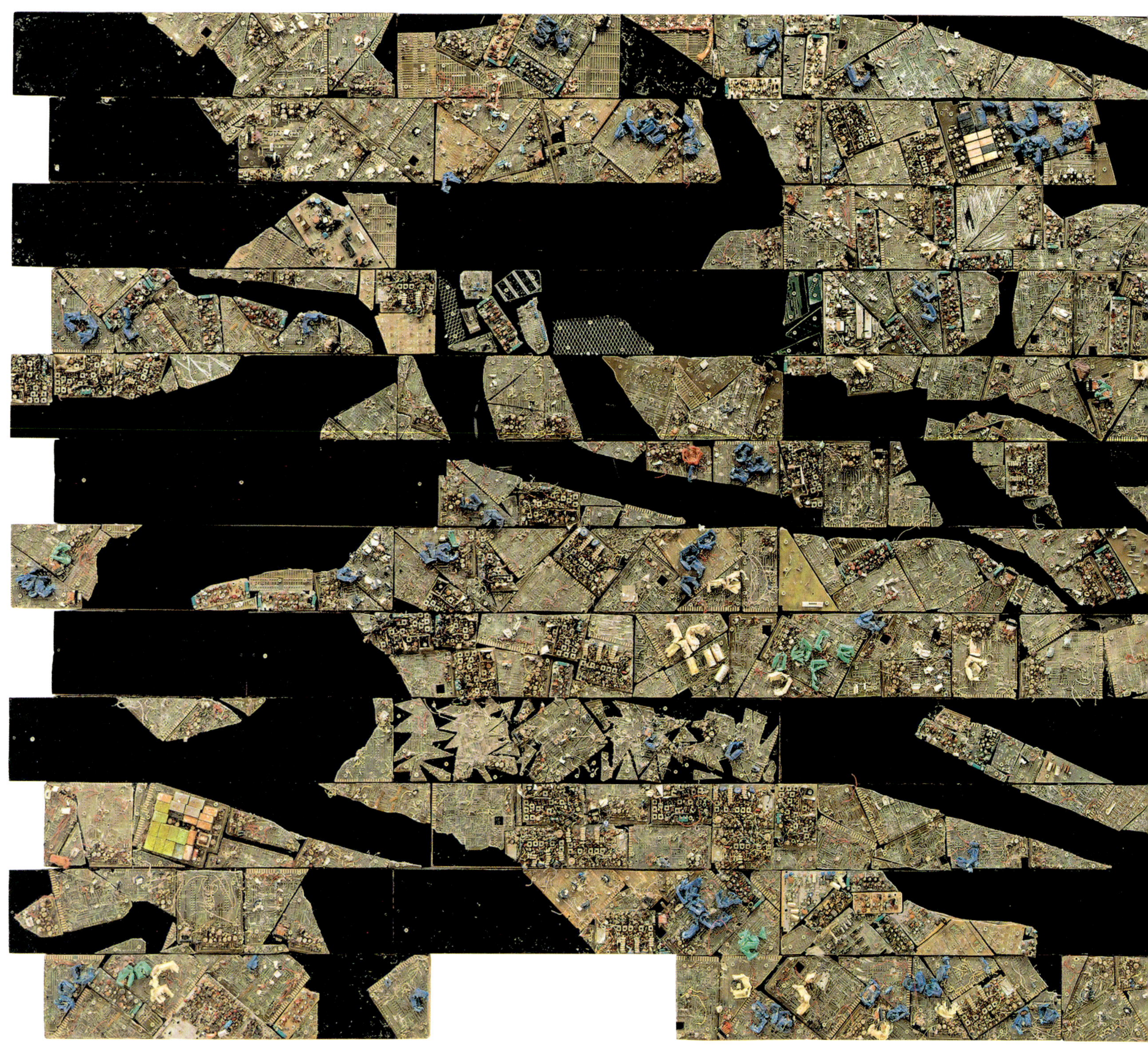

PLATE 8

Tightrope 3

2009–14 | Reclaimed electronic components and fiberglass on panel | 81 ½ in. × 16 ft. 3 in. (207 × 495.3 cm)
Private collection, New York

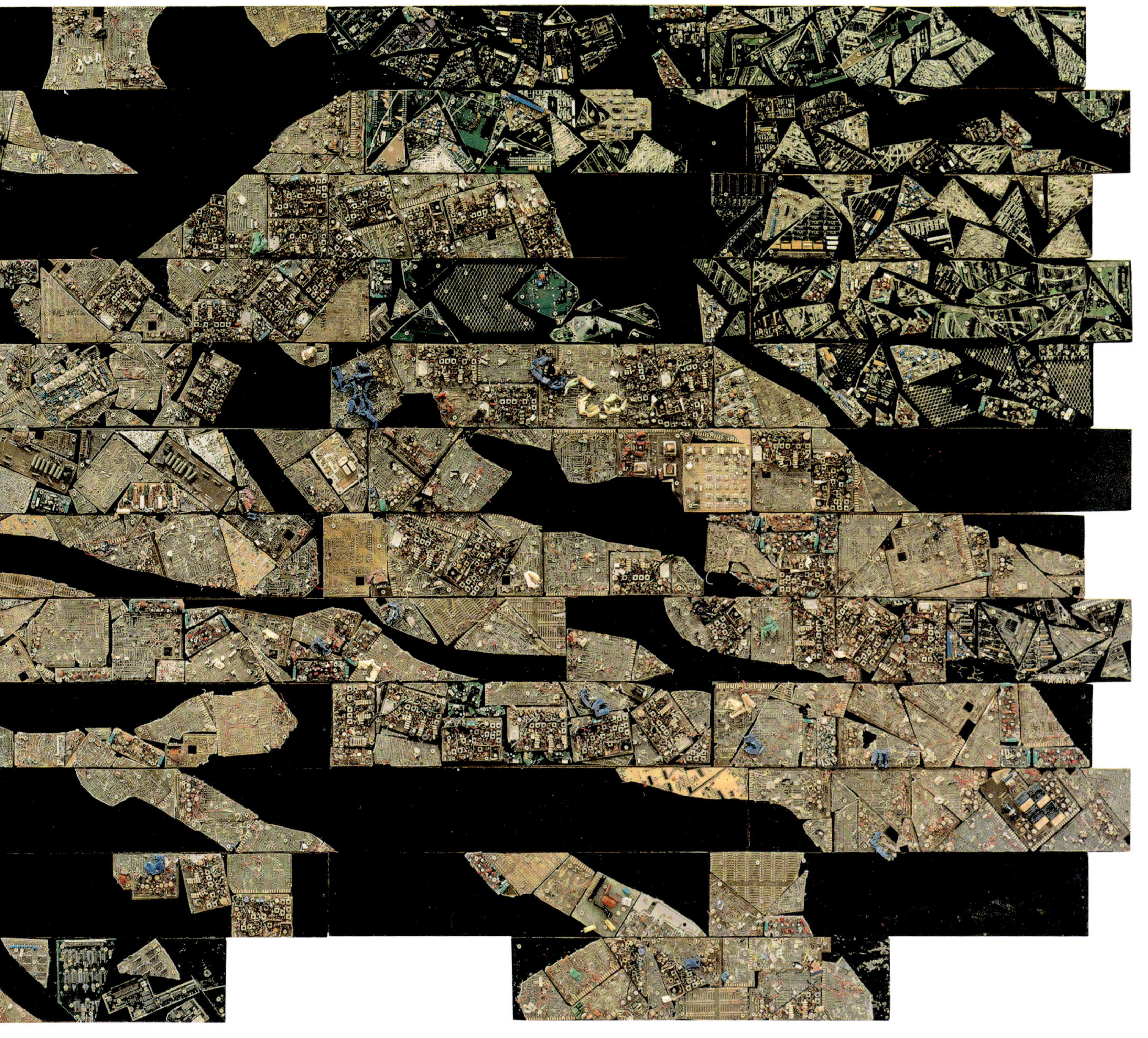

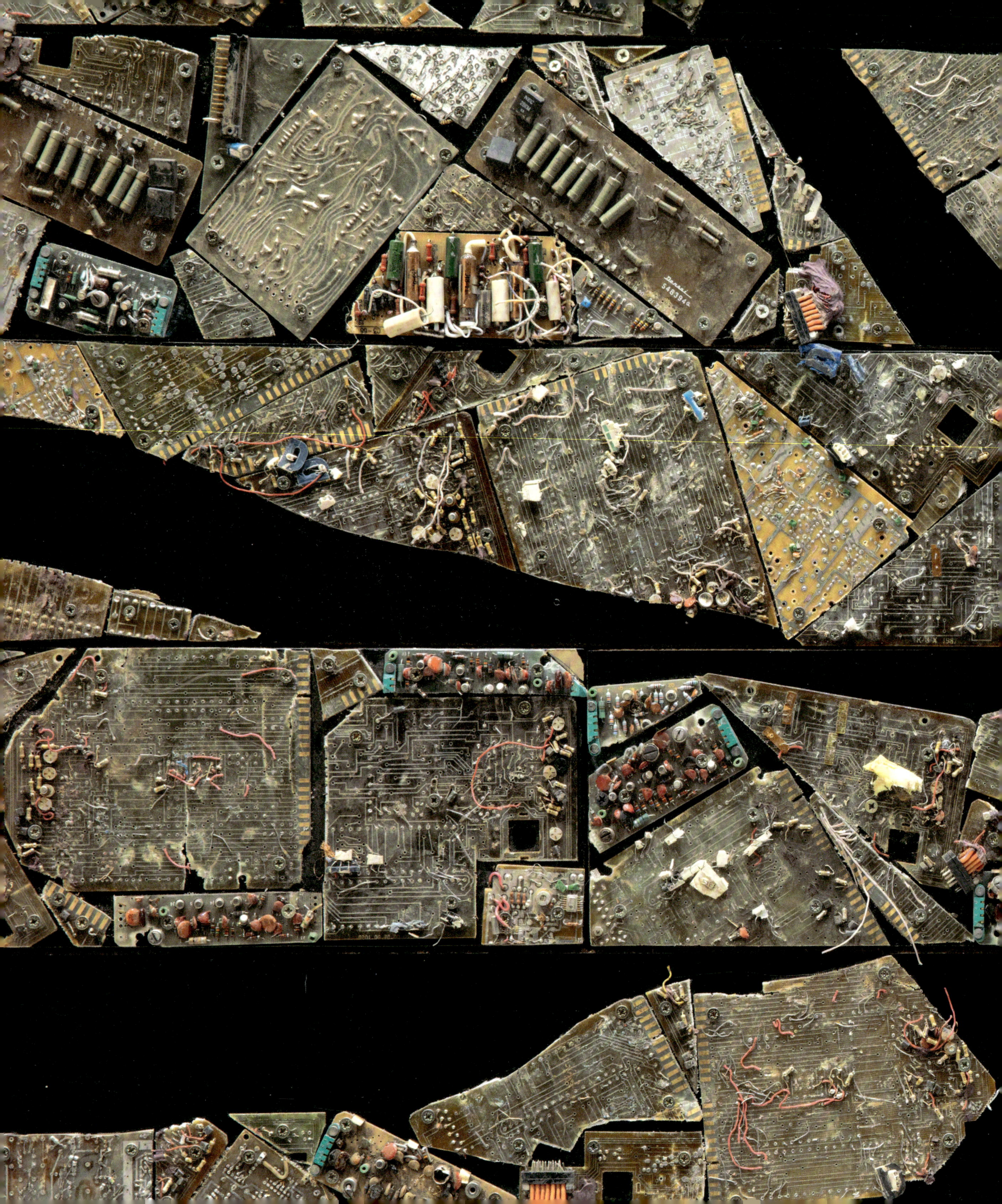

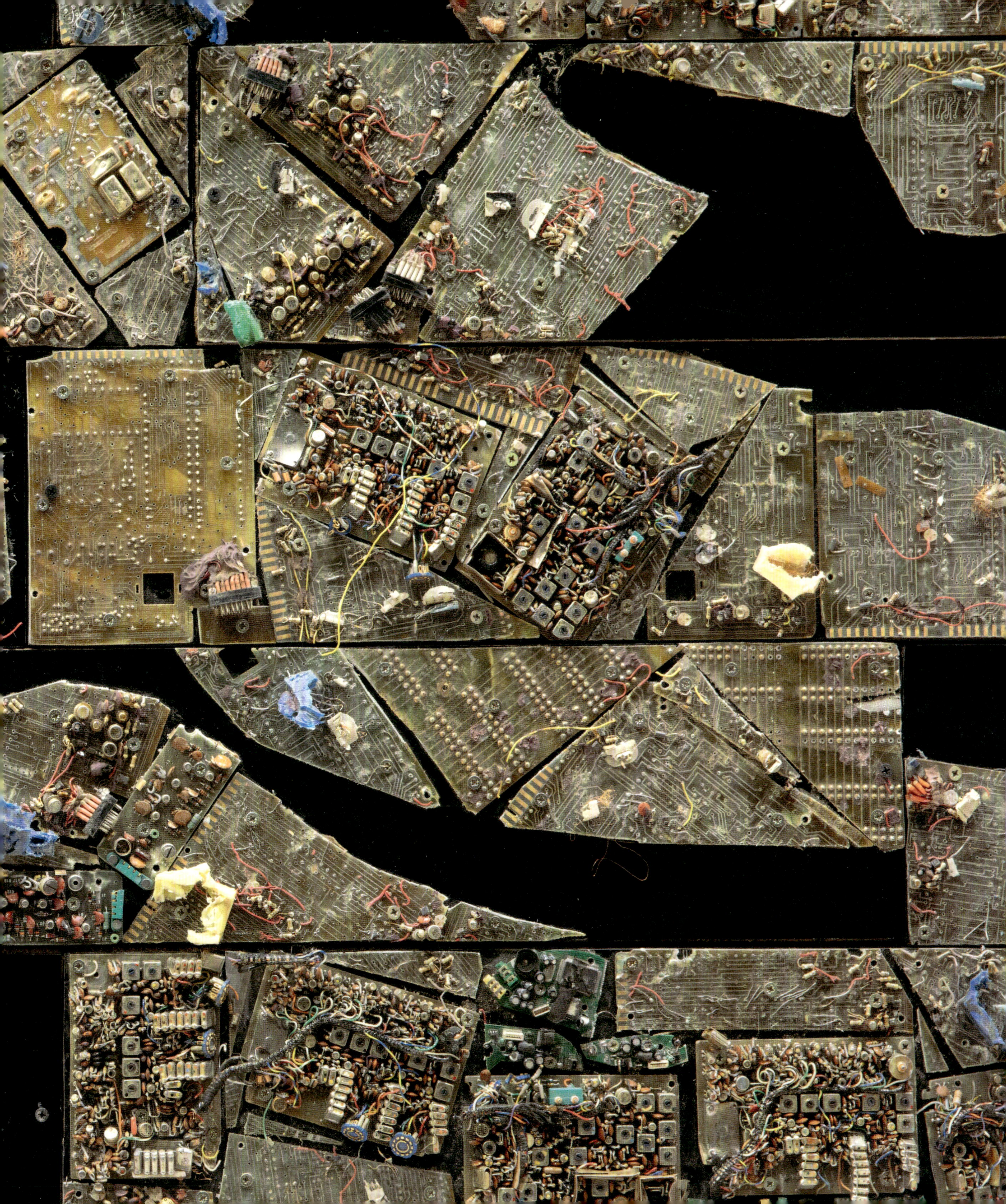

PLATE 9

Tightrope 8

2009–14 | Reclaimed electronic components on panel | 44 1⁄16 × 70 13⁄16 in. (112 × 180 cm)
Private collection, New York

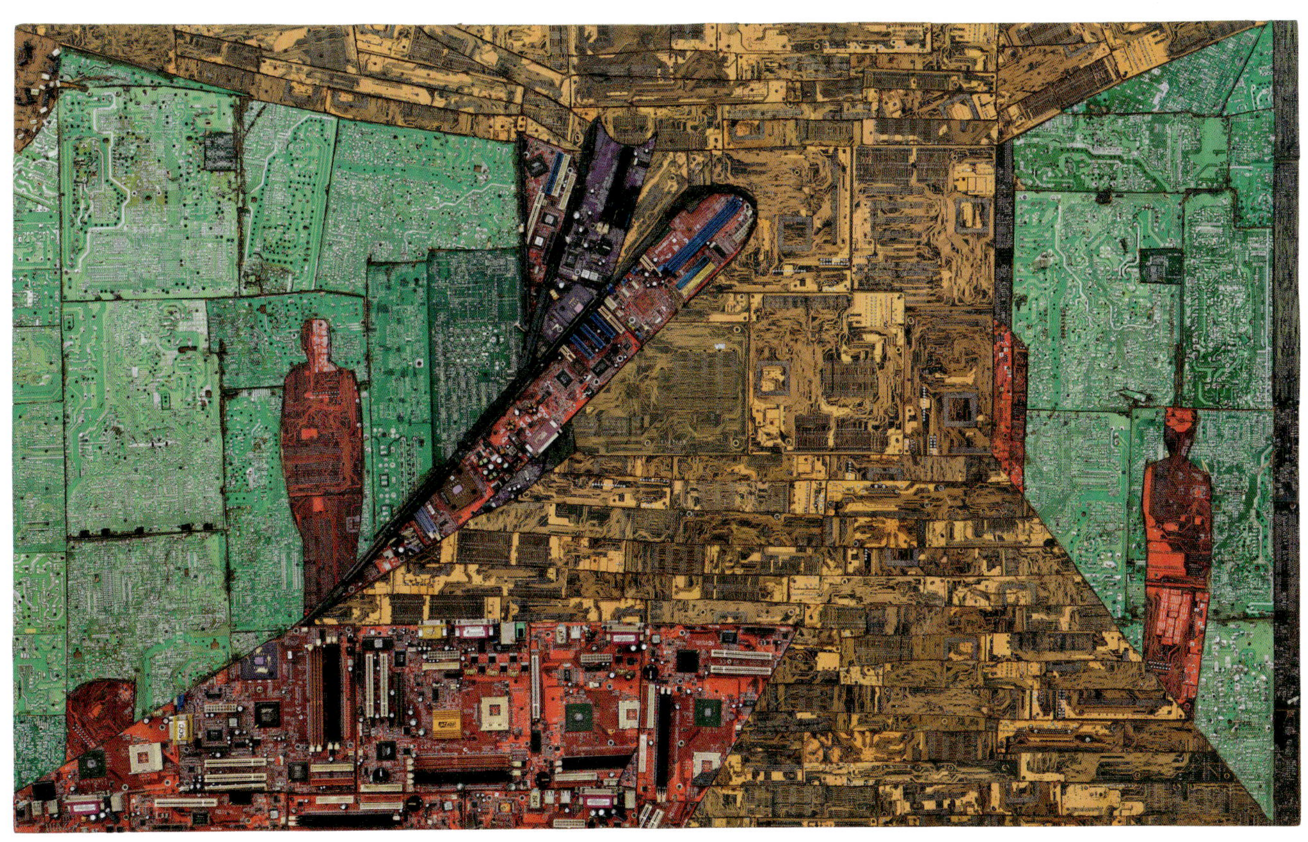

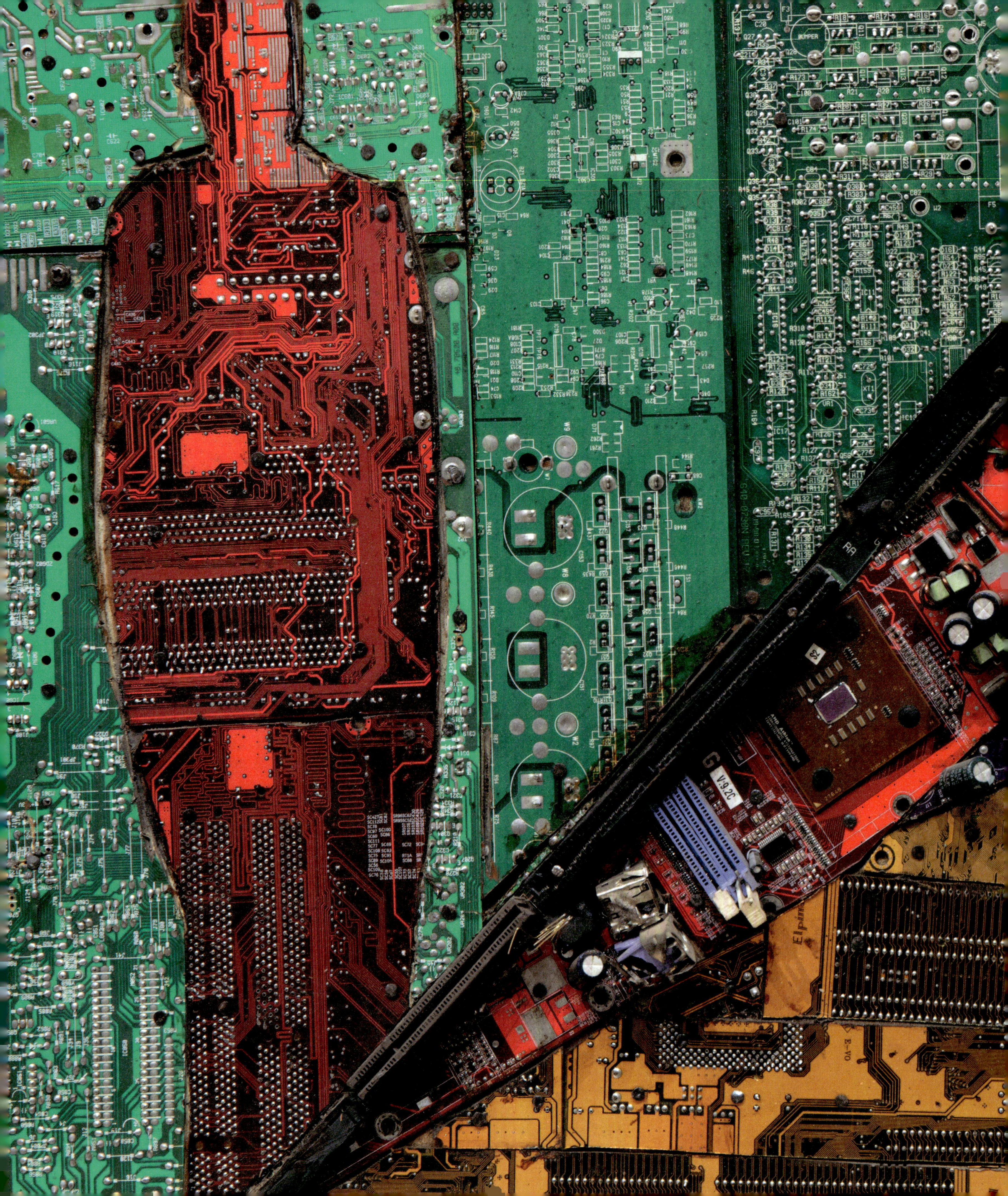

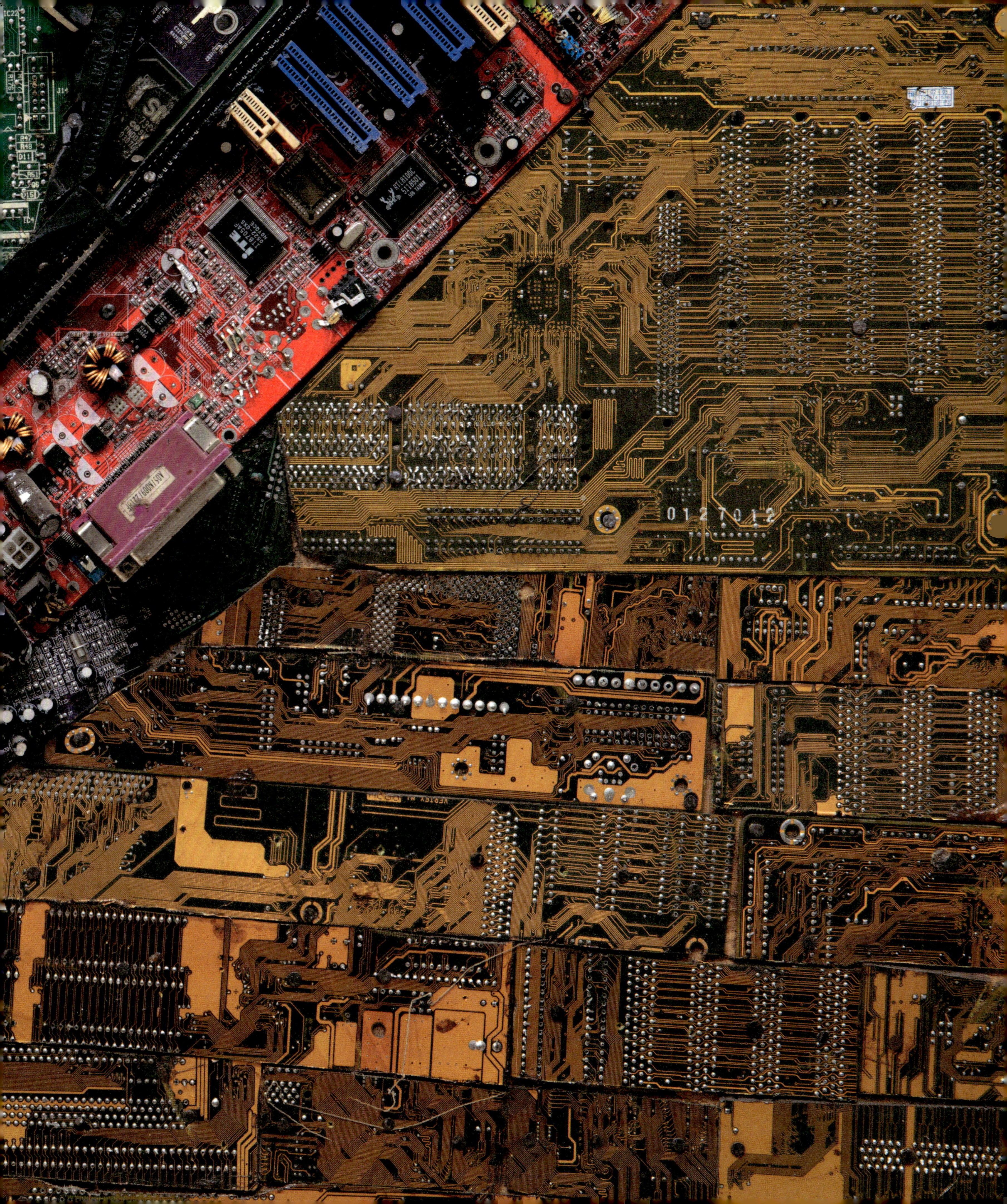

PLATE 10

Tightrope: Hands and Feet

2009–14 | Reclaimed electronic components and insulated wire on panel | 71 in. × 10 ft. 10 ¼ in. (180.3 × 330.8 cm)
Collection of Nancy and Joseph Chetrit, New York

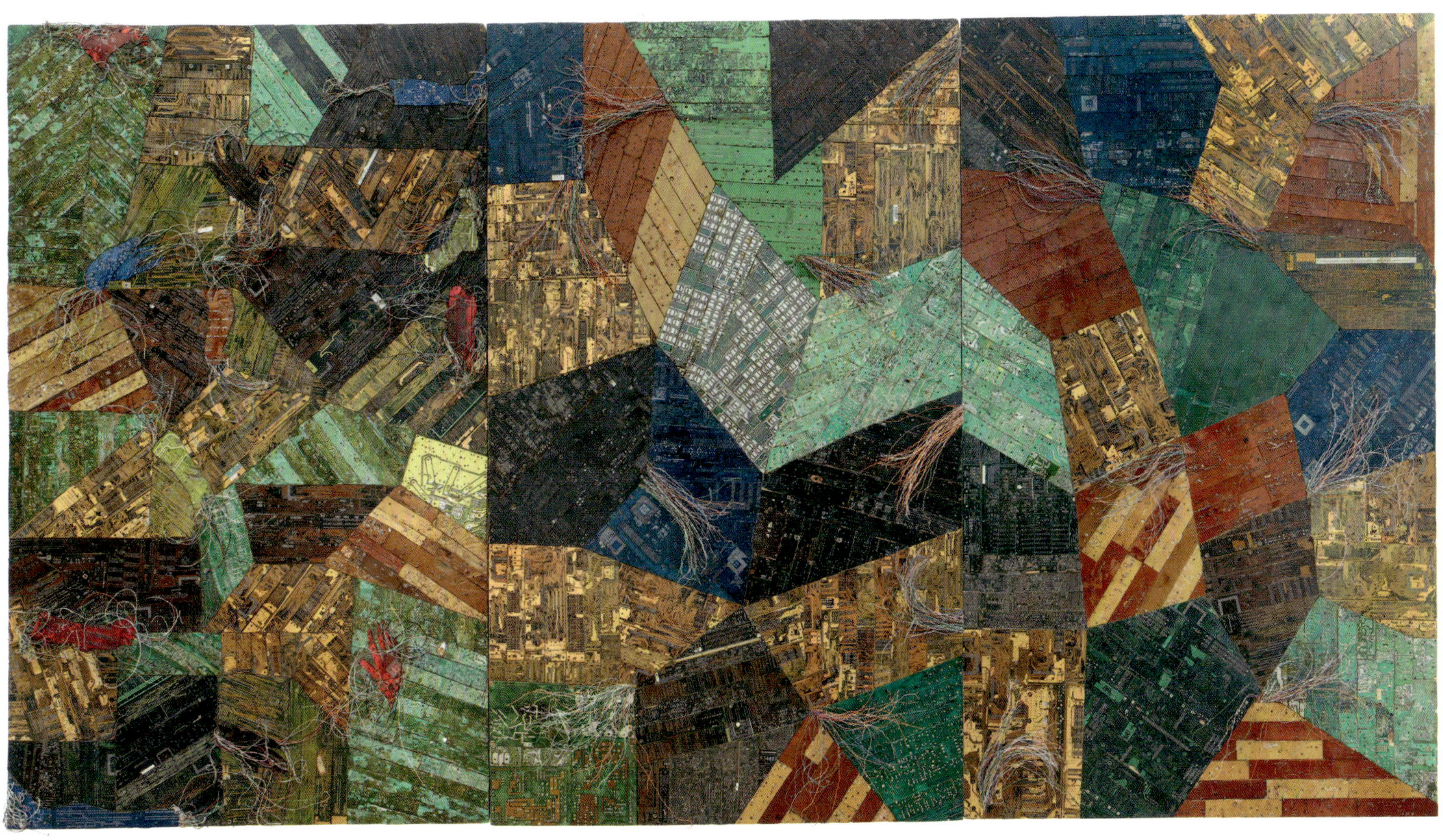

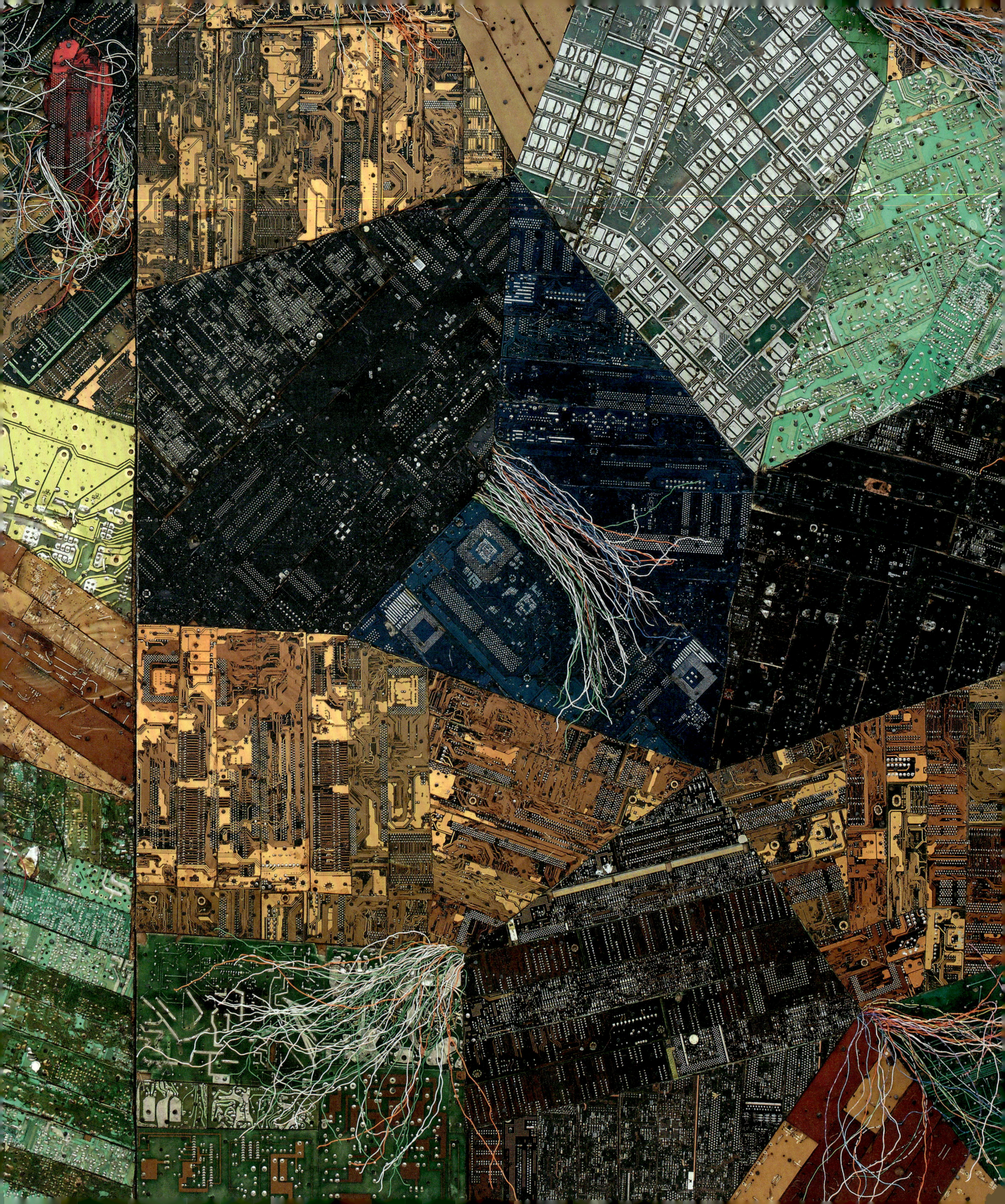

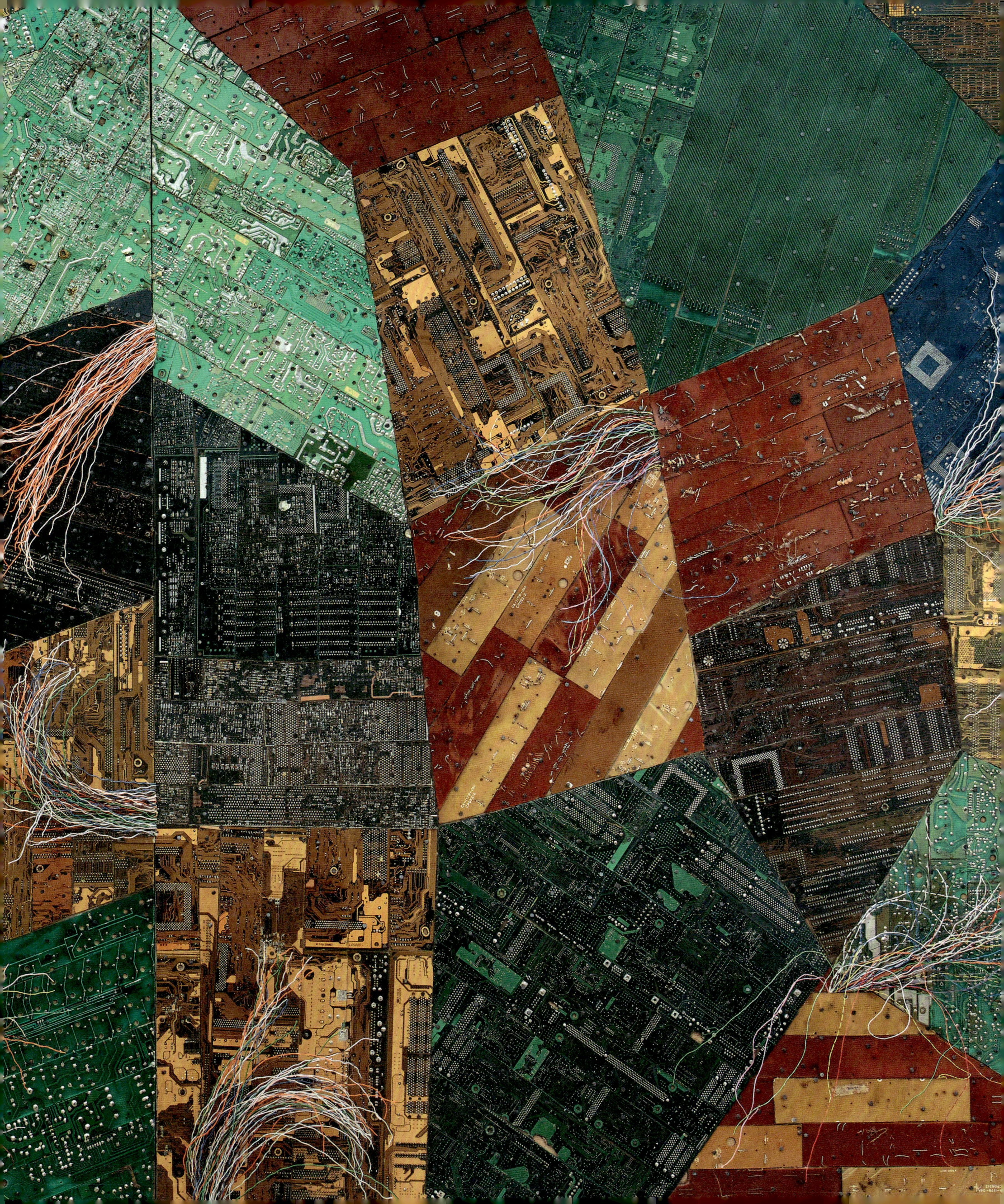

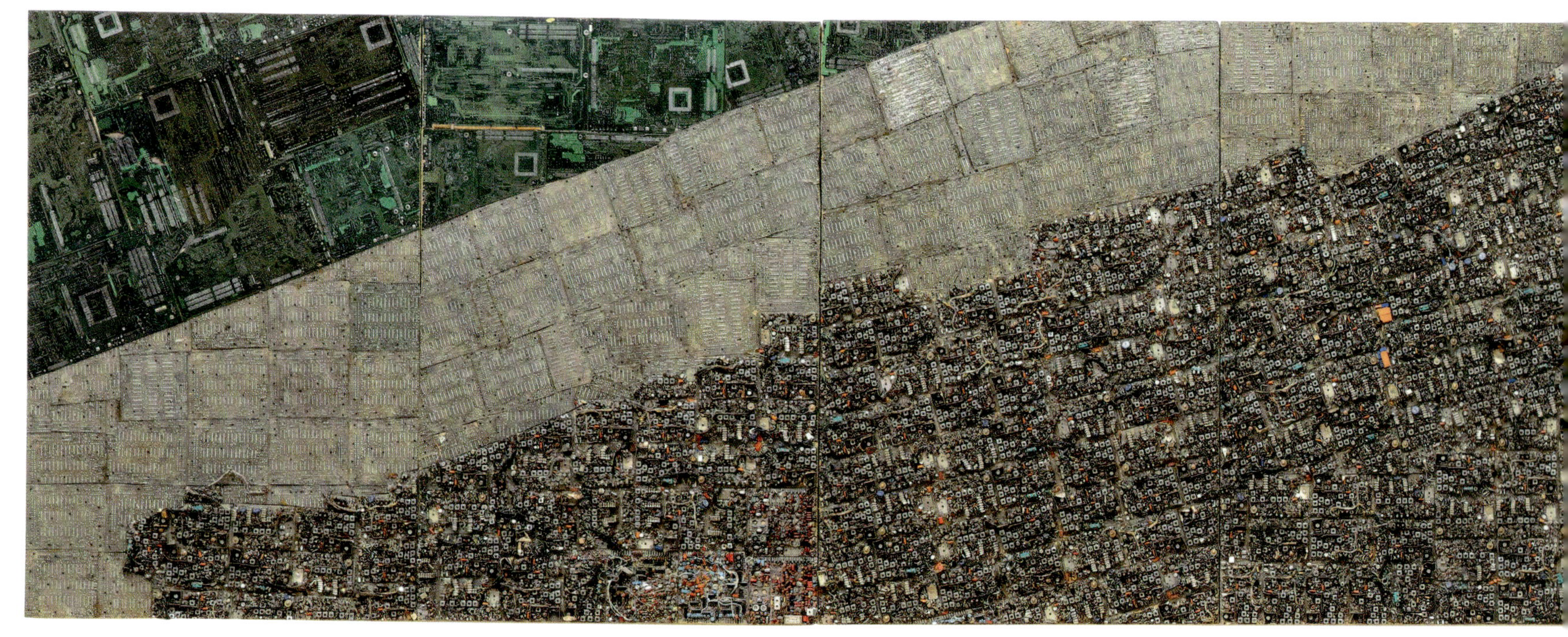

PLATE 11

Tightrope: On the Edge

2015 | Reclaimed electronic components on panel | 48 in. × 21 ft. 6 ¾ in. (121.9 × 657.2 cm)
Kemper Museum of Contemporary Art, Kansas City, MO | Bebe and Crosby Kemper Collection,
Museum purchase made possible by a gift from the William T. Kemper Charitable Trust, UMB Bank, n.a., Trustee

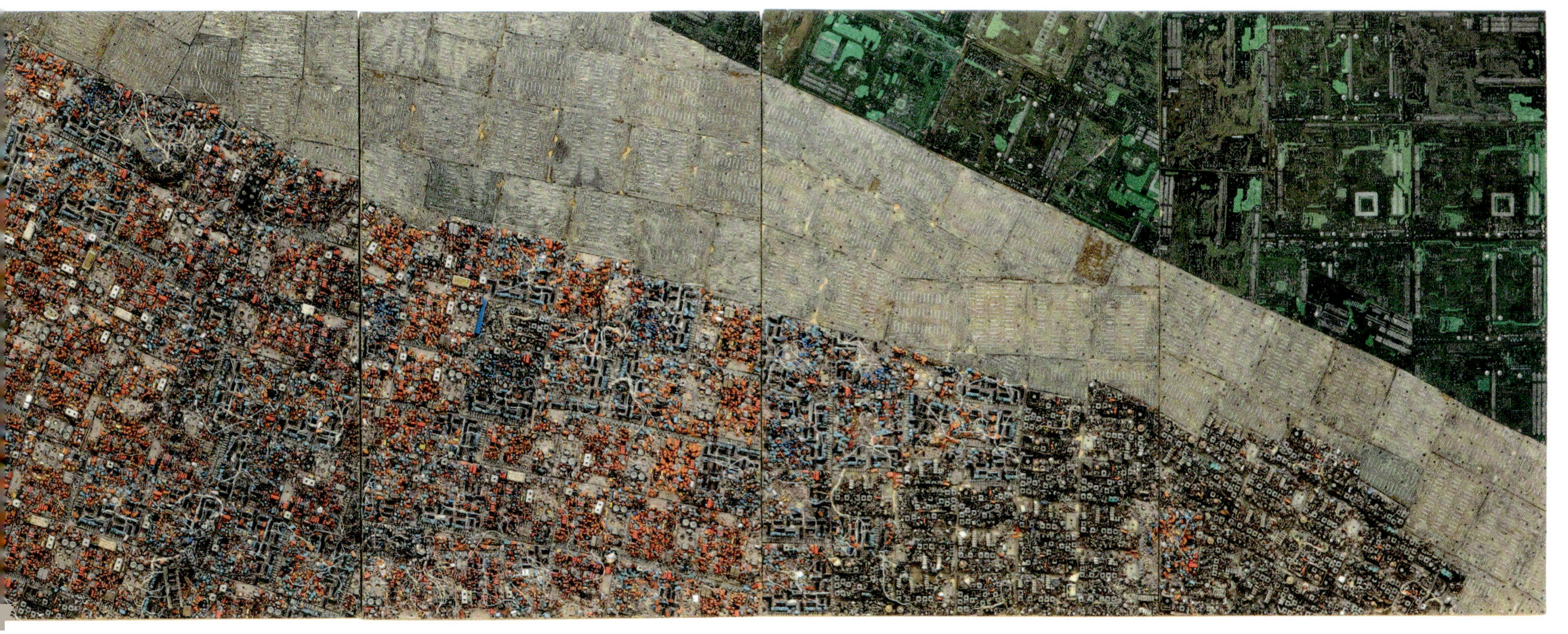

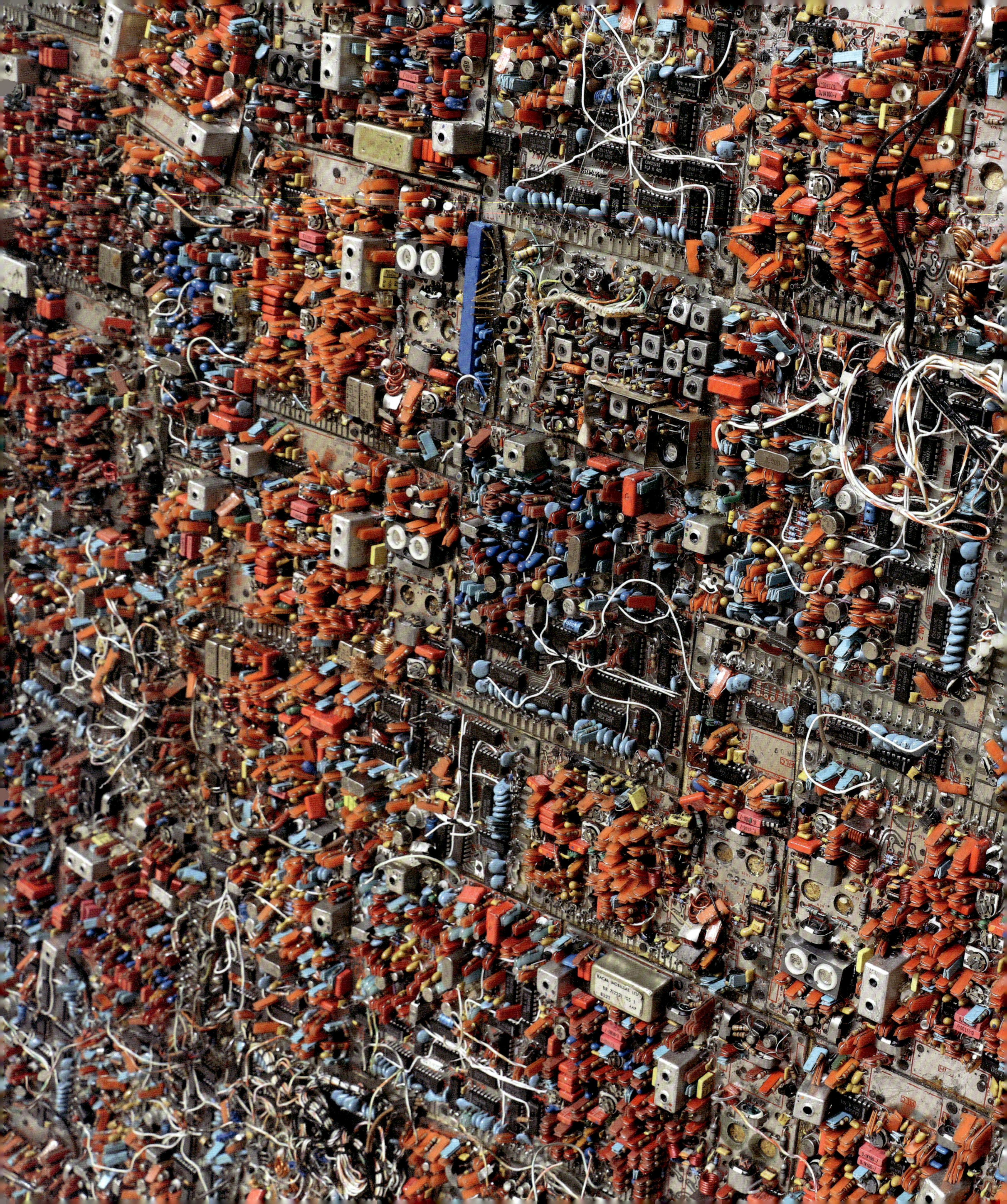

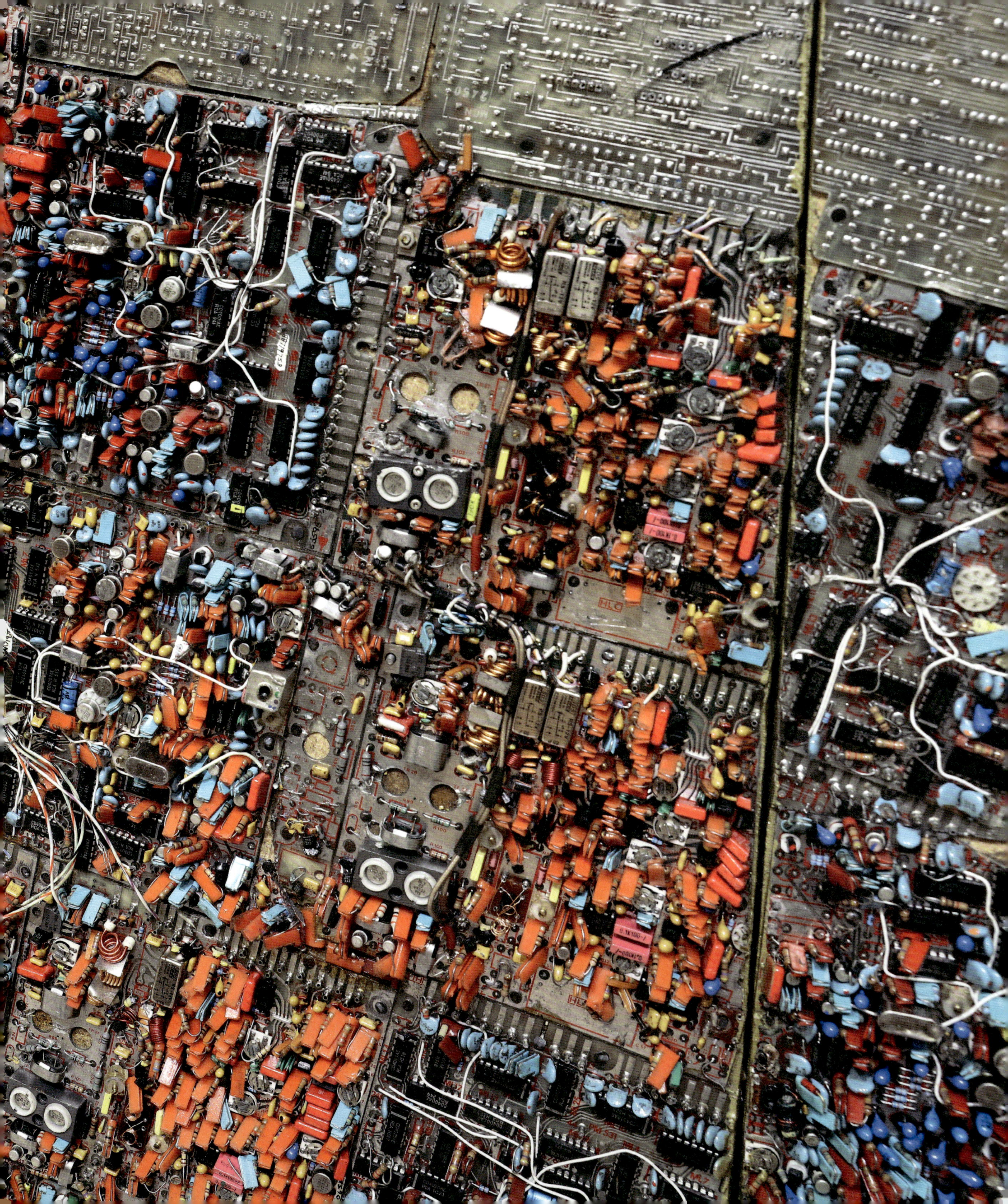

PLATE 12

Tightrope: Familiar Yet Complex 1

2016 | Reclaimed electronic components and insulated wire on panel | 46 × 79 ½ in. (116.8 × 201.9 cm)
Collection of Bill and Christy Gautreaux, Kansas City, MO

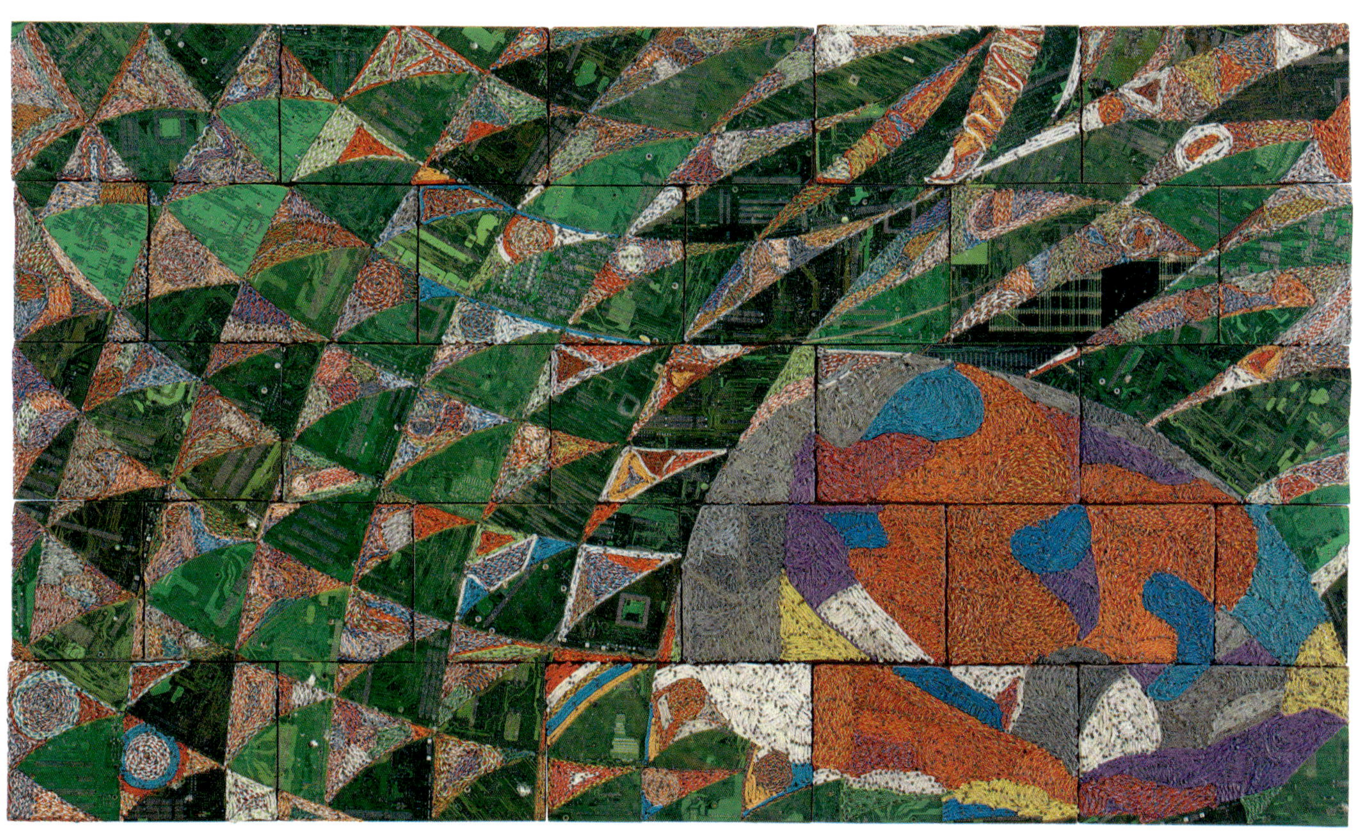

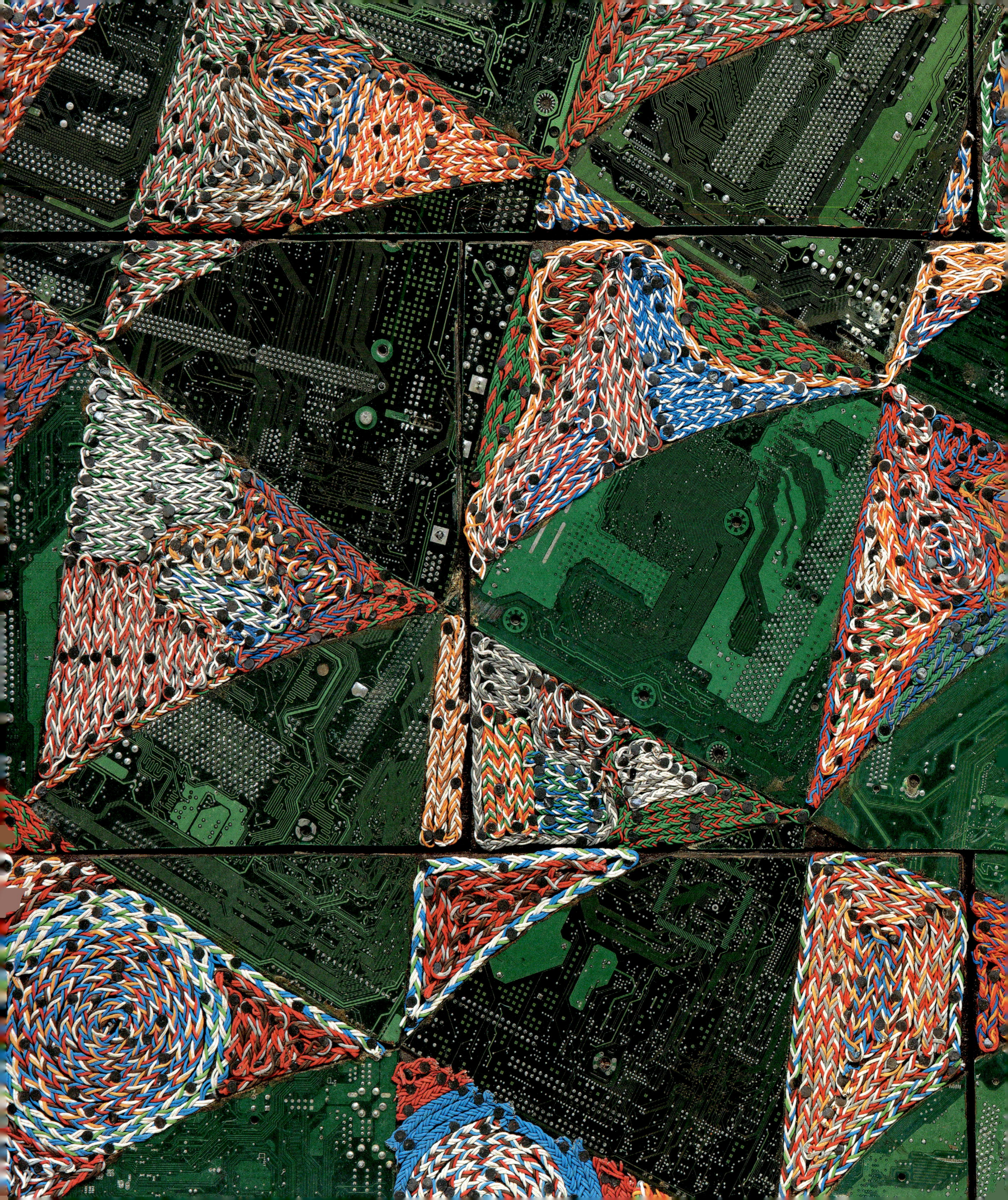

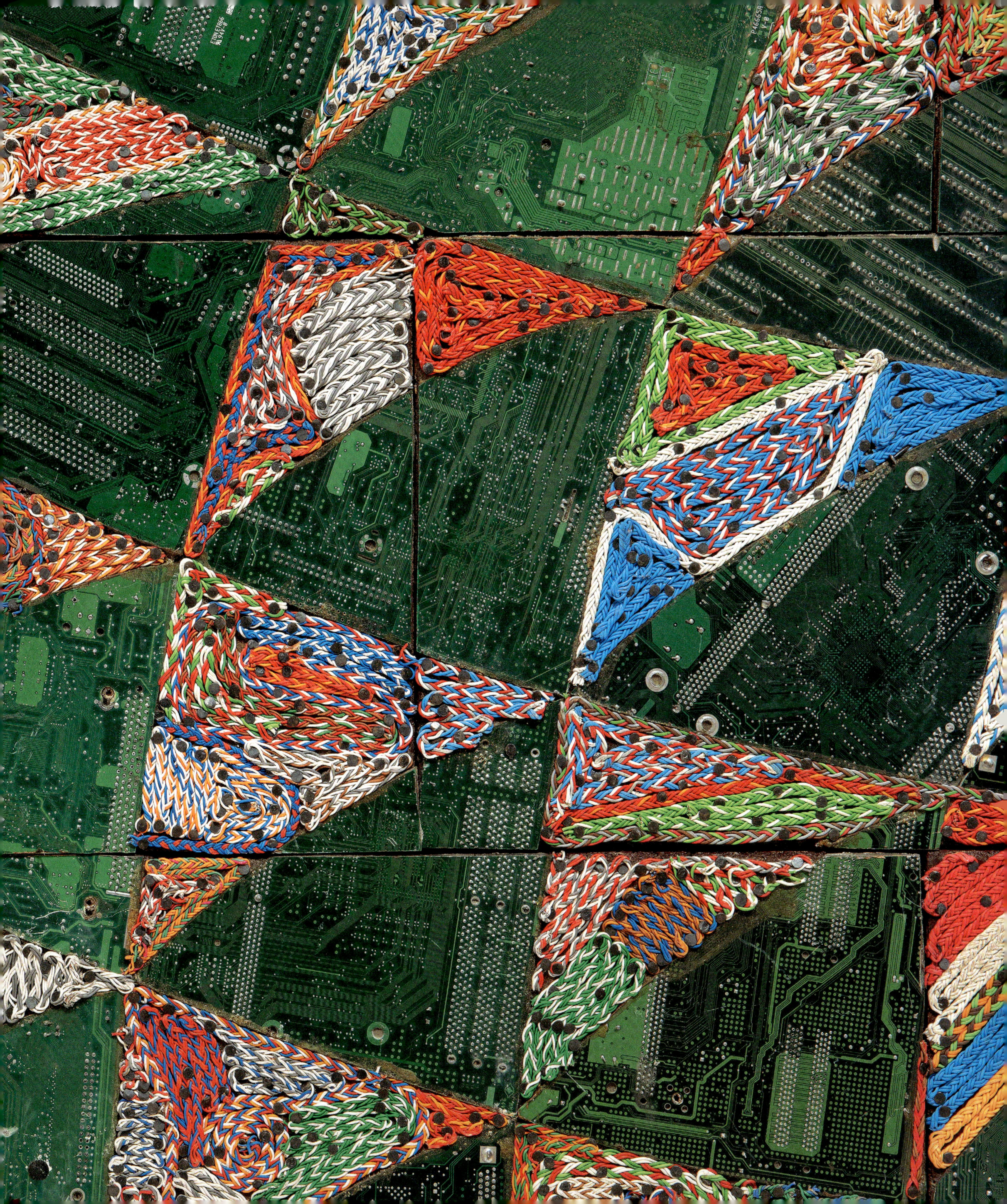

PLATE 13

Tightrope: Familiar Yet Complex 2

2016 | Reclaimed electronic components and insulated wire on panel | 83 × 87 ½ in. (210.8 × 222.3 cm)
Ruth and Elmer Wellin Museum of Art at Hamilton College, Clinton, NY | Purchase, William G. Roehrick '34 Art Acquisition and Preservation Fund

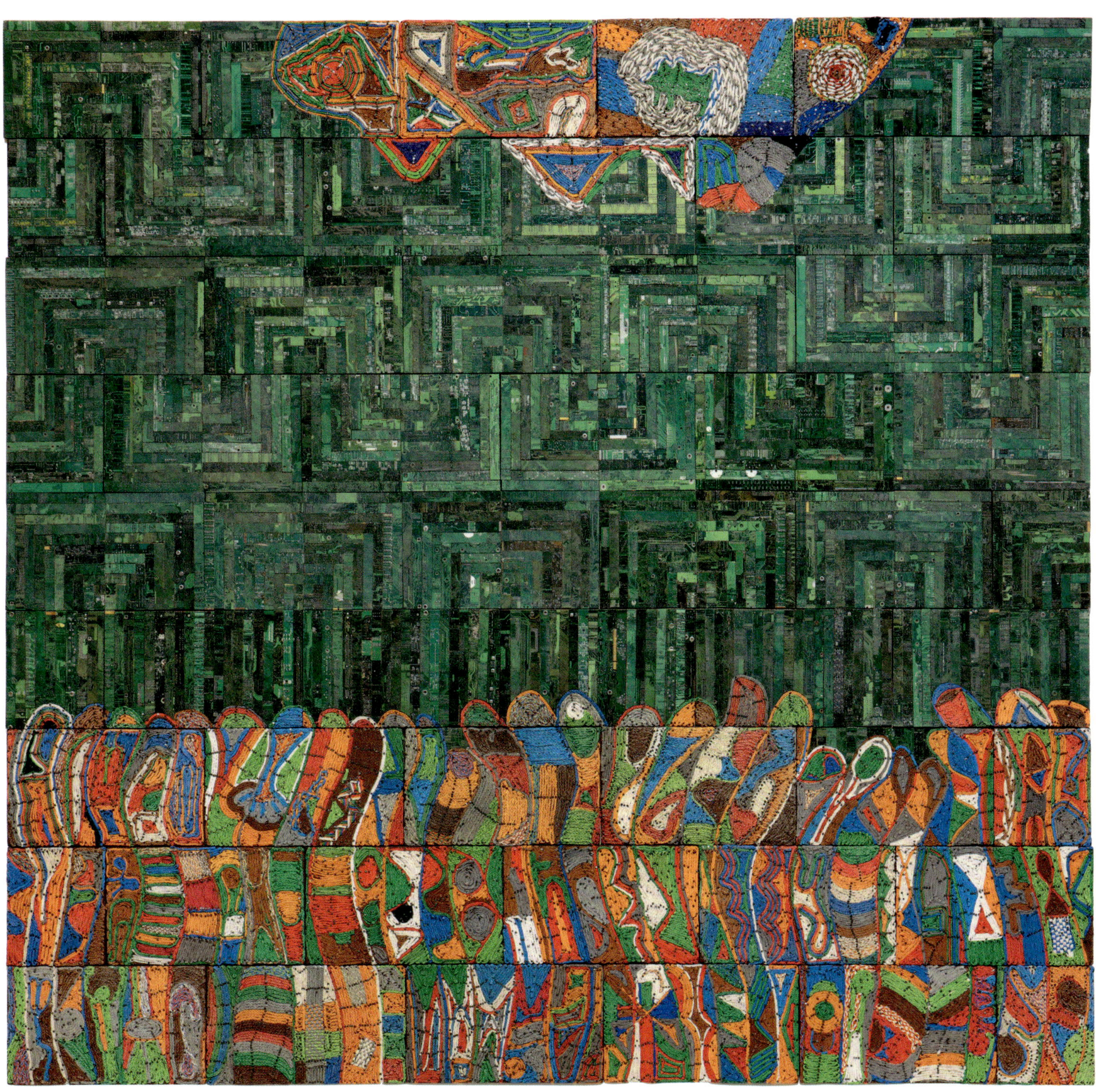

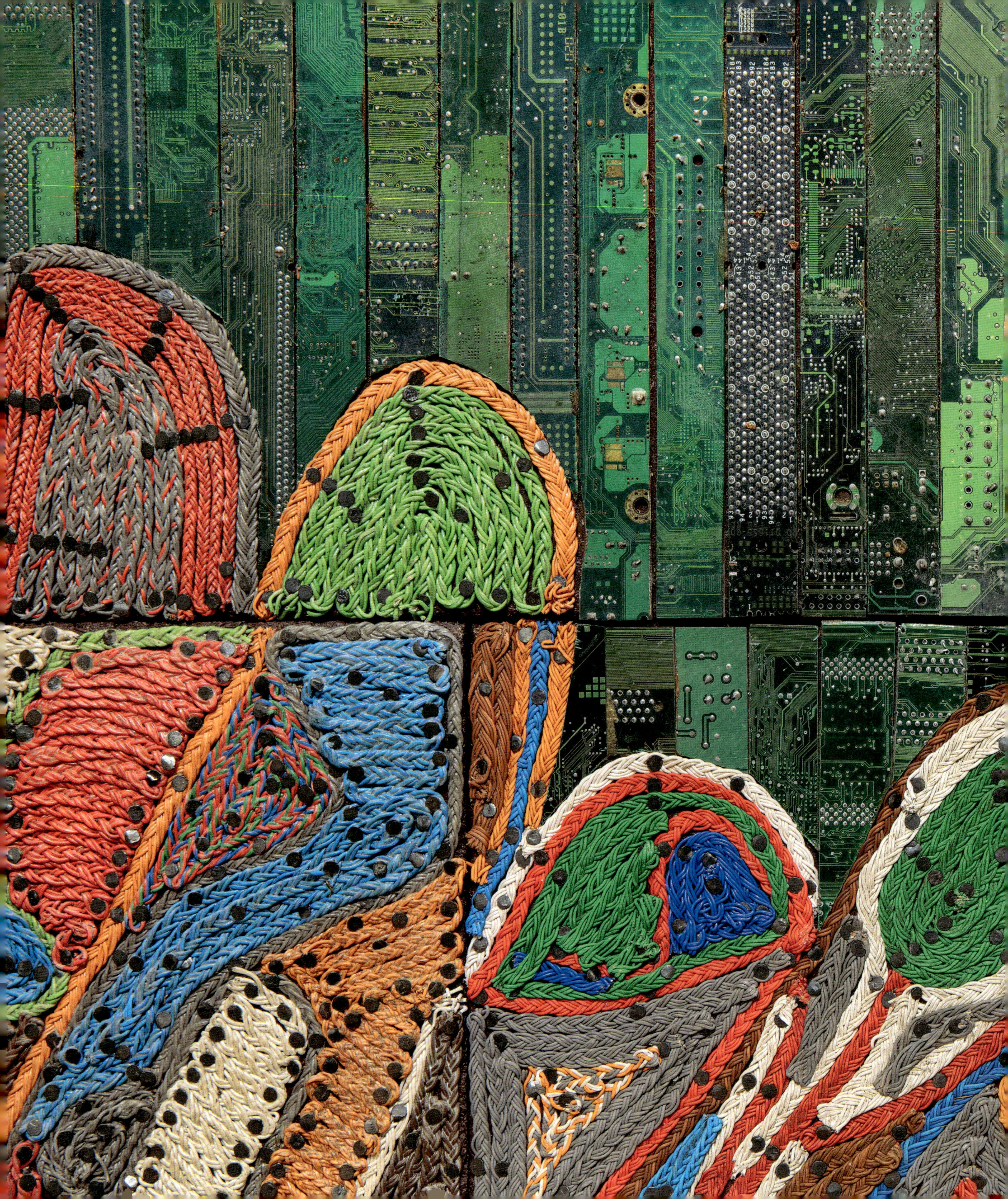

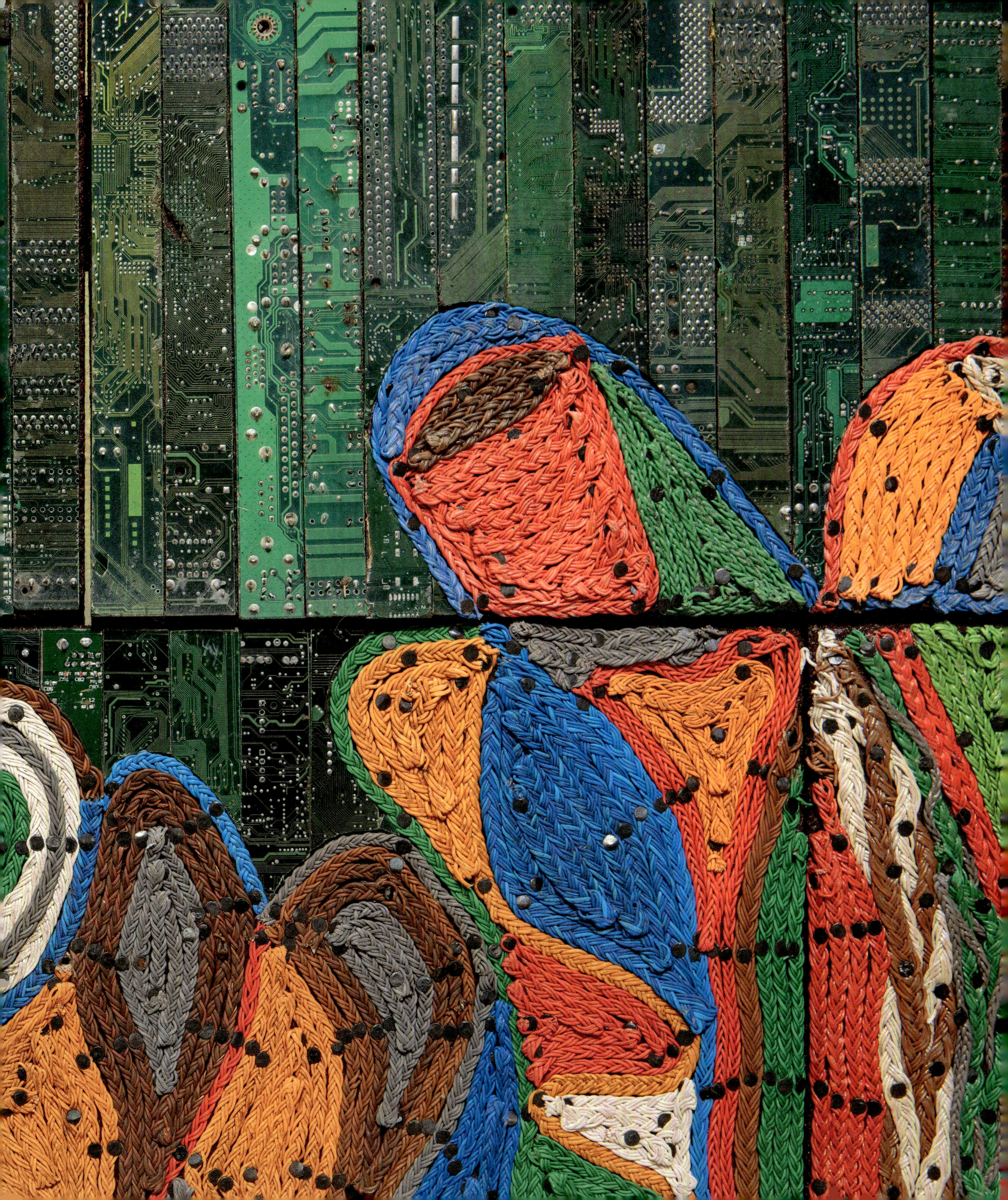

PLATE 14

Tightrope: Familiar Yet Complex 6

2016 | Reclaimed electronic components and insulated wire on panel | 55 ¼ × 79 ½ in. (140.3 × 201.9 cm)
Collection of Jane and James Cohan, New York

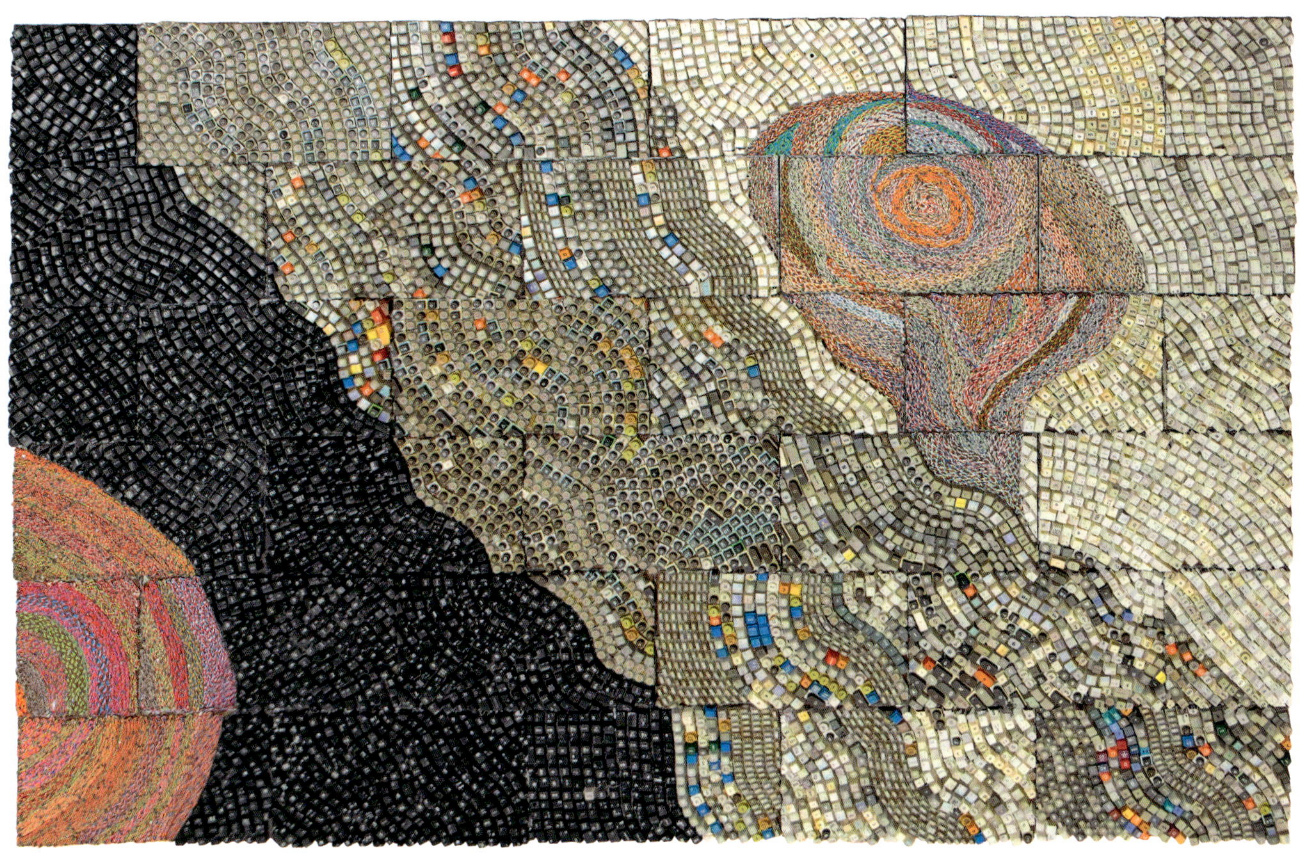

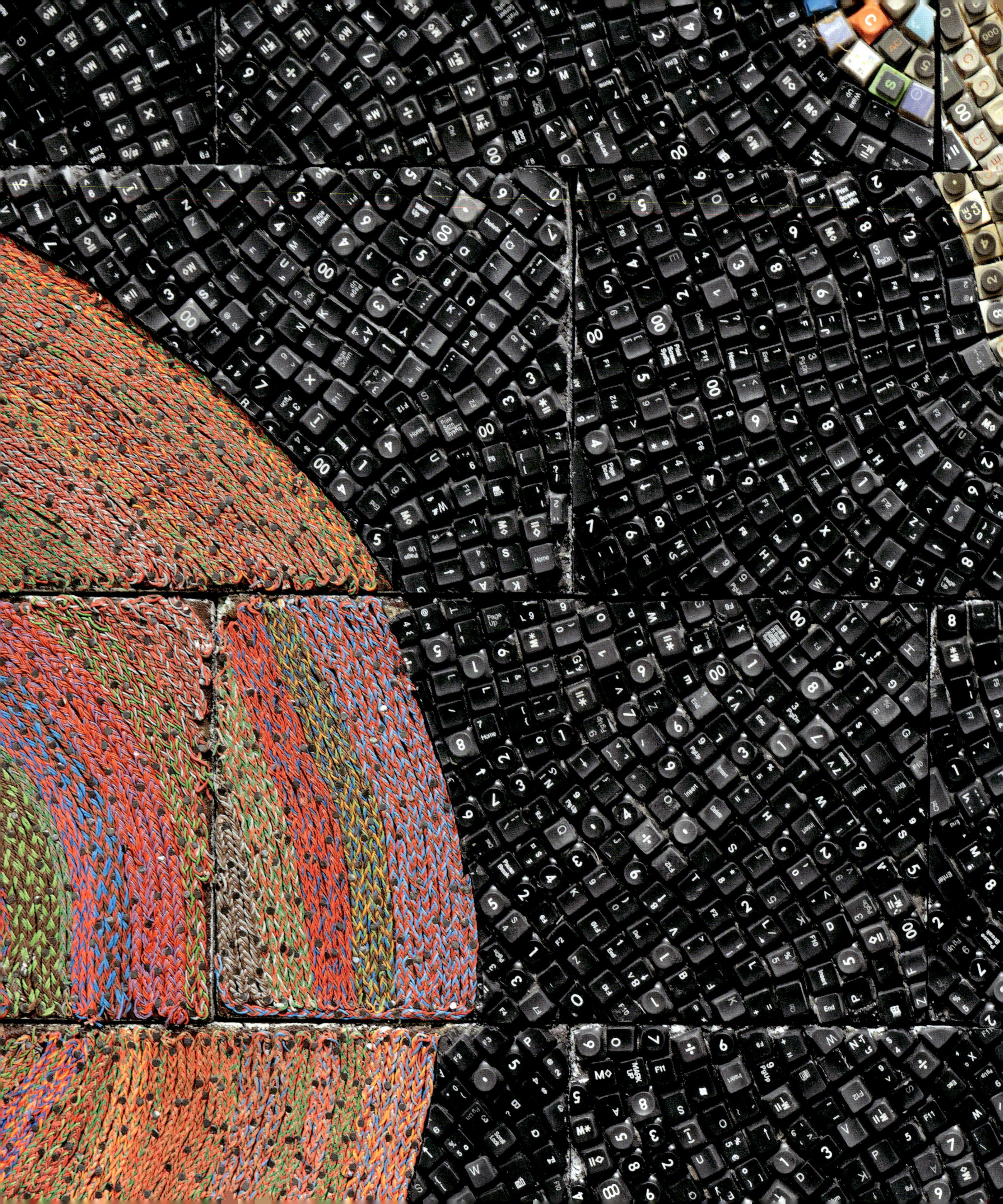

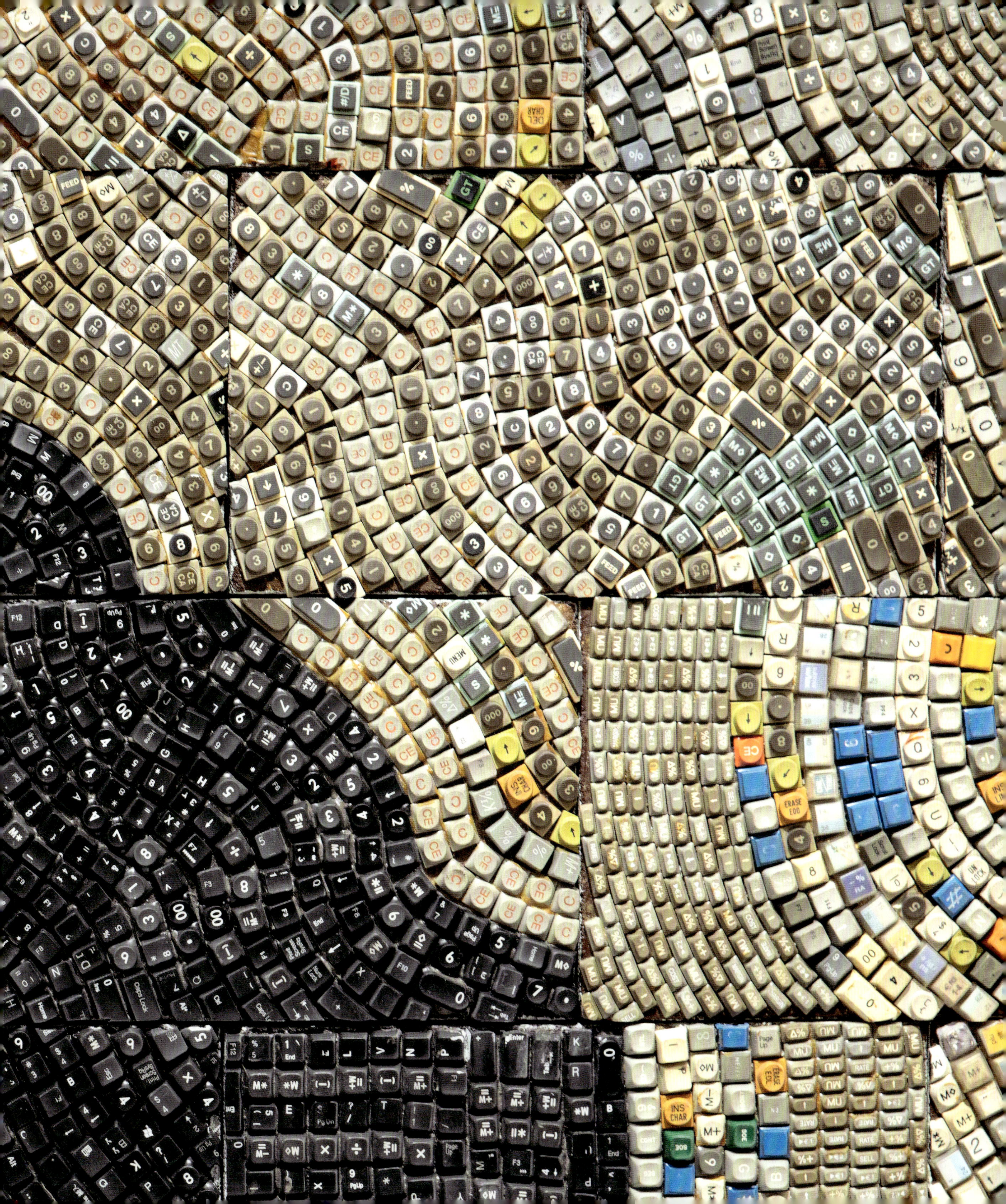

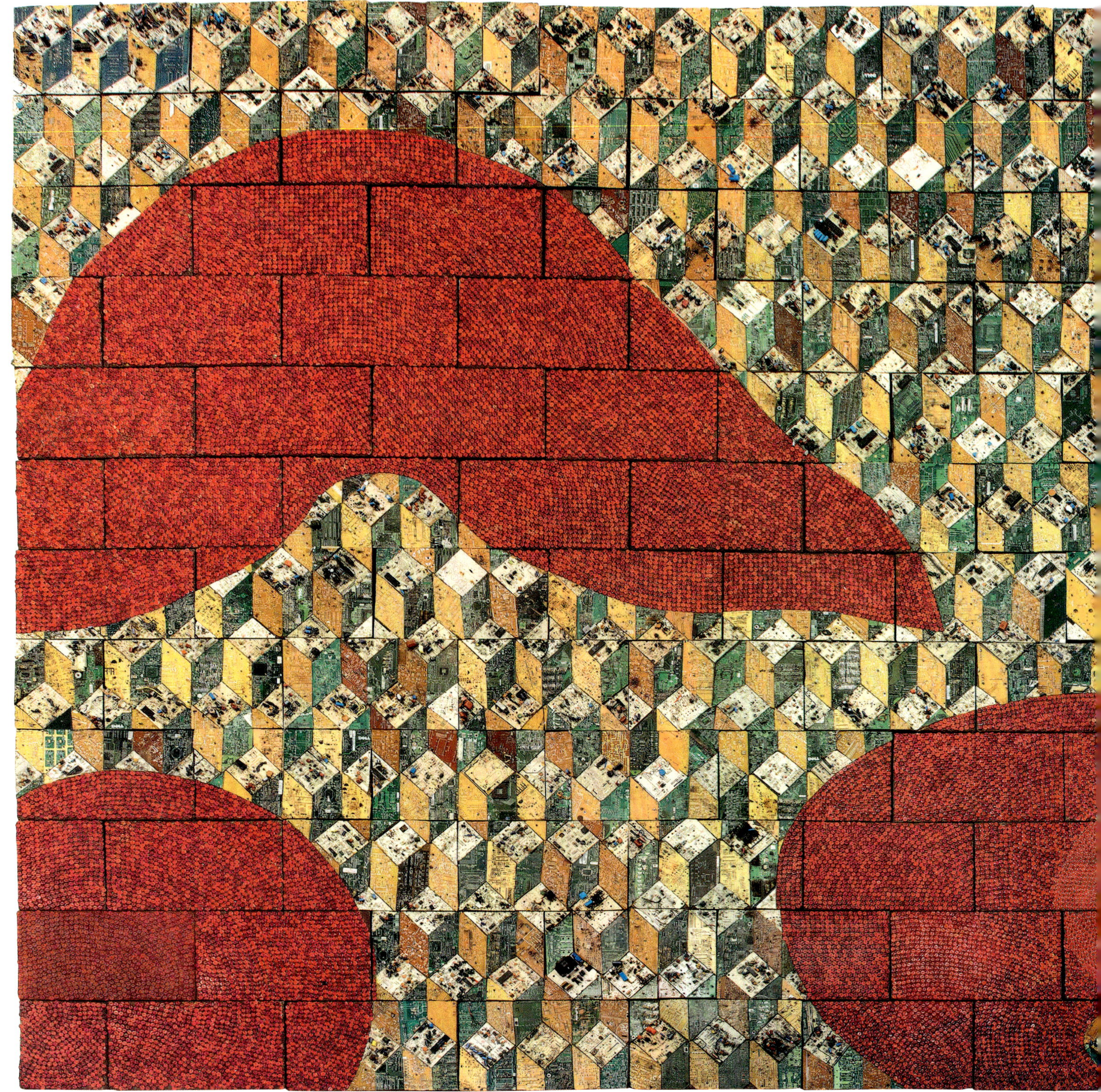

PLATE 15

Tightrope: Surface and Shadow 2

2016 | Reclaimed electronic components and buttons on panel | 9 ft. ⅝ in. × 17 ft. ⅝ in. (275.9 × 519.8 cm)
Pizzuti Collection, Columbus, OH

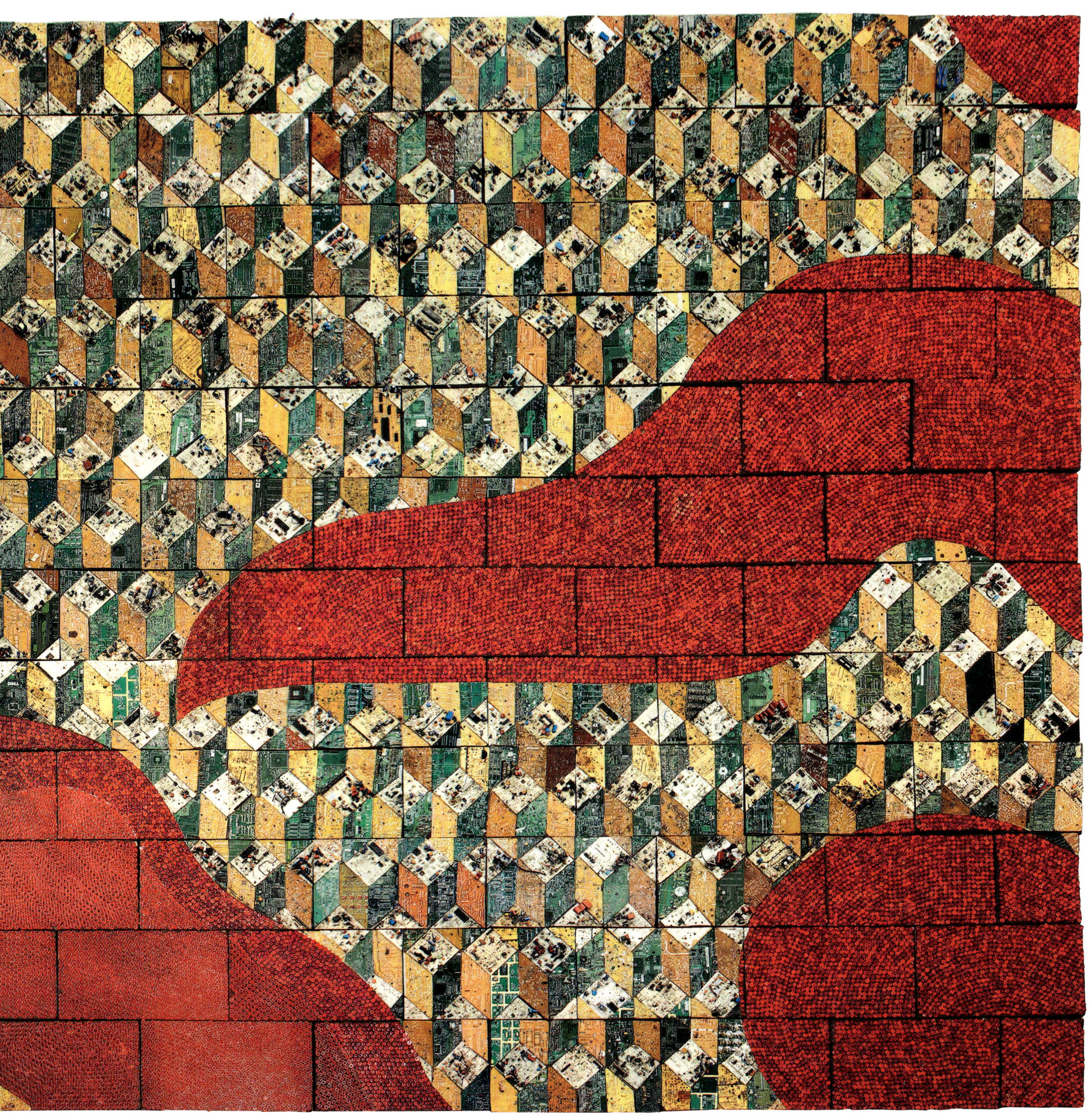

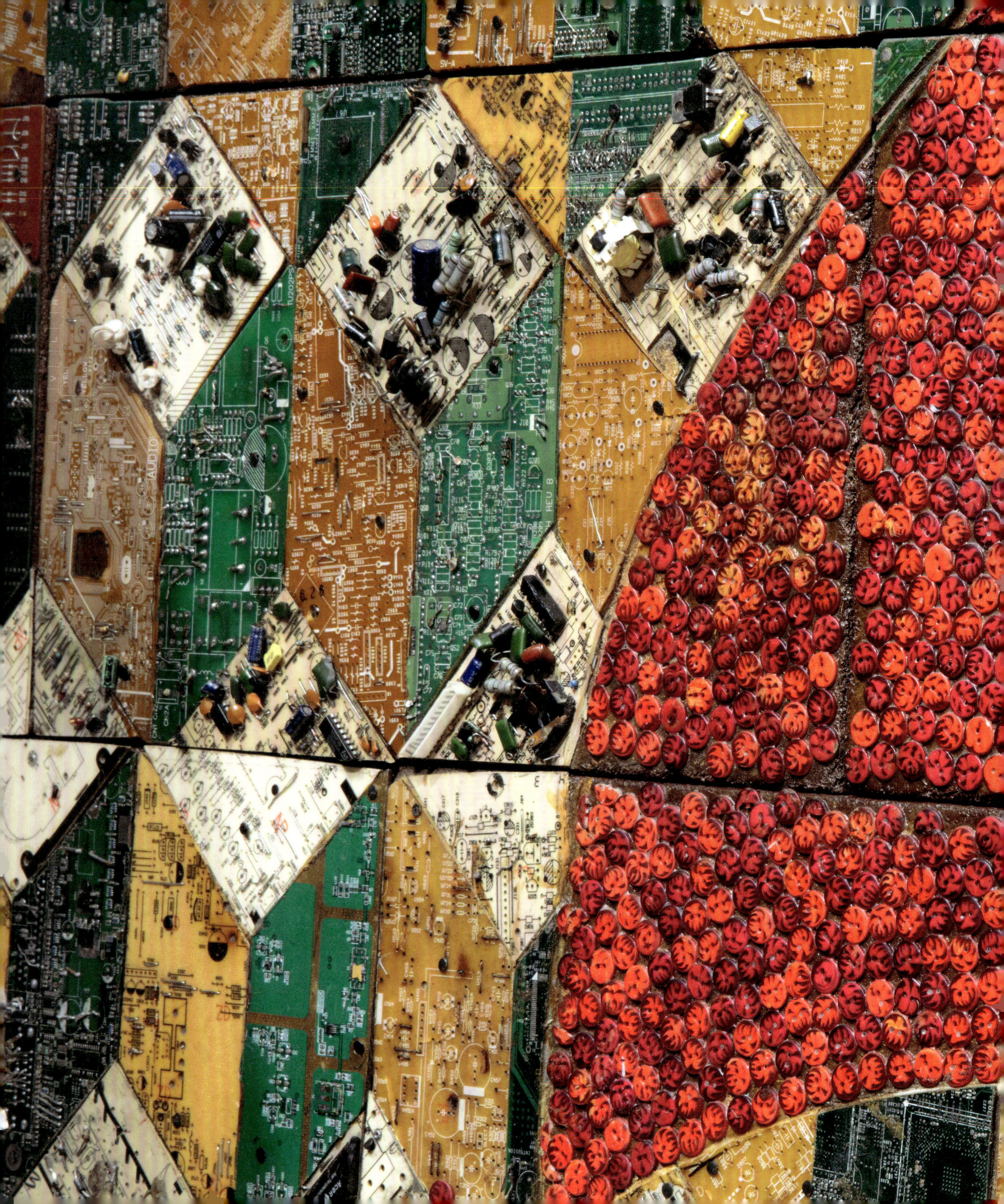

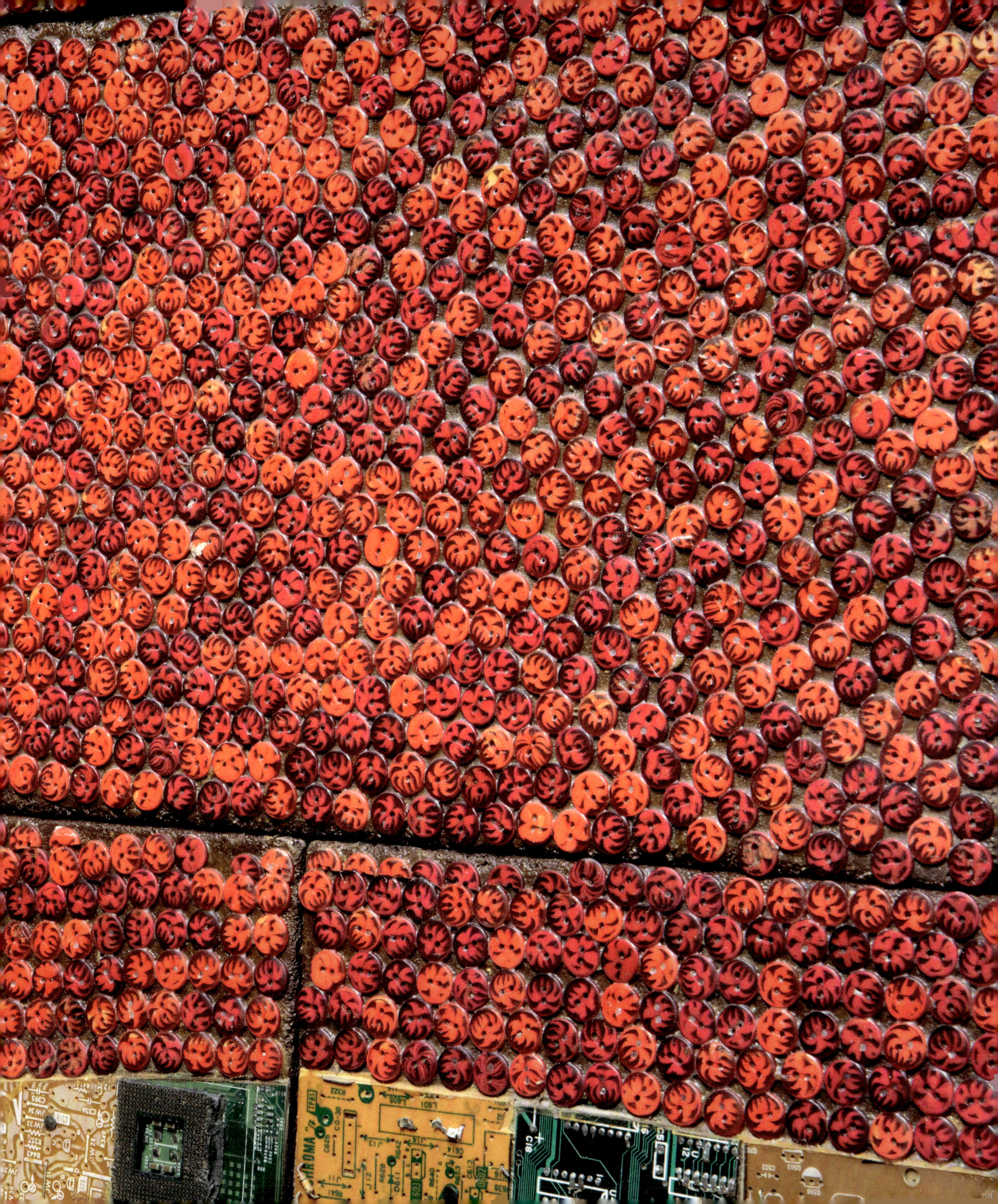

PLATE 16

Tightrope: Behind the Beauty

2017 | Reclaimed insulated wire on panel | 91 ¼ in. × 10 ft. 7 ¼ in. (231.8 × 323.2 cm)
Collection of Scott Mueller, Cleveland, OH

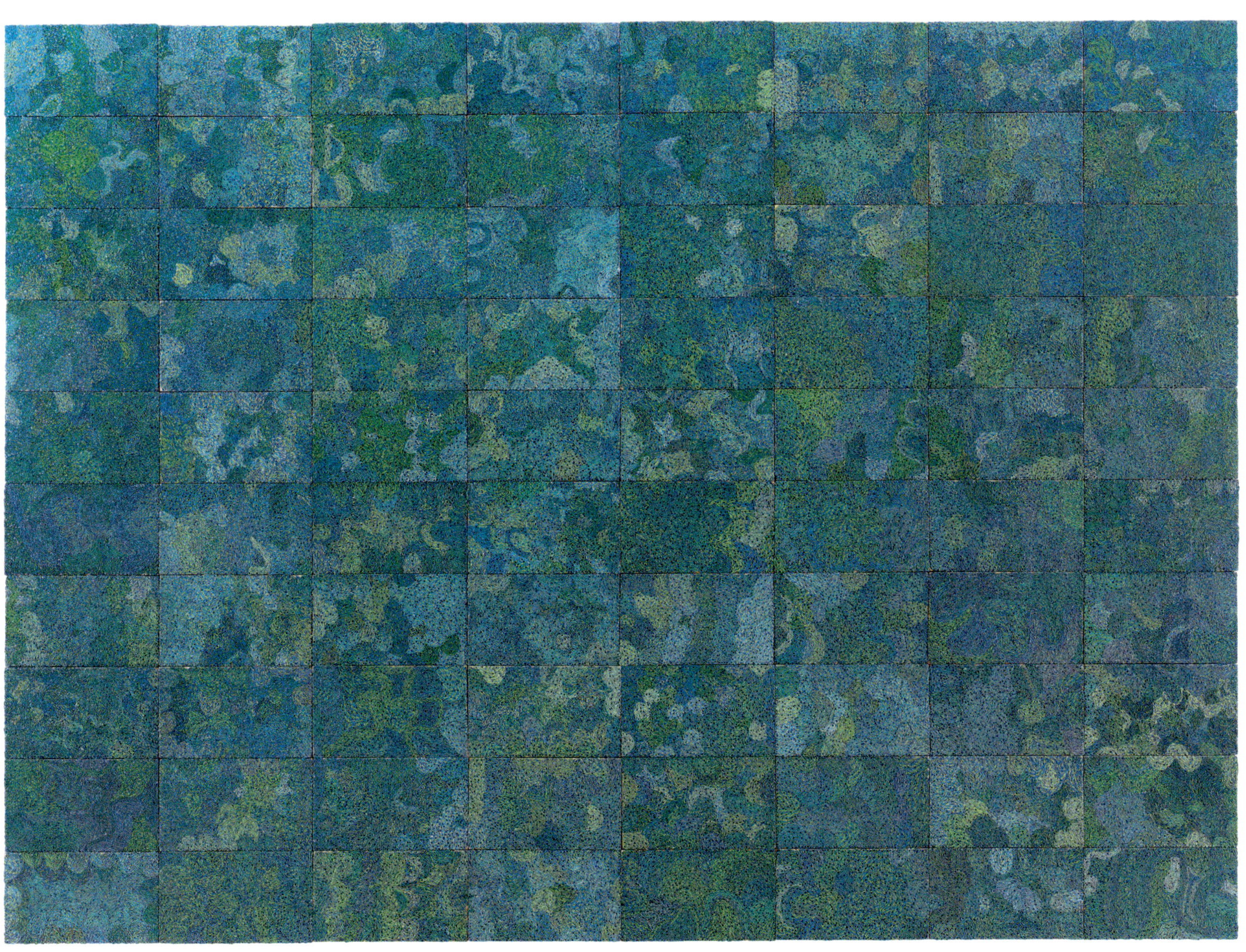

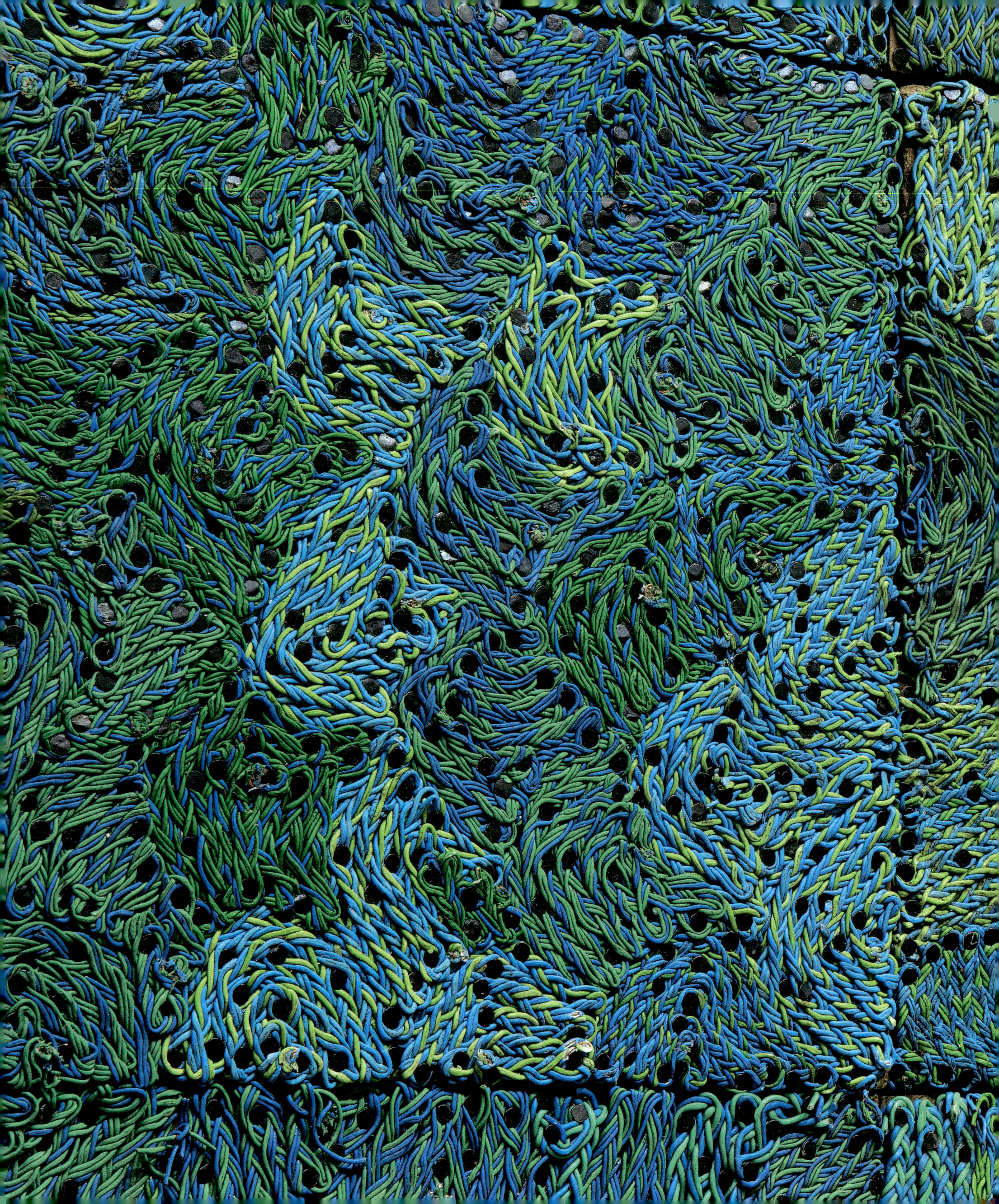

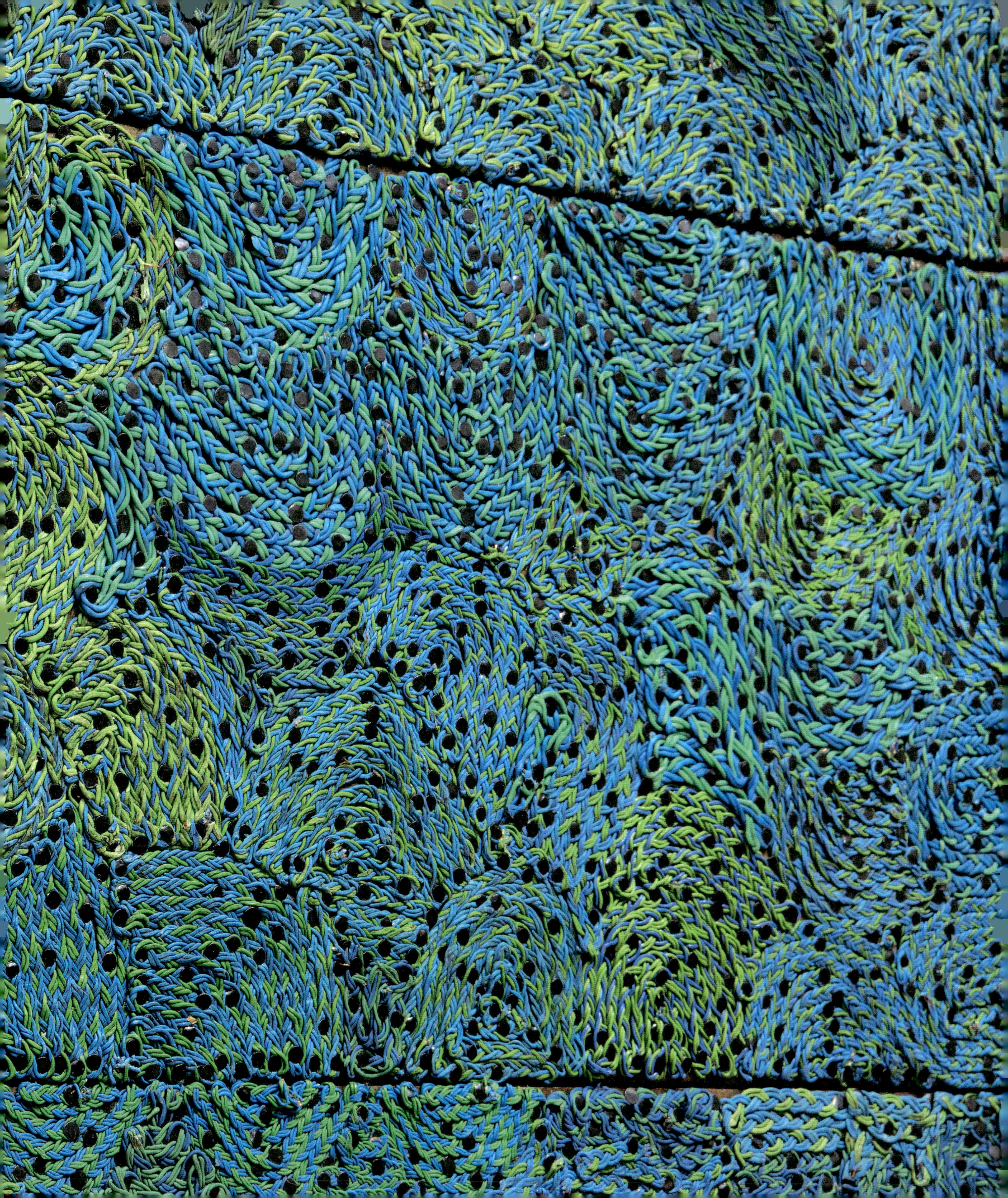

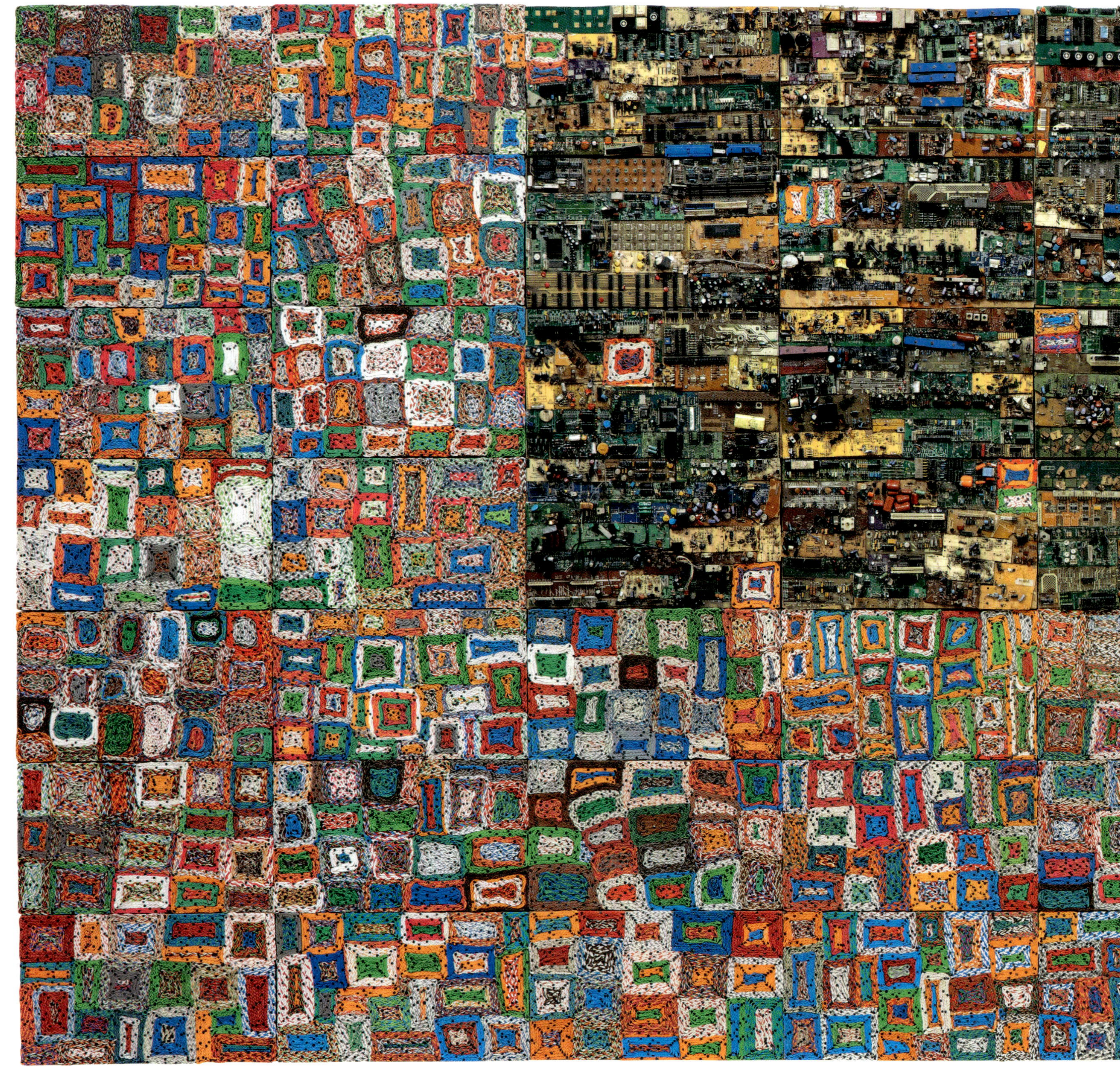

PLATE 17

Tightrope: In Boxes

2017 | Reclaimed electronic components and insulated wire on panel | 64 in. × 11 ft. 10 ⅝ in. (162.6 × 362.3 cm)
Royal Ontario Museum, Toronto | Acquisition made possible by the generous support of the Louise Hawley Stone Charitable Trust

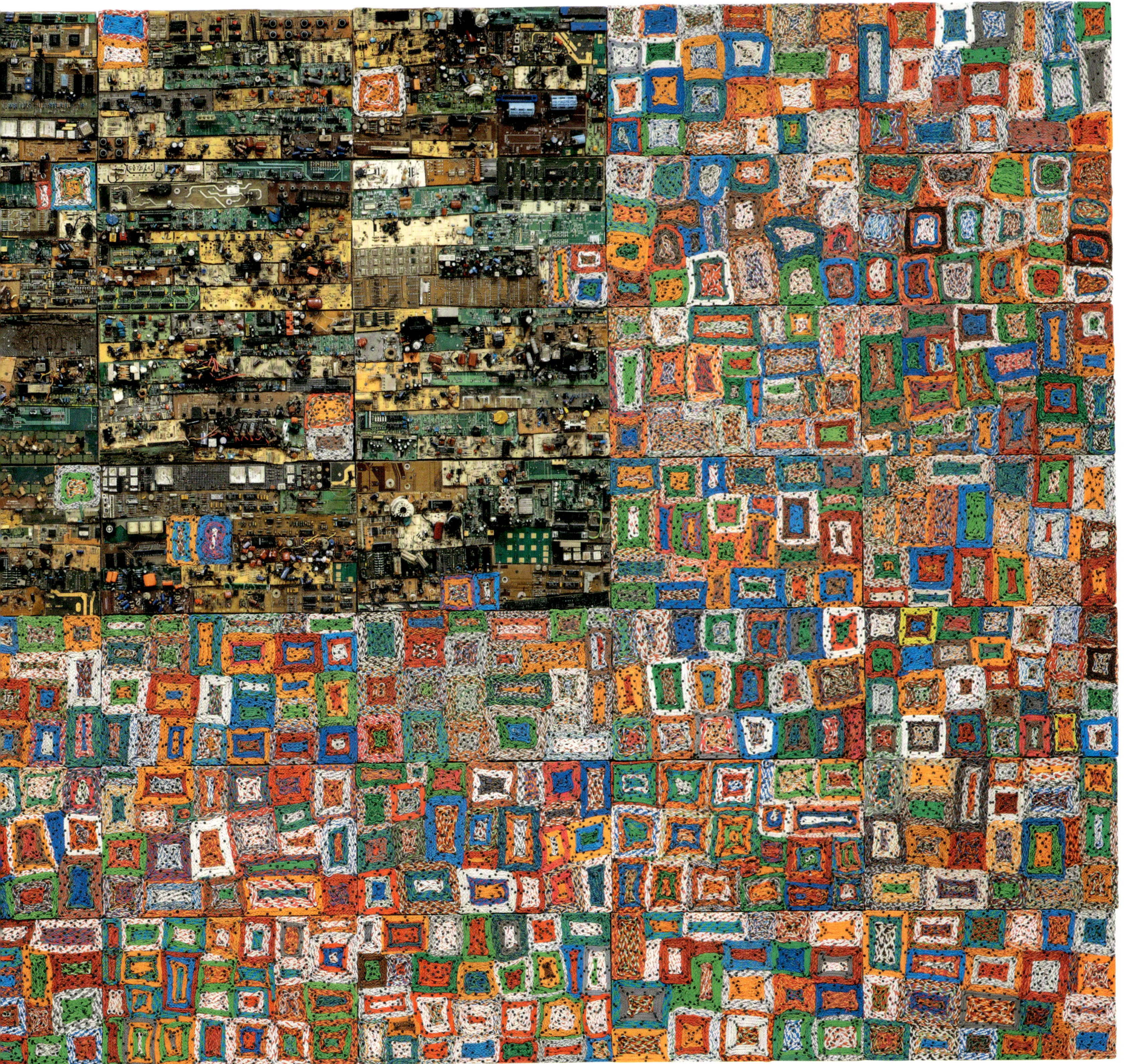

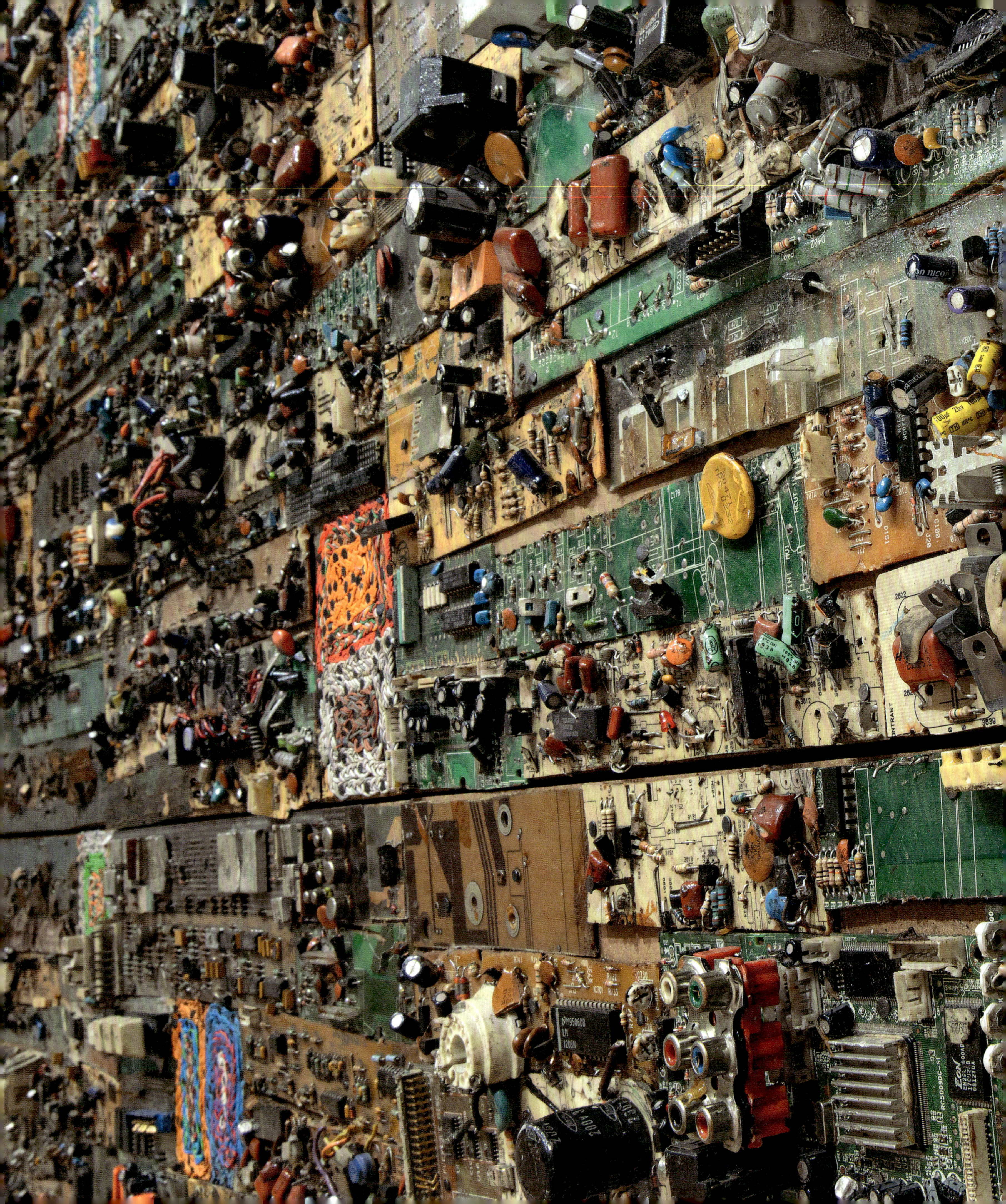

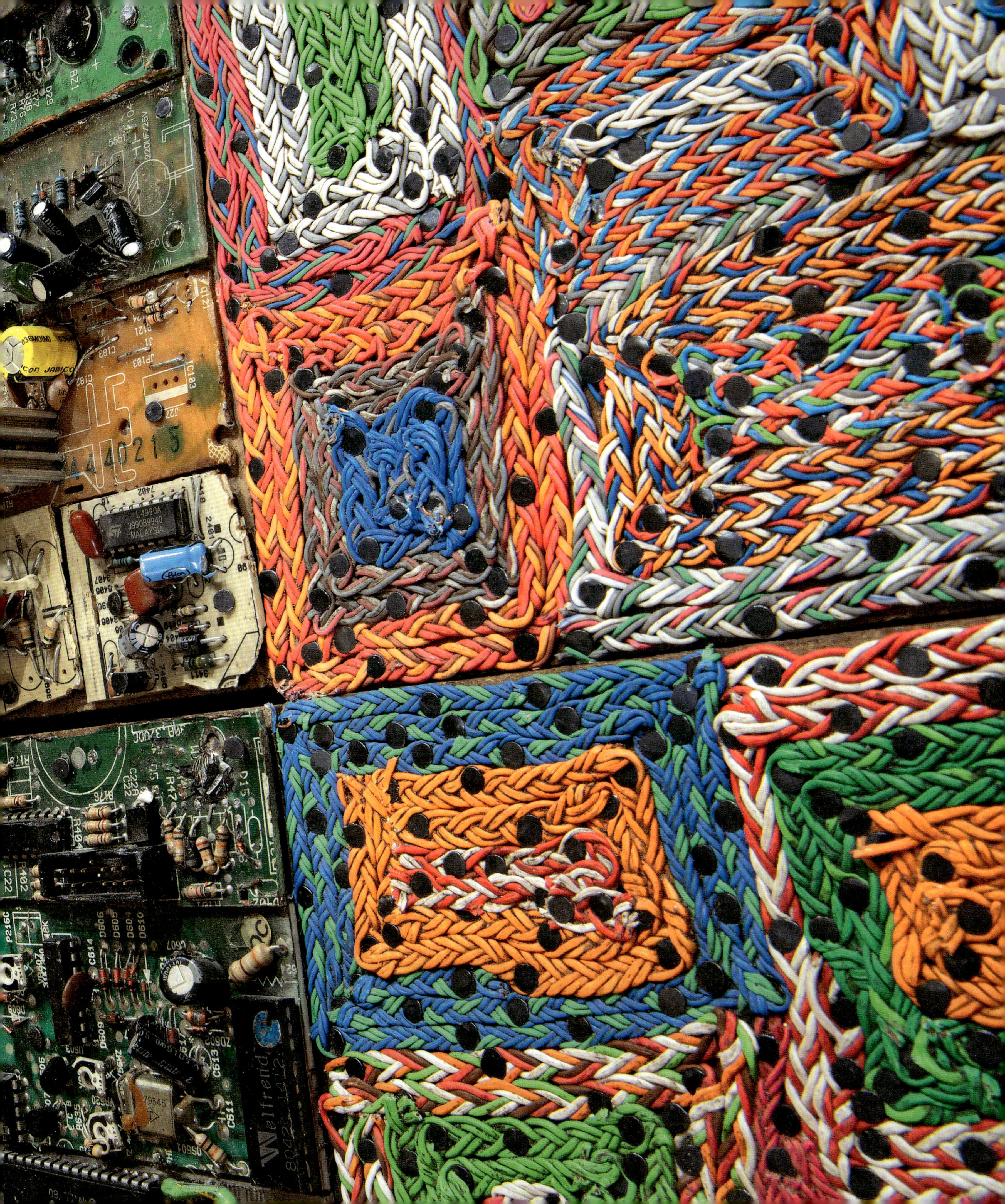

PLATE 18

Tightrope: Internalized

2017 | Reclaimed electronic components and insulated wire on panel | 63 ⅜ × 94 ⅜ in. (161 × 239.7 cm)
Private collection

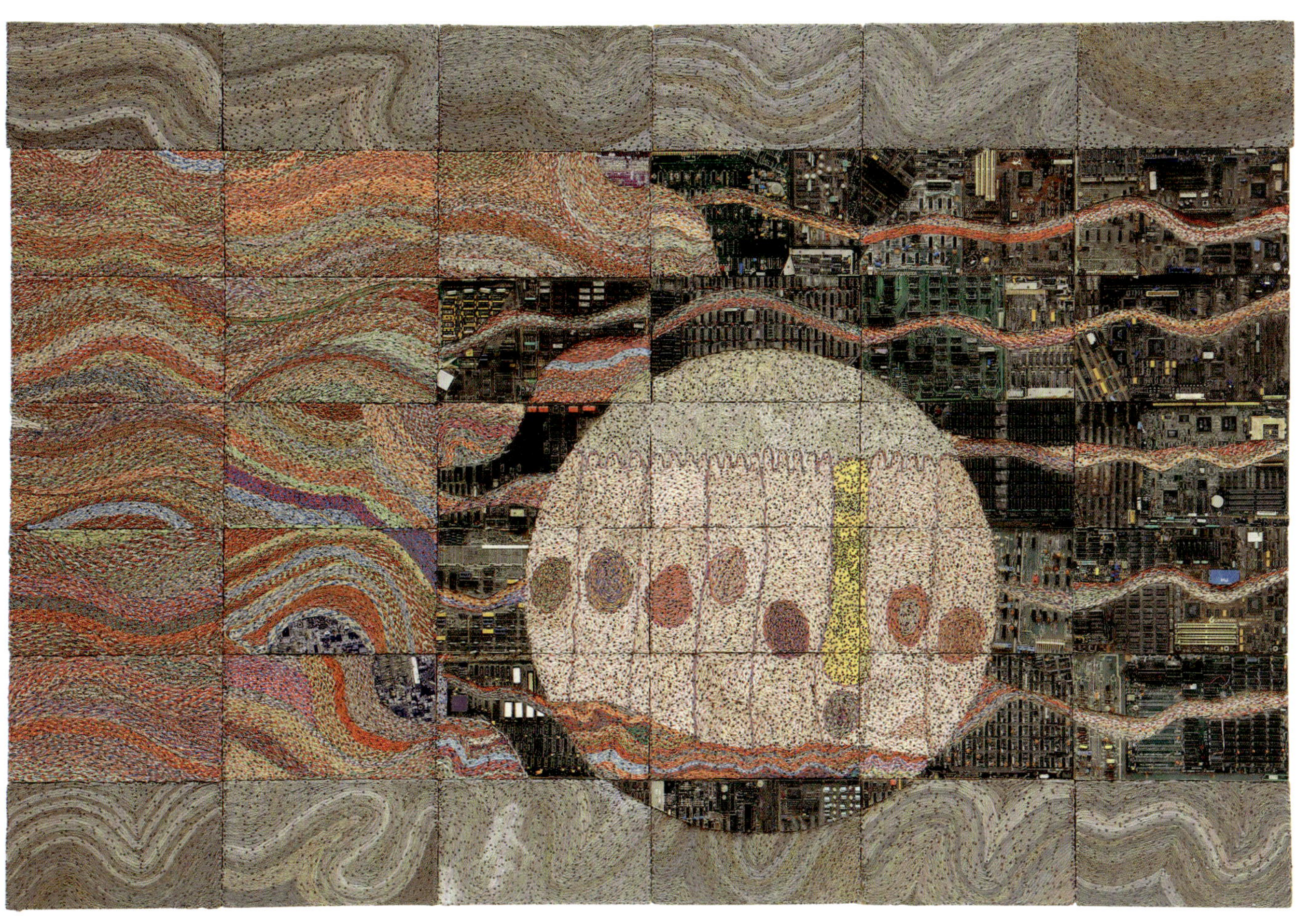

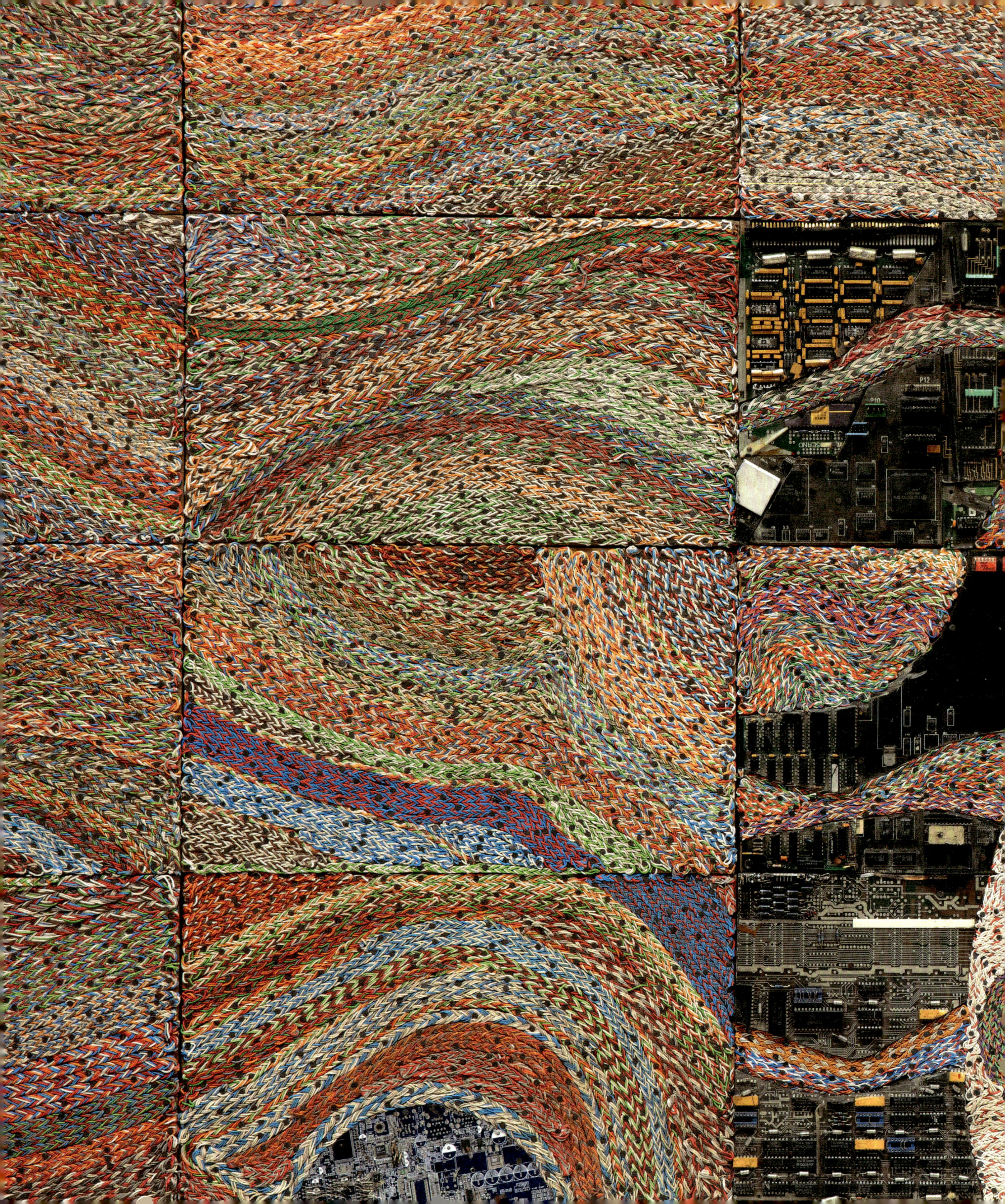

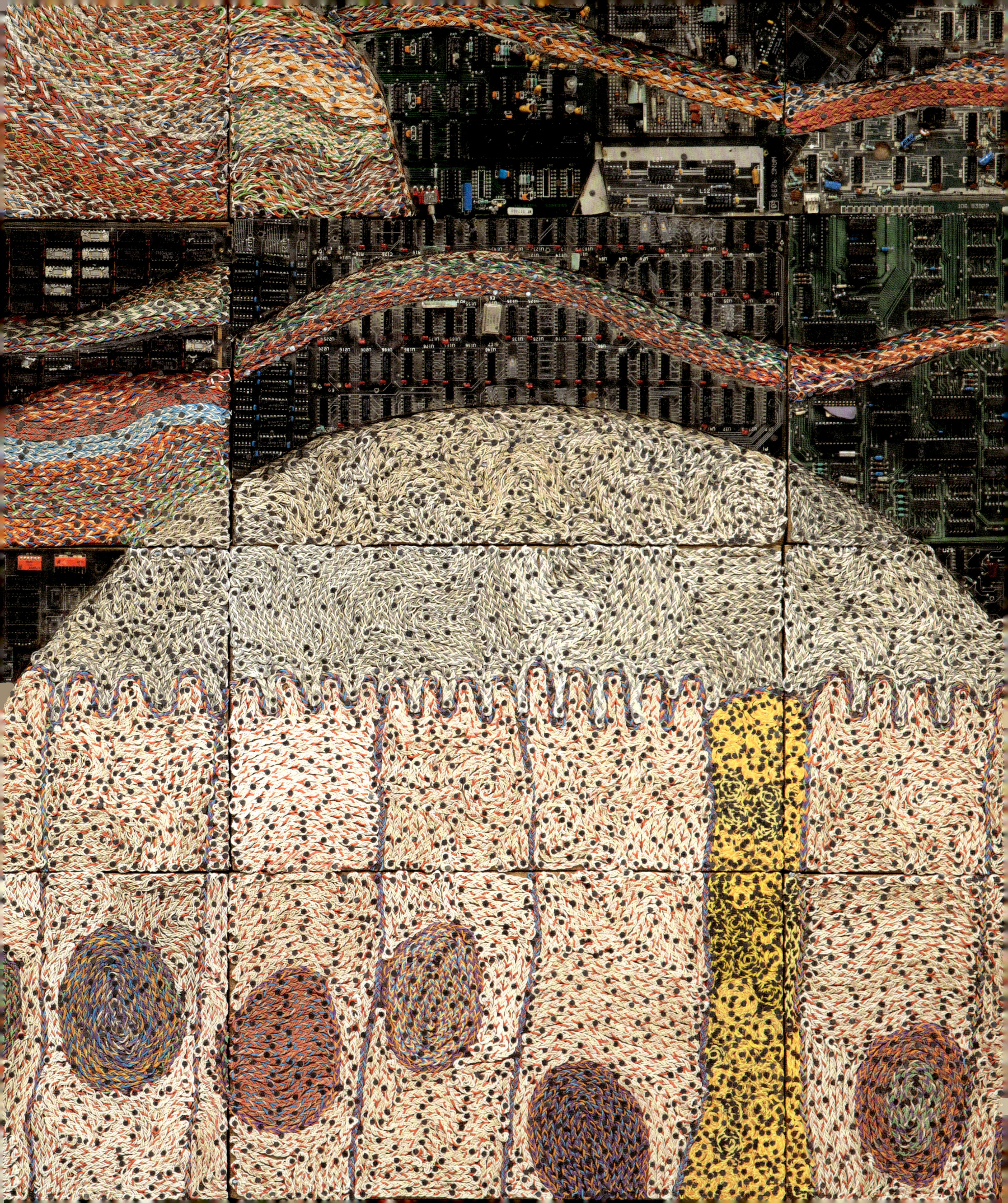

PLATE 19

Tightrope: The Dominant

2017 | Reclaimed insulated wire on panel | 81 ⅜ in. × 10 ft. 6 in. (206.7 × 320 cm)
Collection of Erica Tennenbaum and Alex Friedman, New York

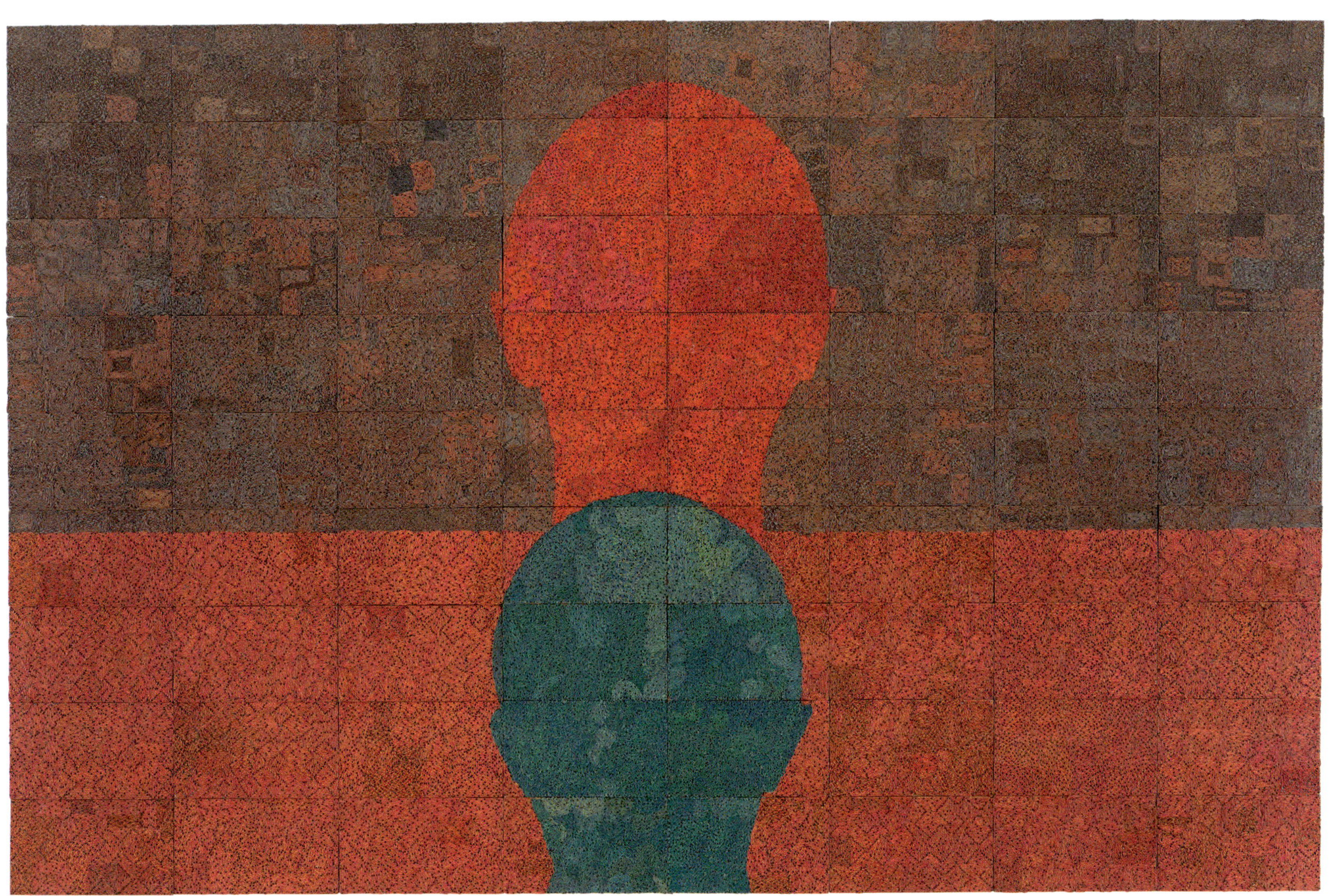

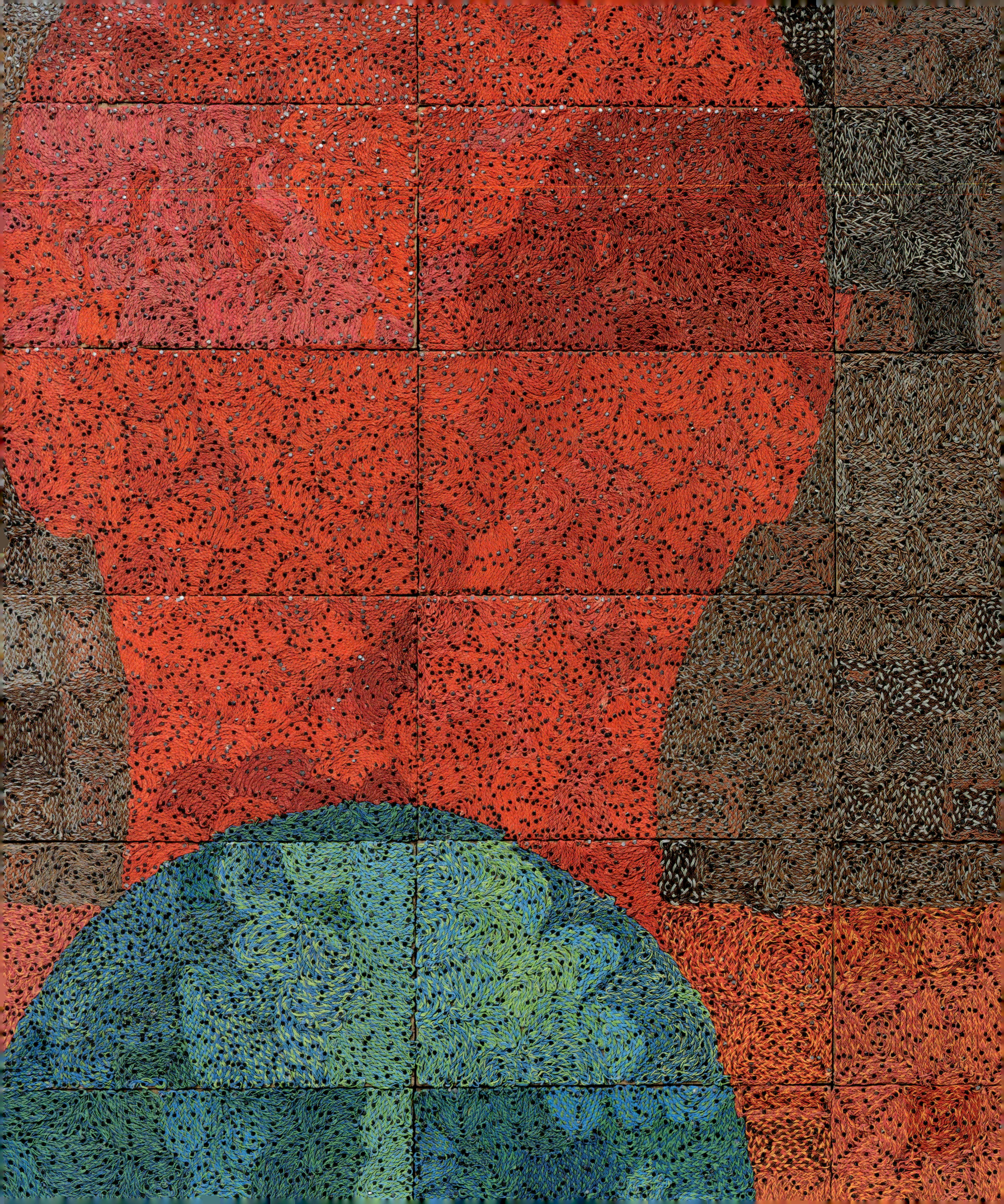

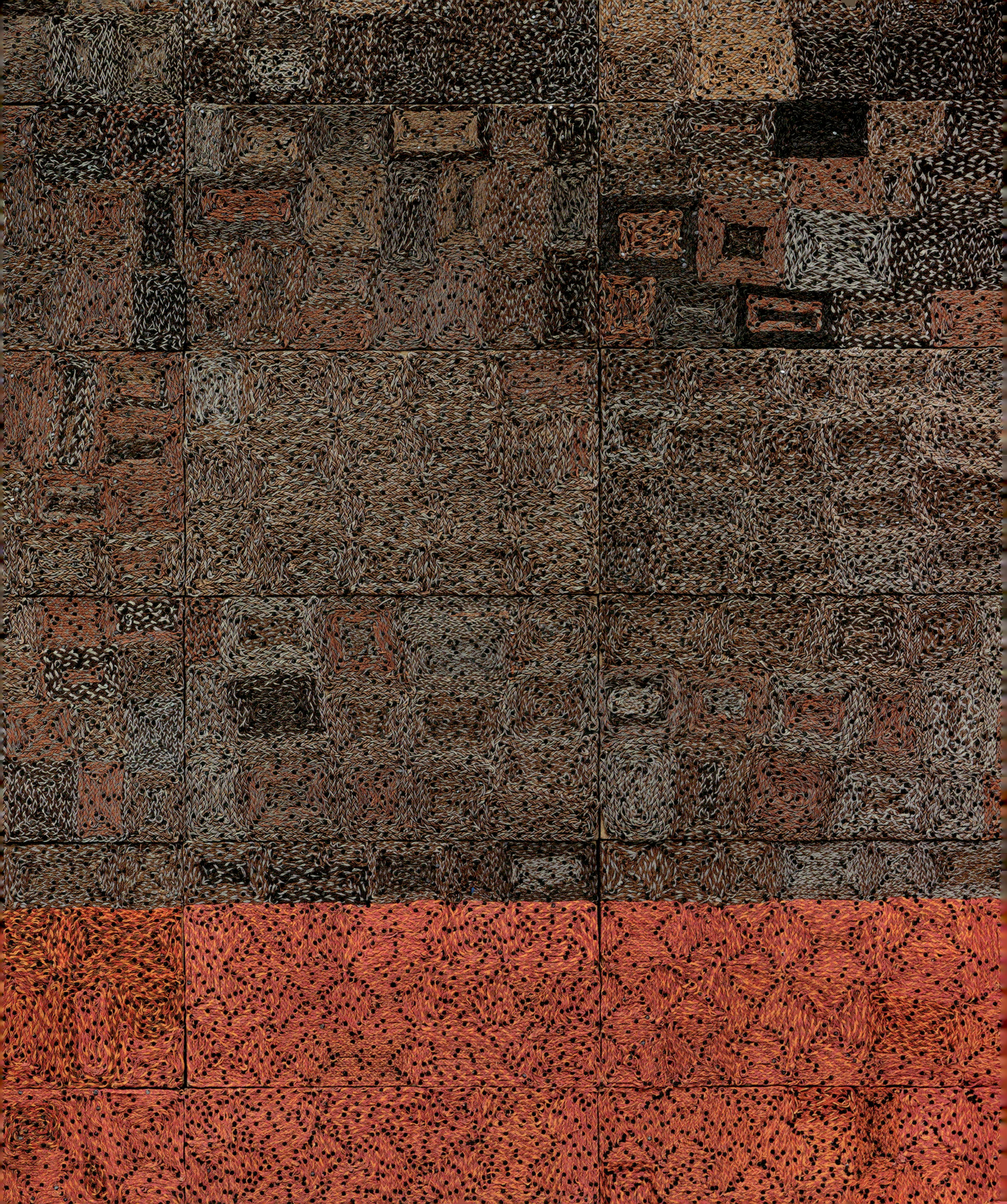

PLATE 20

Tightrope: Whirlwind

2017 | Reclaimed insulated wire on panel | 9 ft. 1 ¾ in. × 11 ft. 10 ½ in. (278.8 × 362 cm)
Courtesy of the artist and James Cohan, New York

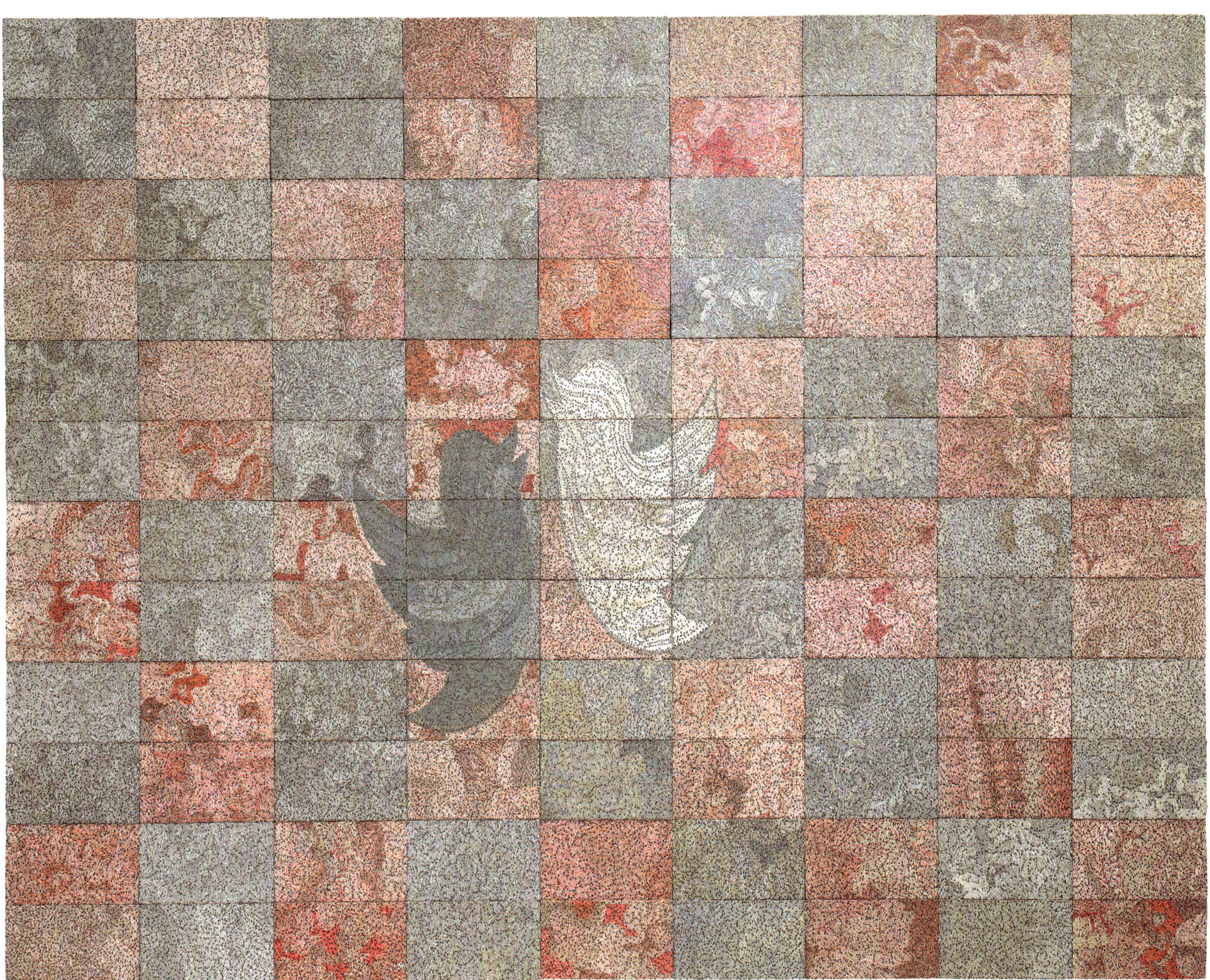

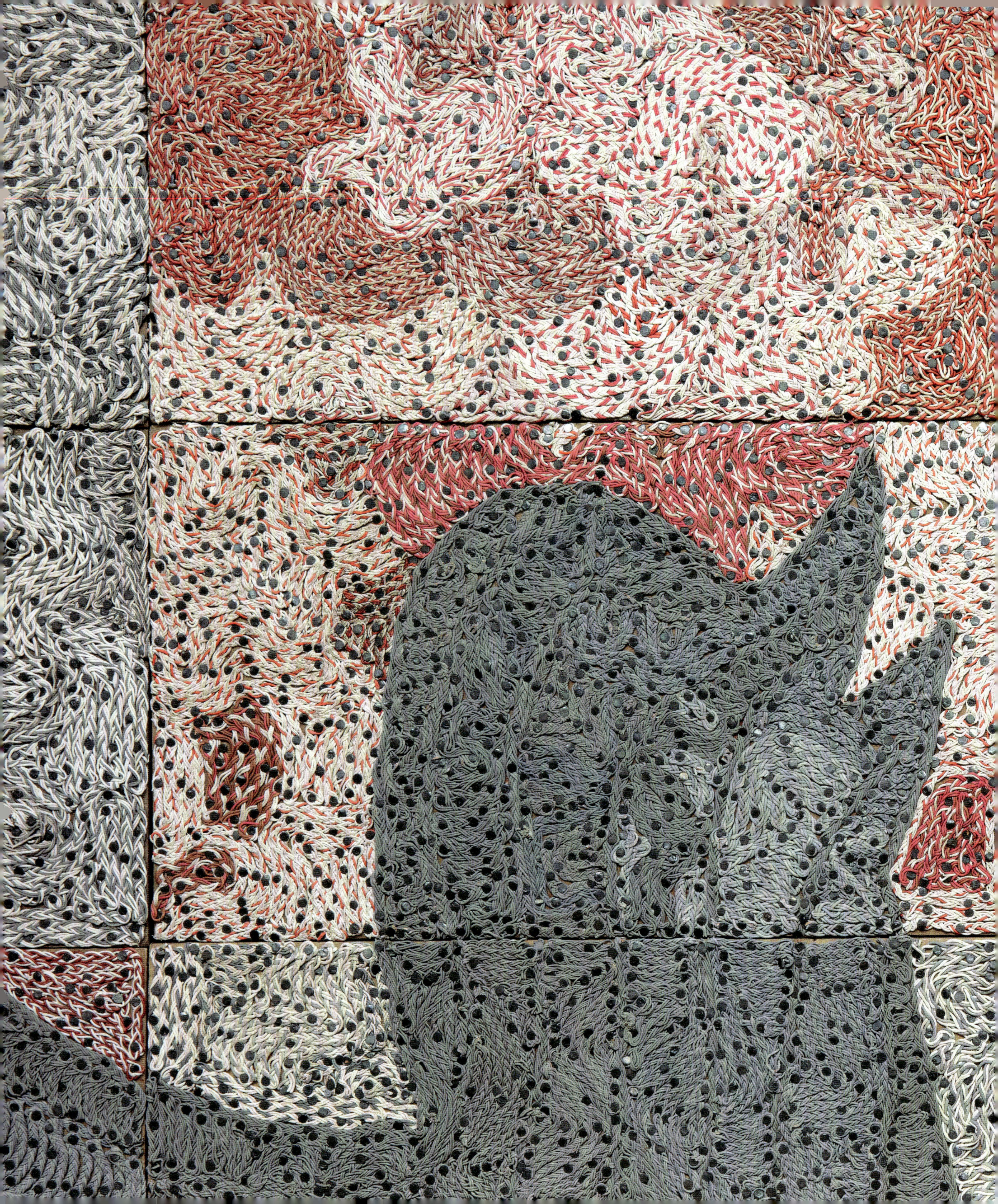

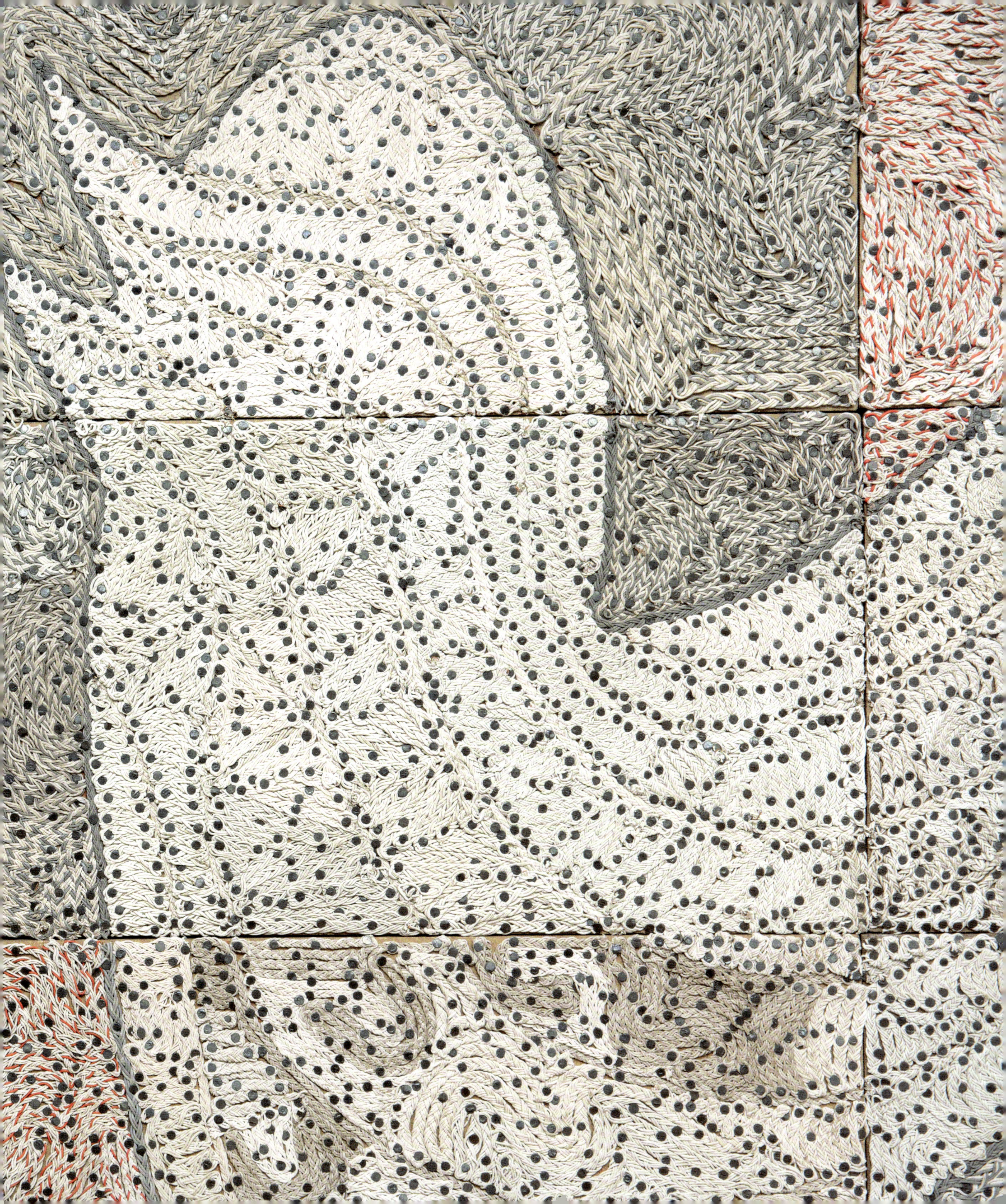

PLATE 21

Tightrope: (1) While Observing . . .

2018 | Reclaimed electronic components on panel | 72 ½ × 31 ⅝ in. (184.2 × 80.3 cm)
Carl & Marilynn Thoma Art Foundation, Chicago, IL, and Santa Fe, NM

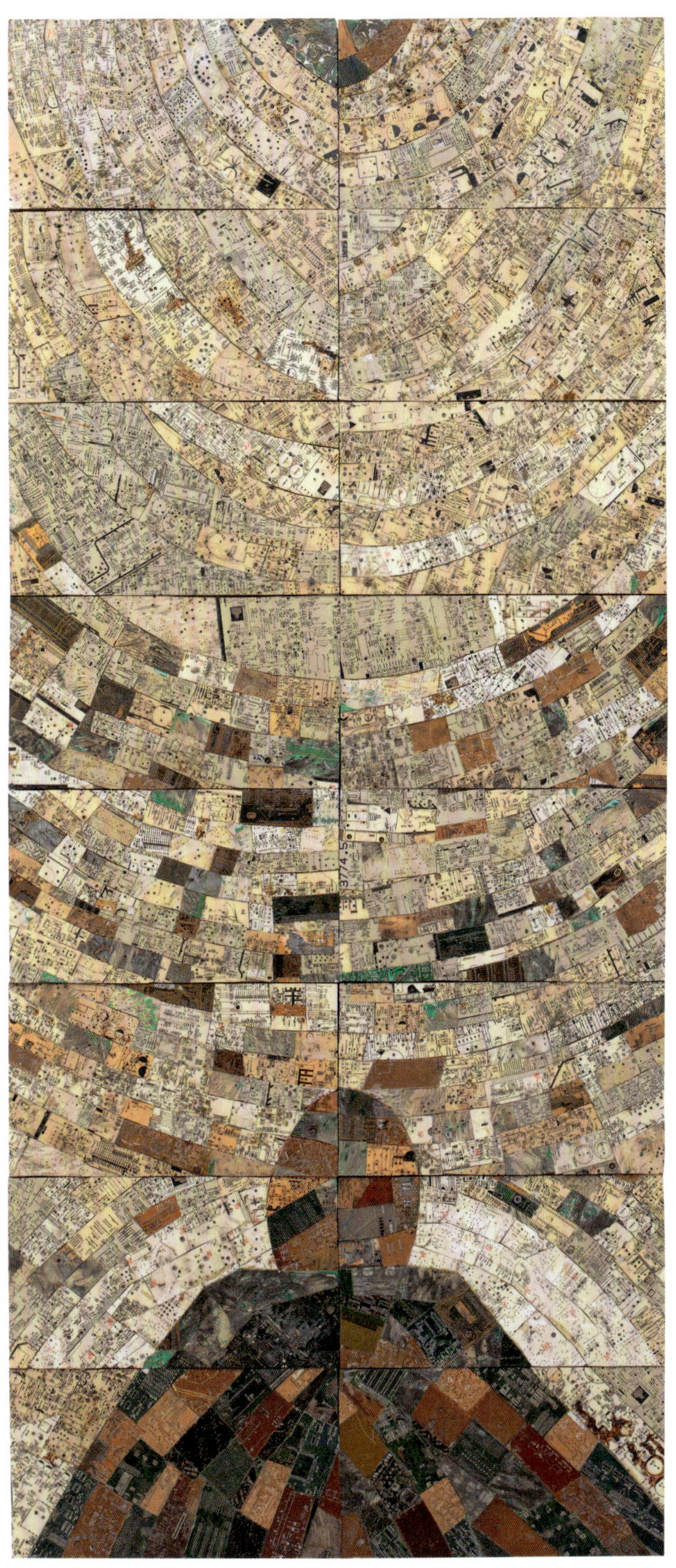

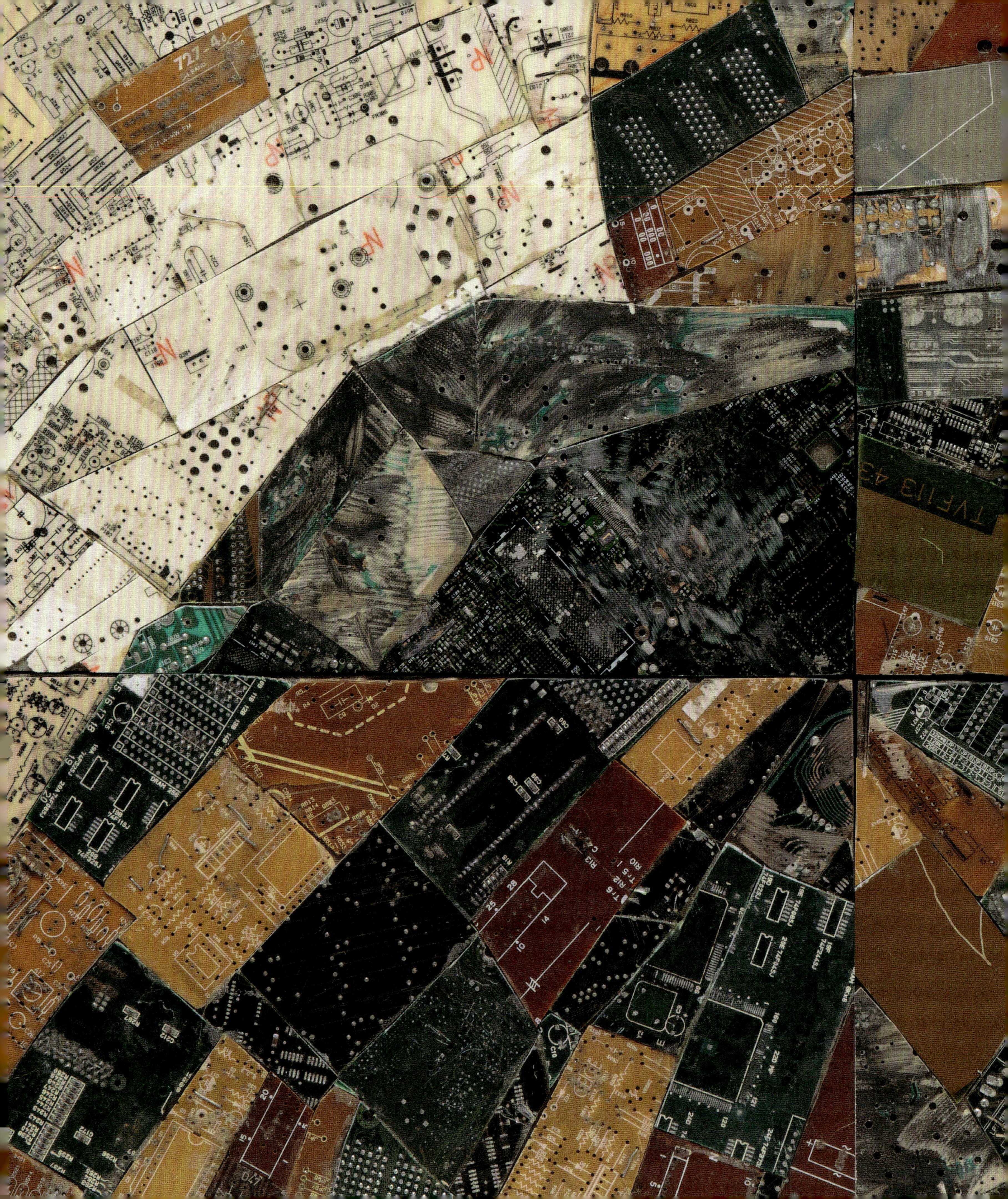

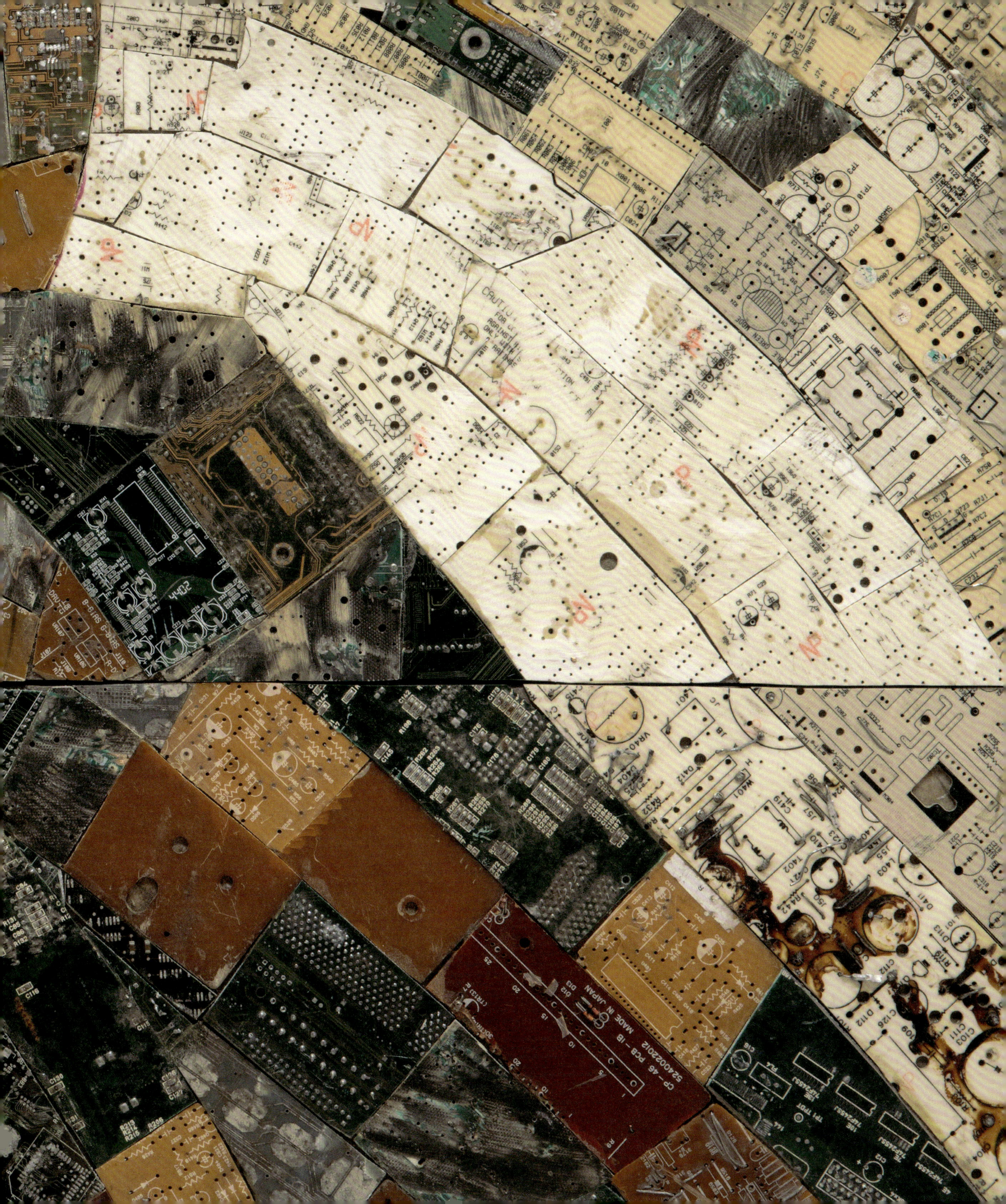

PLATE 22

Tightrope: (5) While Observing . . .

2018 | Reclaimed electronic components and insulated wire on panel | 54 ¼ × 63 in. (137.8 × 160 cm)
Collection of Chris and Heather Kempczinski, Boston

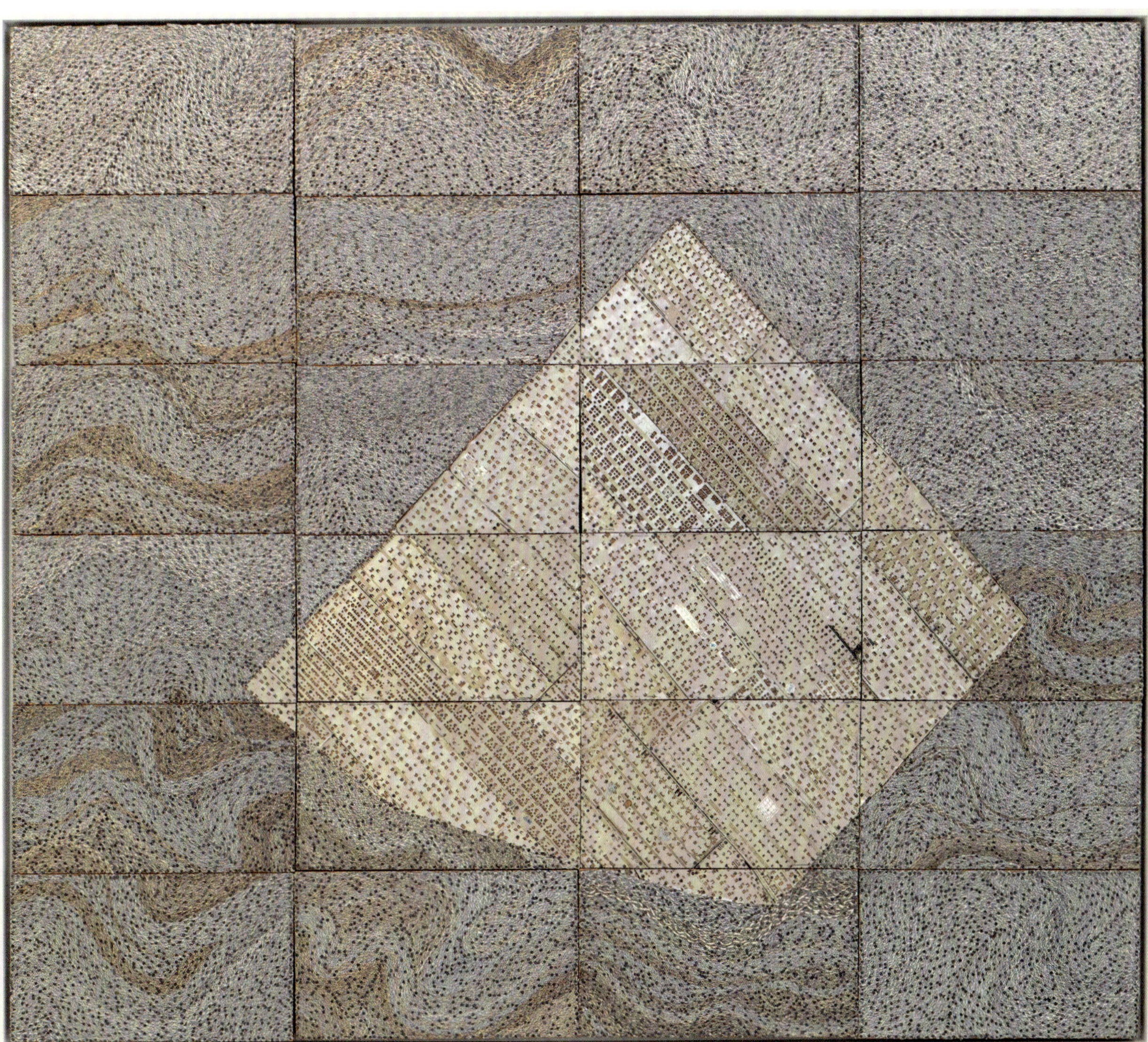

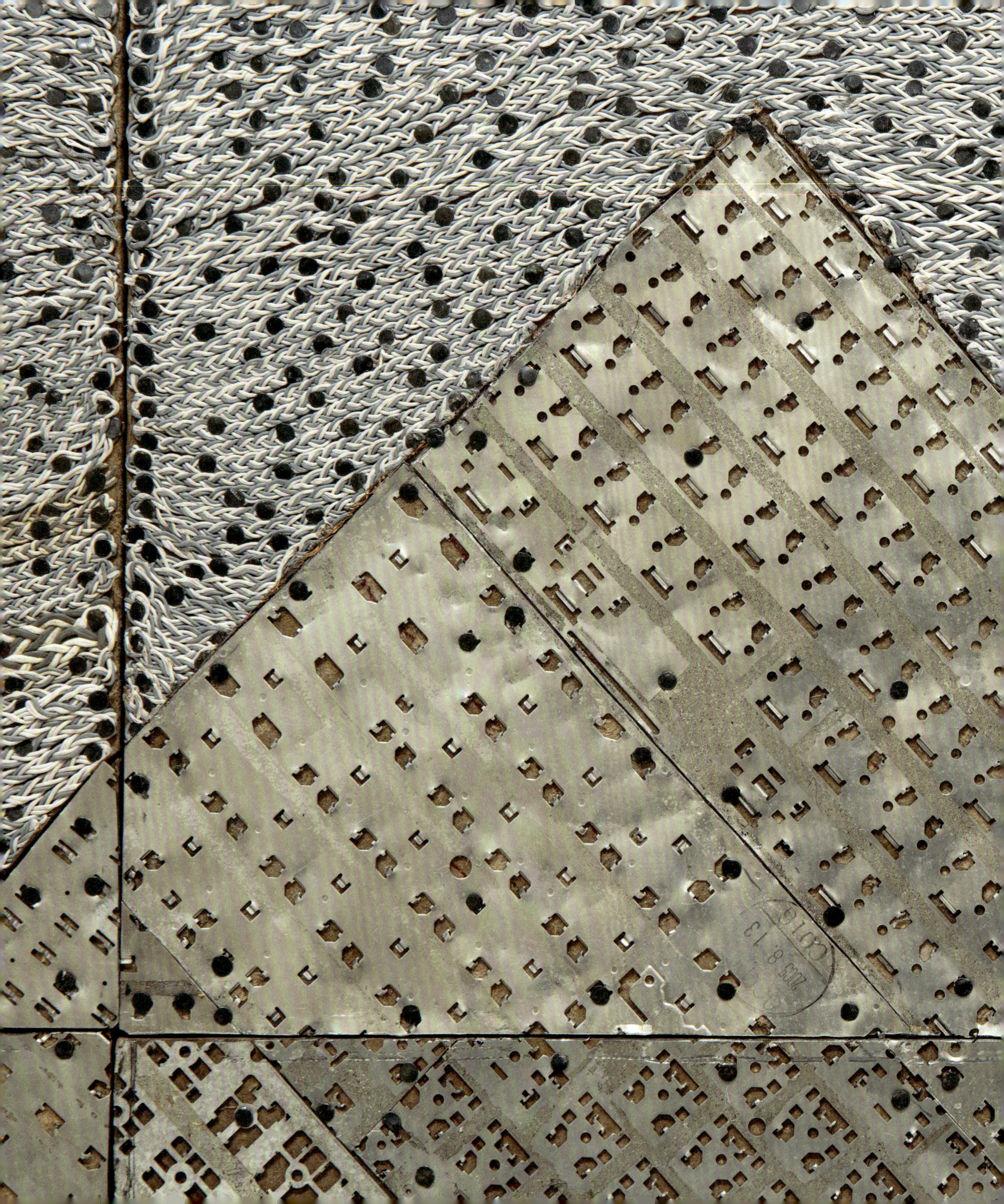

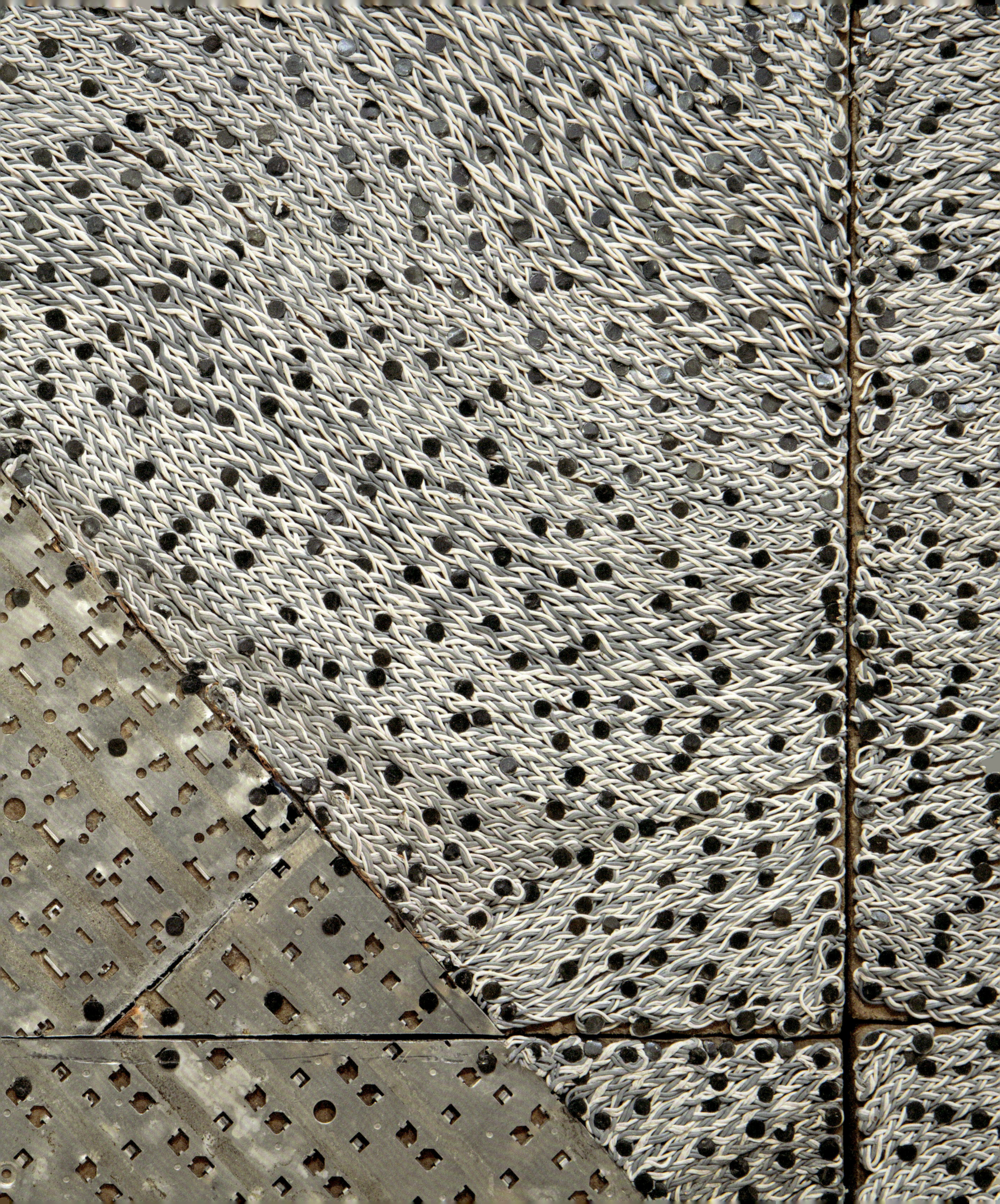

PLATE 23

Tightrope: (8) While Observing . . .

2018 | Reclaimed electronic components and insulated wire on panel | 86 ¾ × 46 ⅝ in. (220.4 × 118.4 cm)
Courtesy of the artist and James Cohan, New York

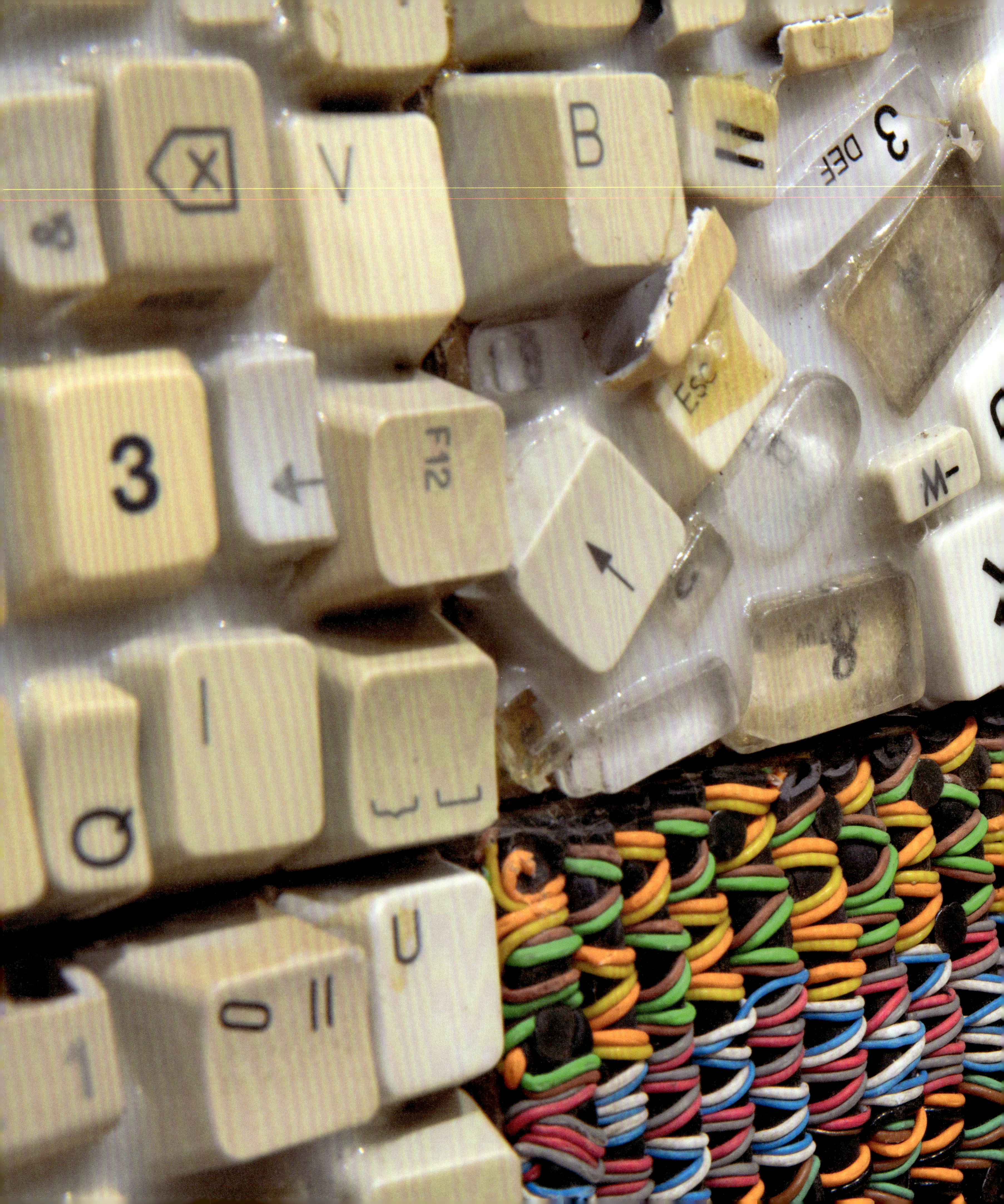

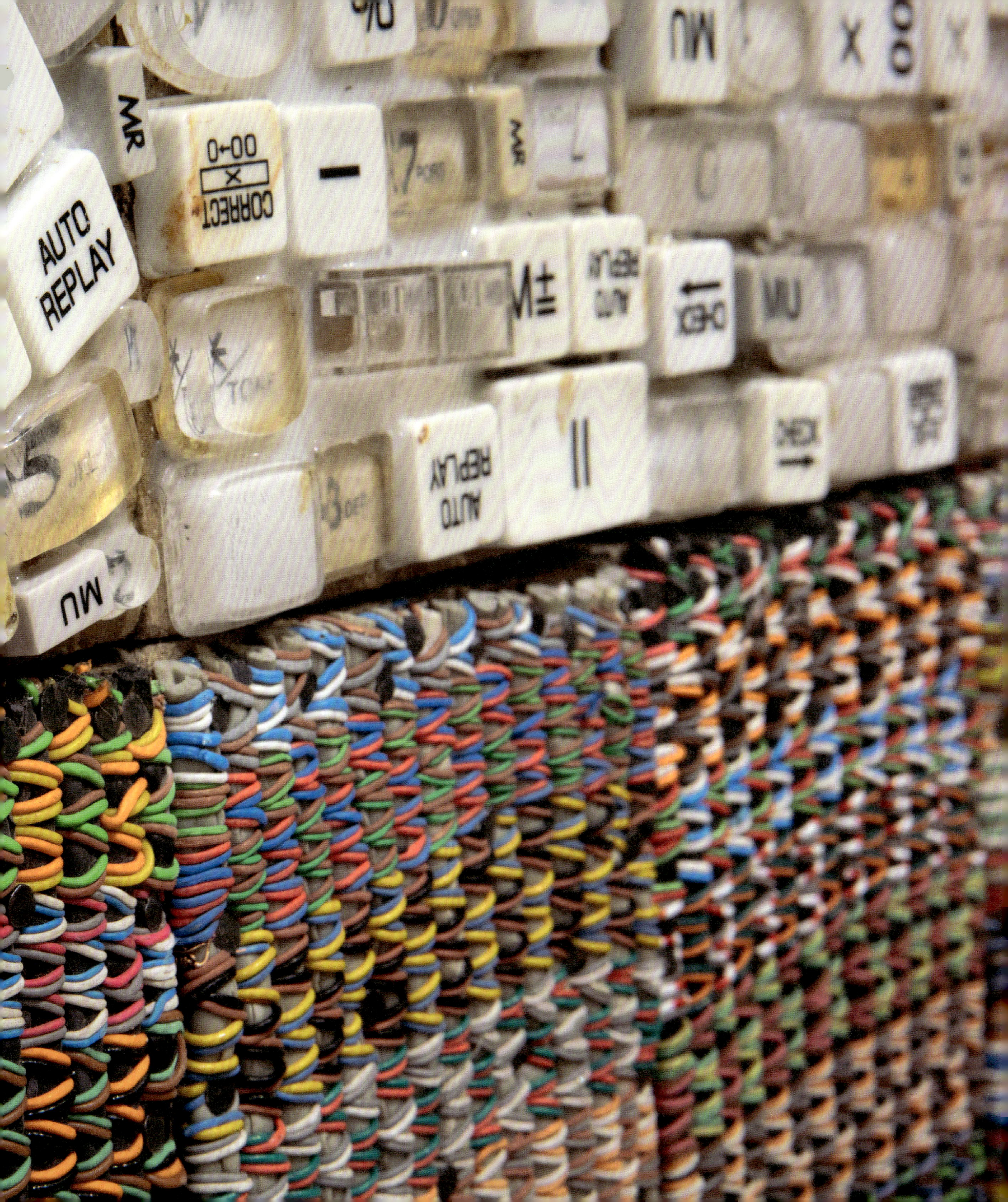

MR
AUTO REPLAY
CORRECT
MU
M±
AUTO REPLAY
CHECK
MR
MU
AUTO REPLAY
CHECK
MU

PLATE 24

Tightrope: (9) While Observing . . .

2018 | Reclaimed electronic components and insulated wire on panel | 94 ⅜ × 63 ⅜ in. (239.7 × 161 cm)
Collection of Robert and Karen Duncan, Lincoln, NE

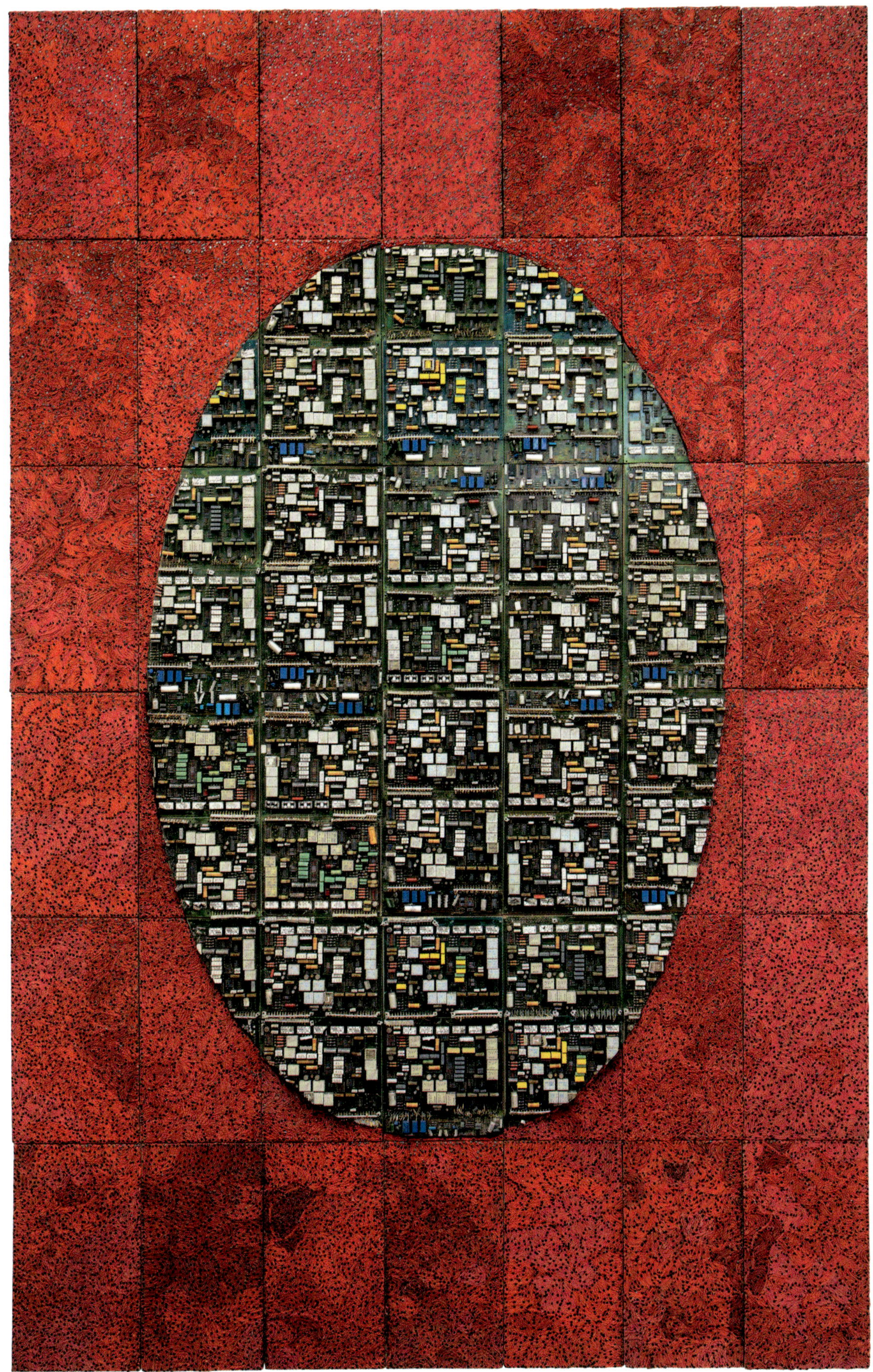

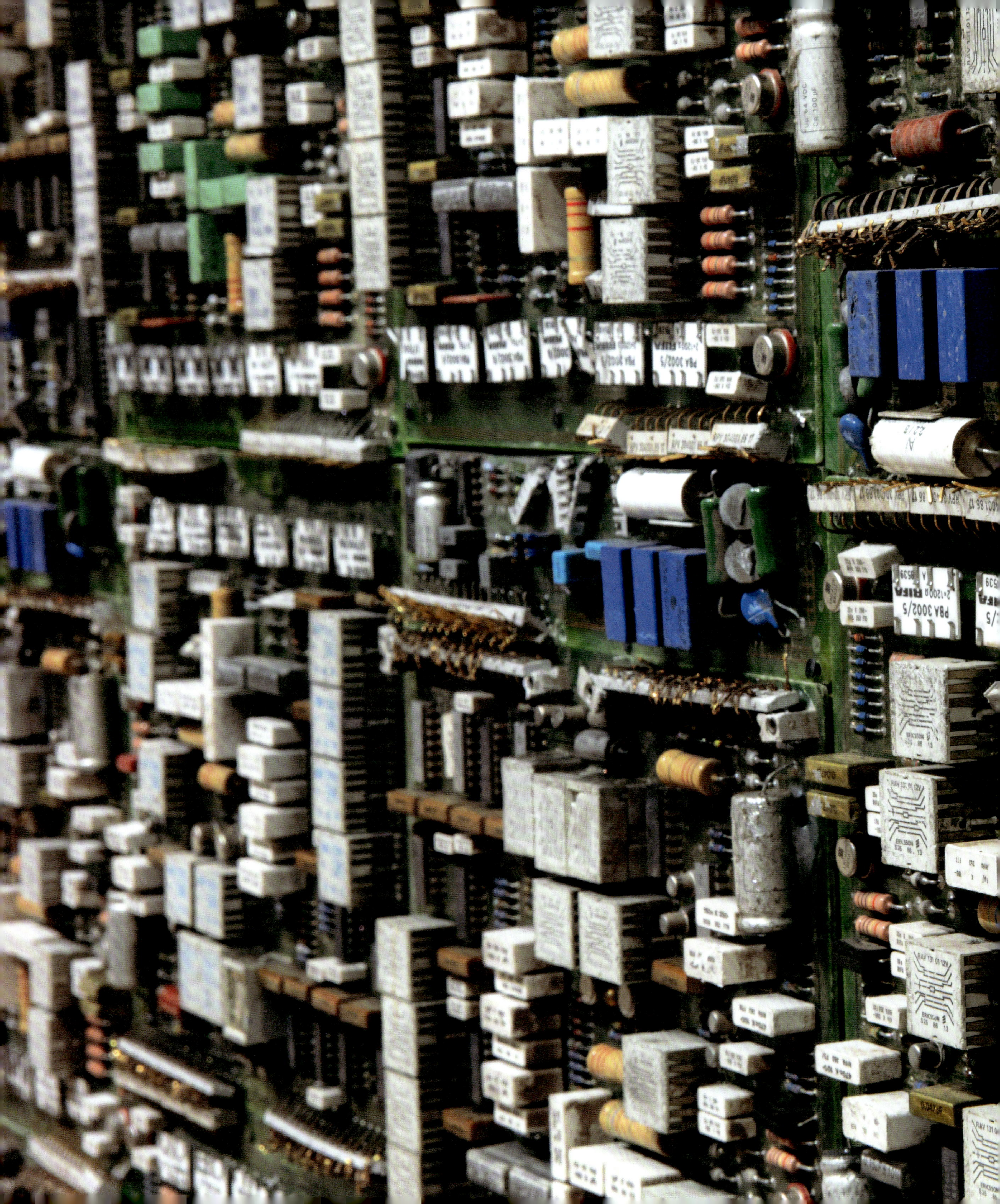
PBA 3002/5

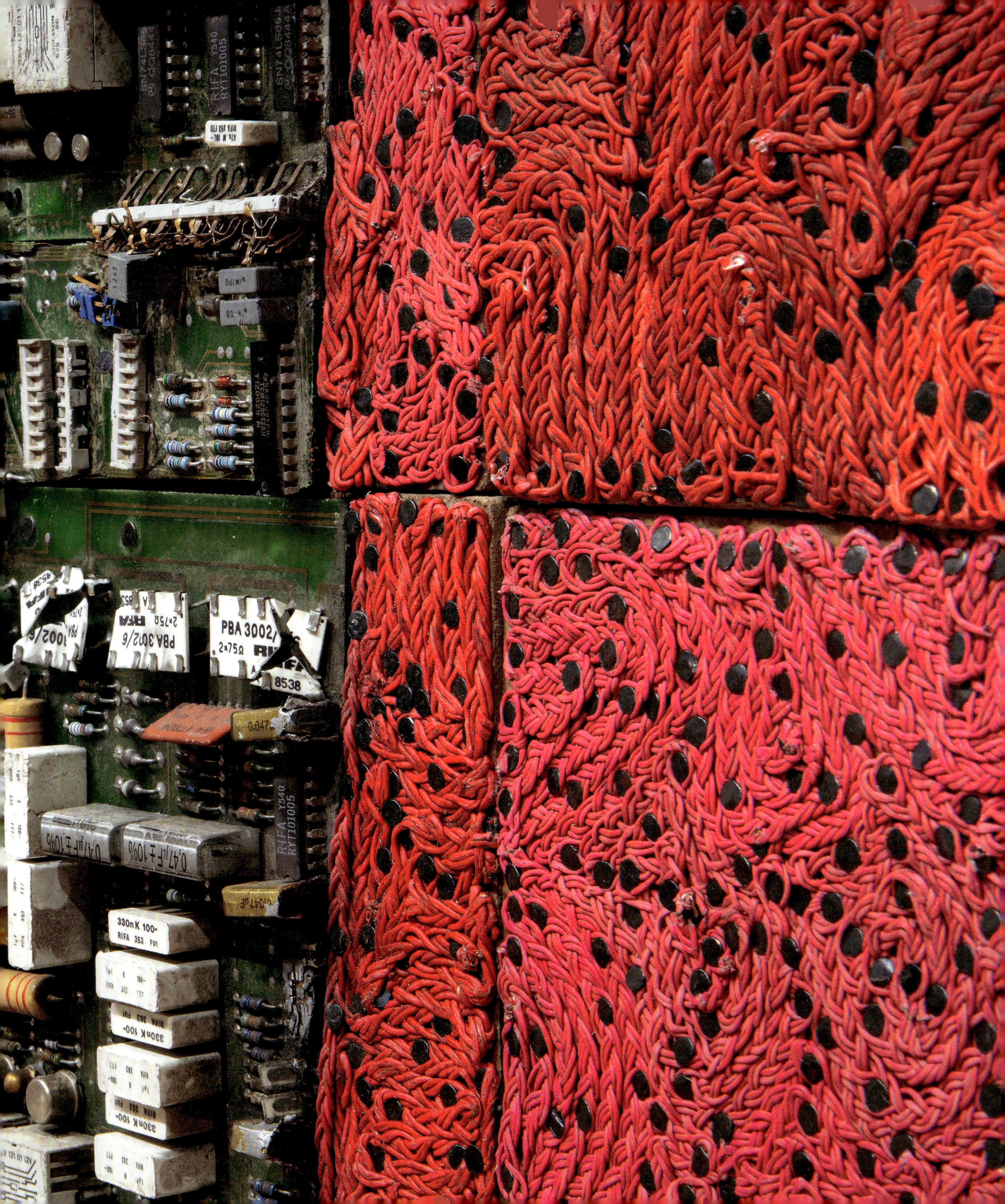

SN74LS86
RIFA Y540
RYT101005
PBA 3002/6
2×75Ω
PBA 3002/
8538
0,47µF ± 10%
330nK 100-
RIFA 353 FU1

PLATE 25

Tightrope: Noiseless 2

2019 | Reclaimed electronic components and insulated wire on panel | 8 ft. 5 in. × 13 ft. 2 in. (256.5 × 401.3 cm)
Courtesy of the artist and James Cohan, New York

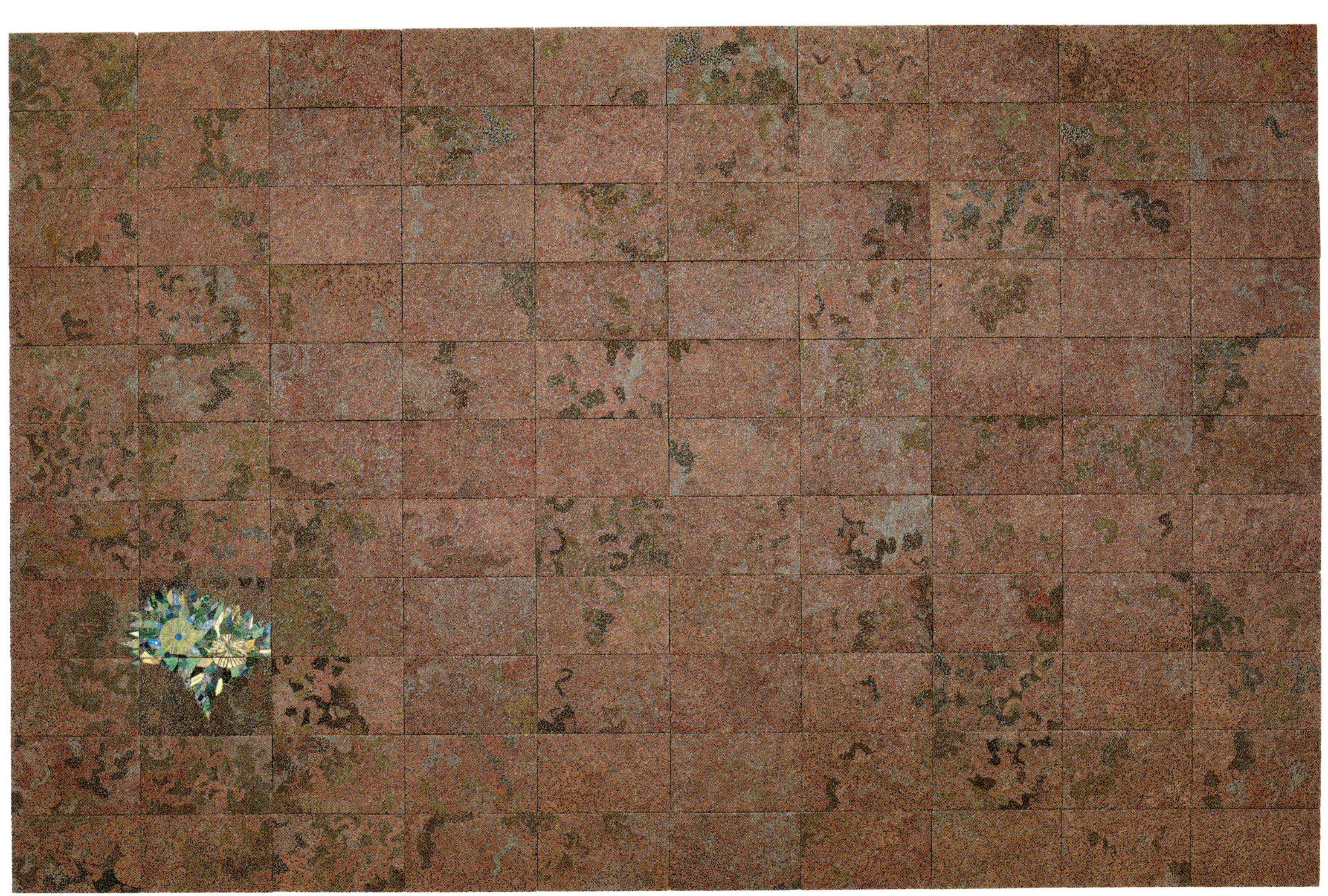

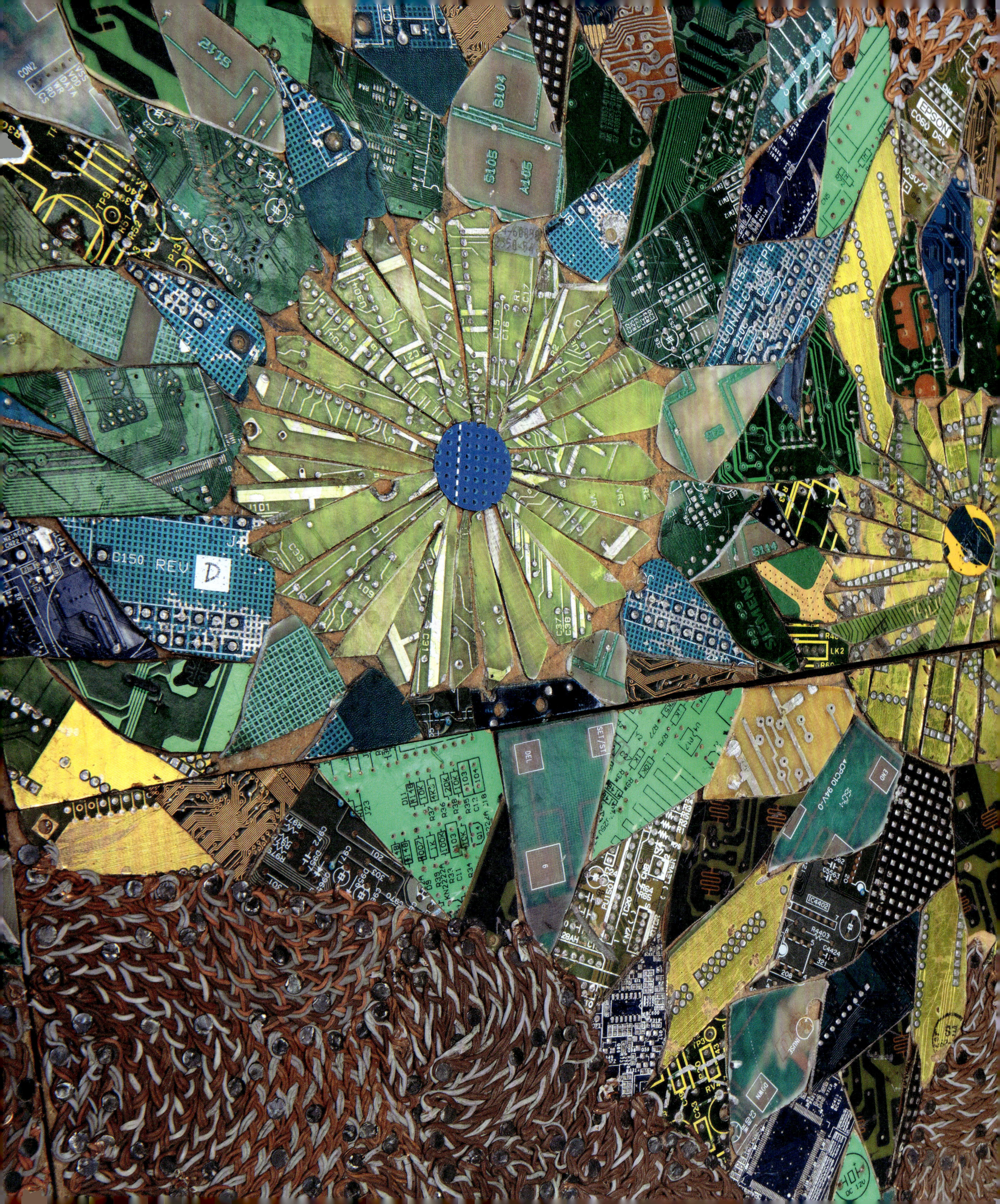
C150 REV D
SIEMENS
EPSON

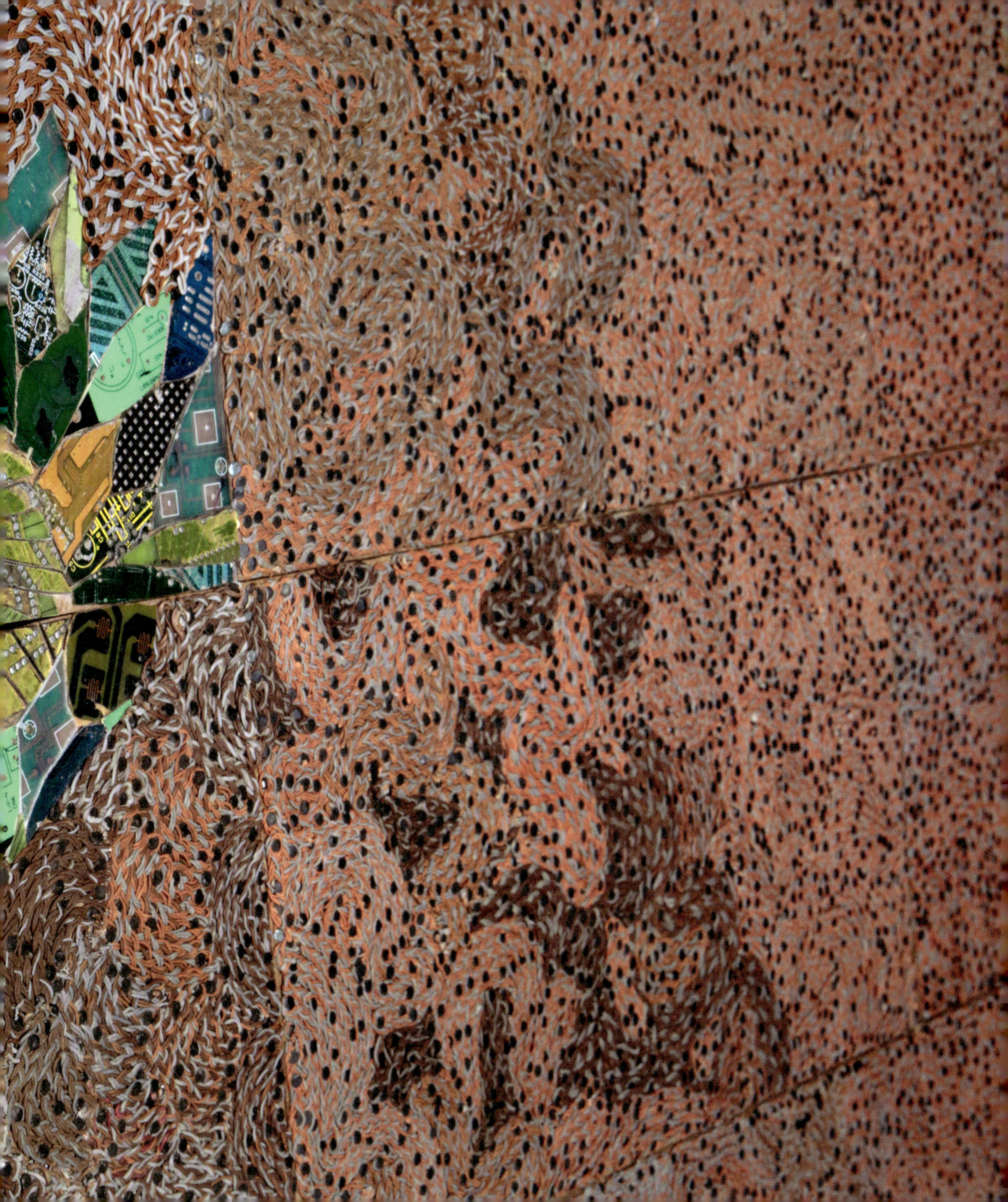

PLATE 26

Tightrope: Noiseless 12

2019 | Reclaimed insulated wire on panel | 9 ft. 9 in. × 63 ½ in. (297.2 × 161.3 cm)
Des Moines Art Center, IA | Purchased with funds from the Edmundson Art Foundation

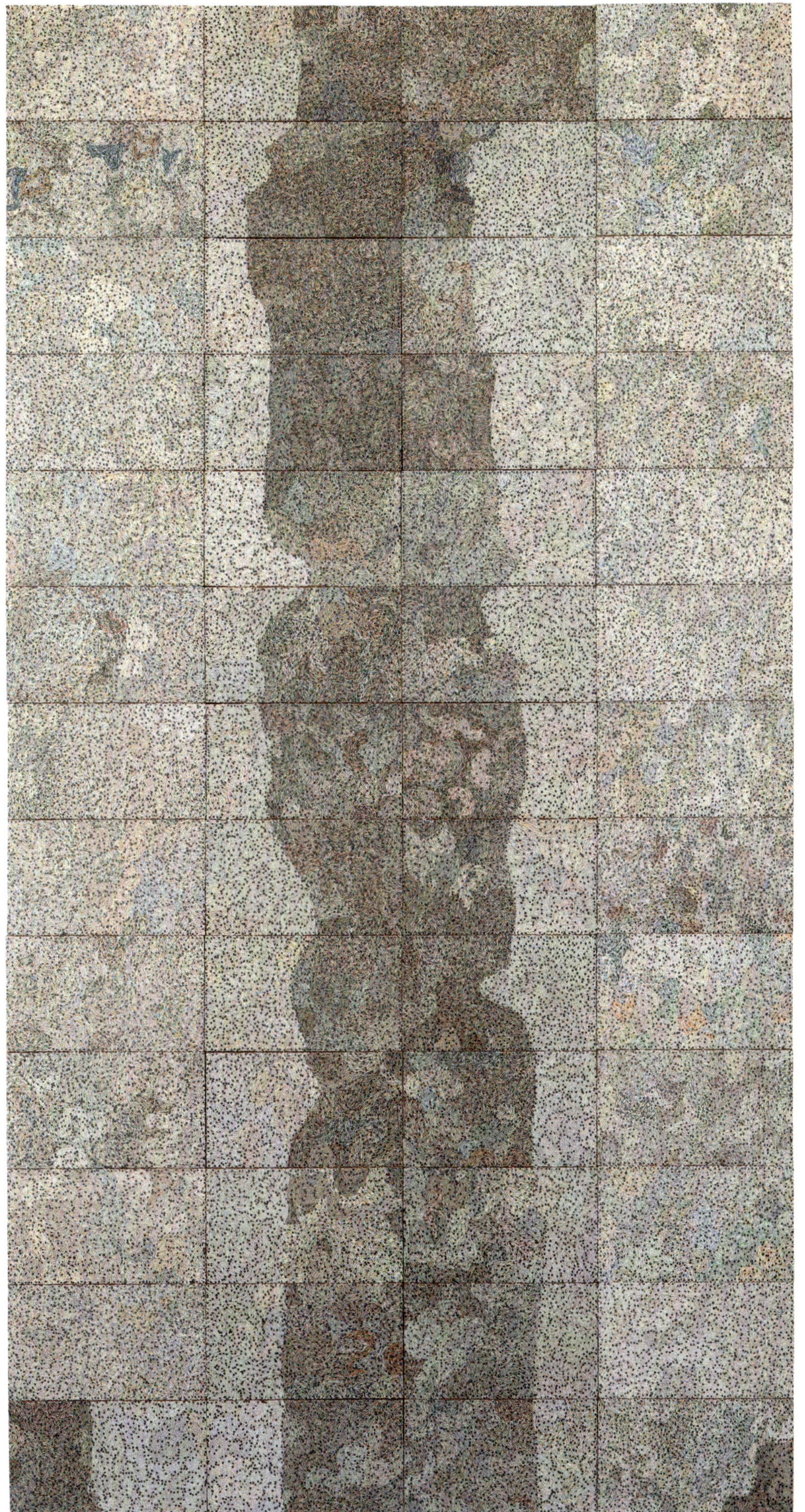

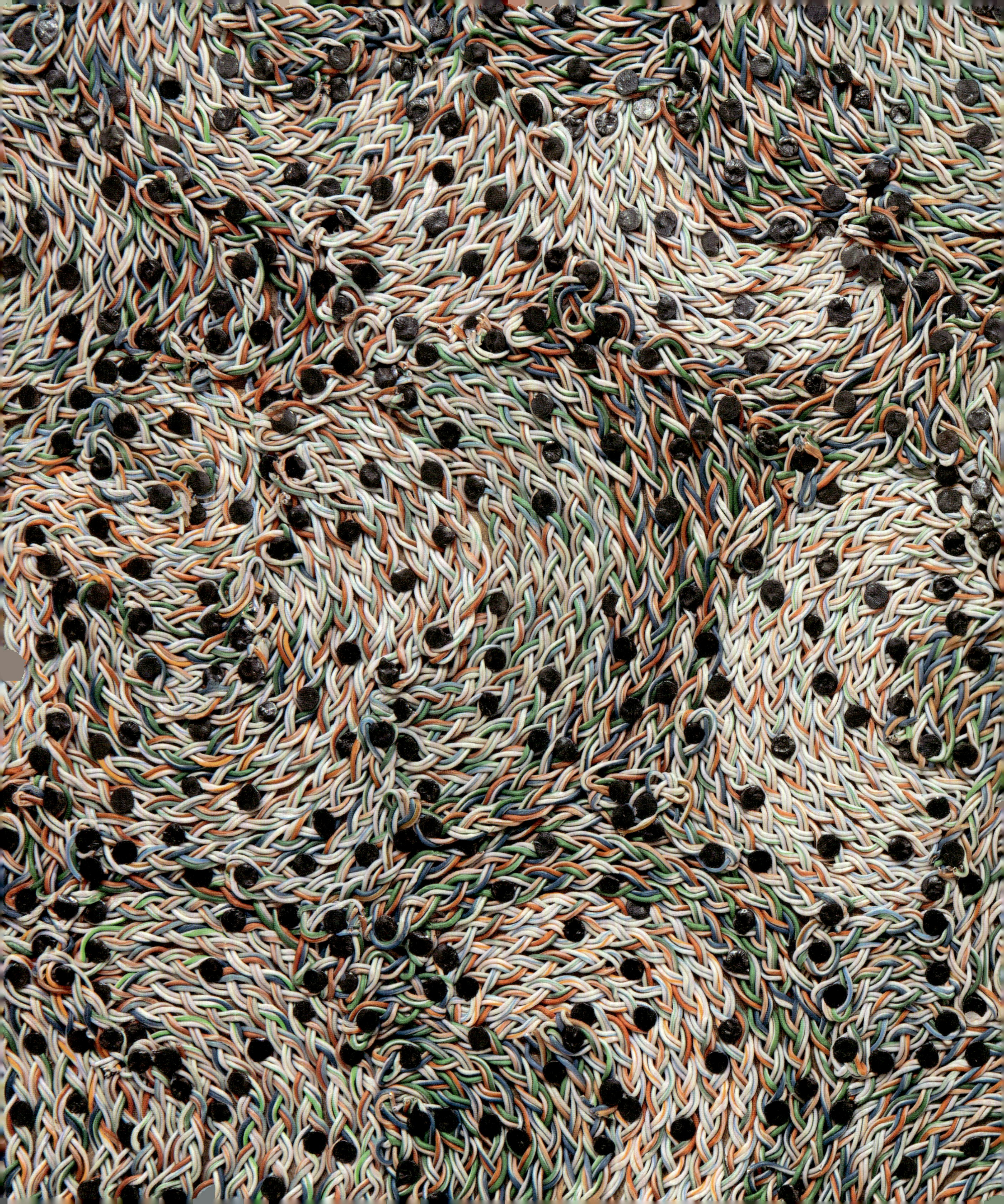

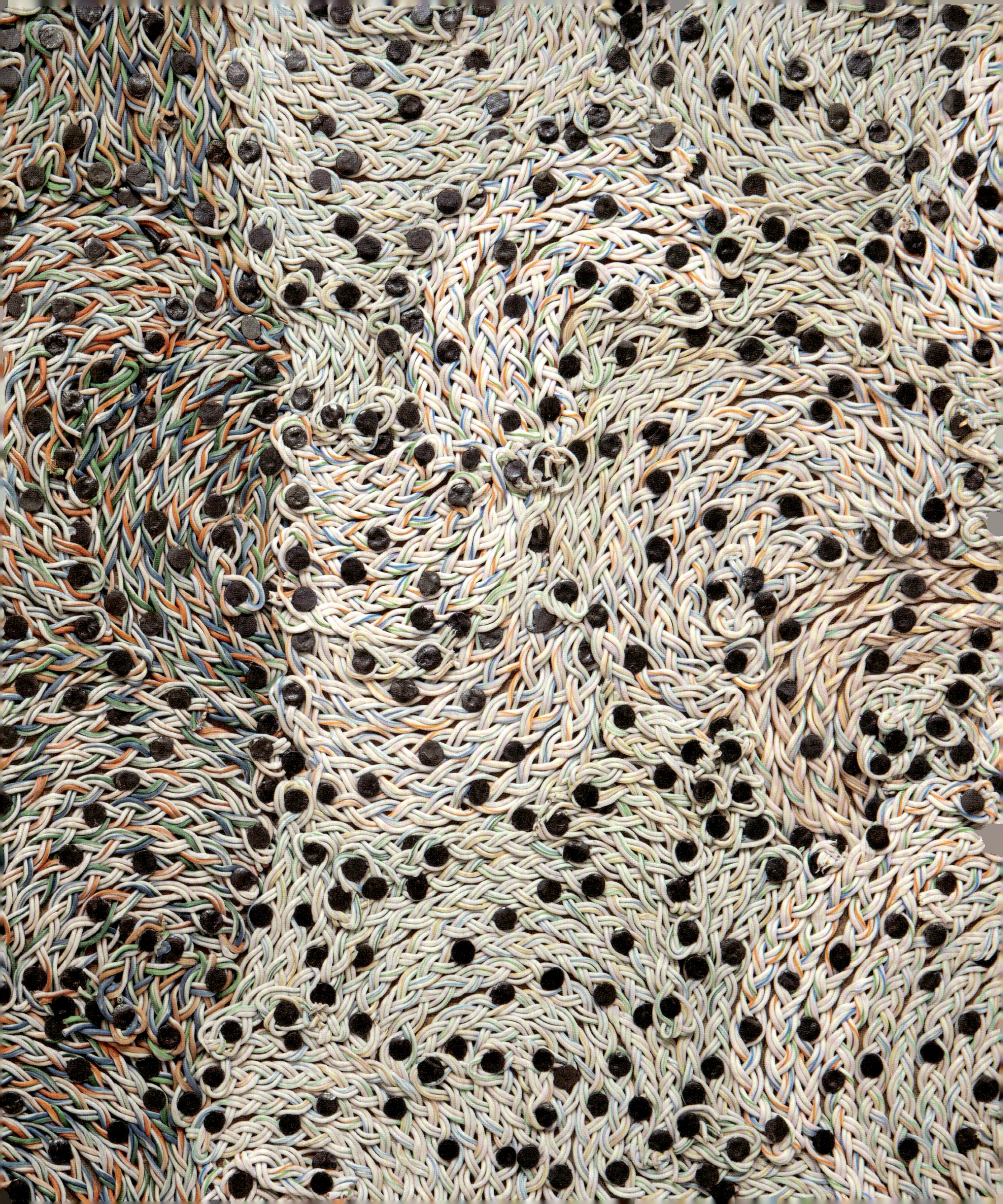

PLATE 27

Tightrope: Noiseless 23

2019 | Reclaimed electronic components and insulated wire on panel | 8 ft. 4 ½ in. × 46 ¾ in. (255.3 × 118.7 cm)
Collection of Charles Banta, Buffalo, NY

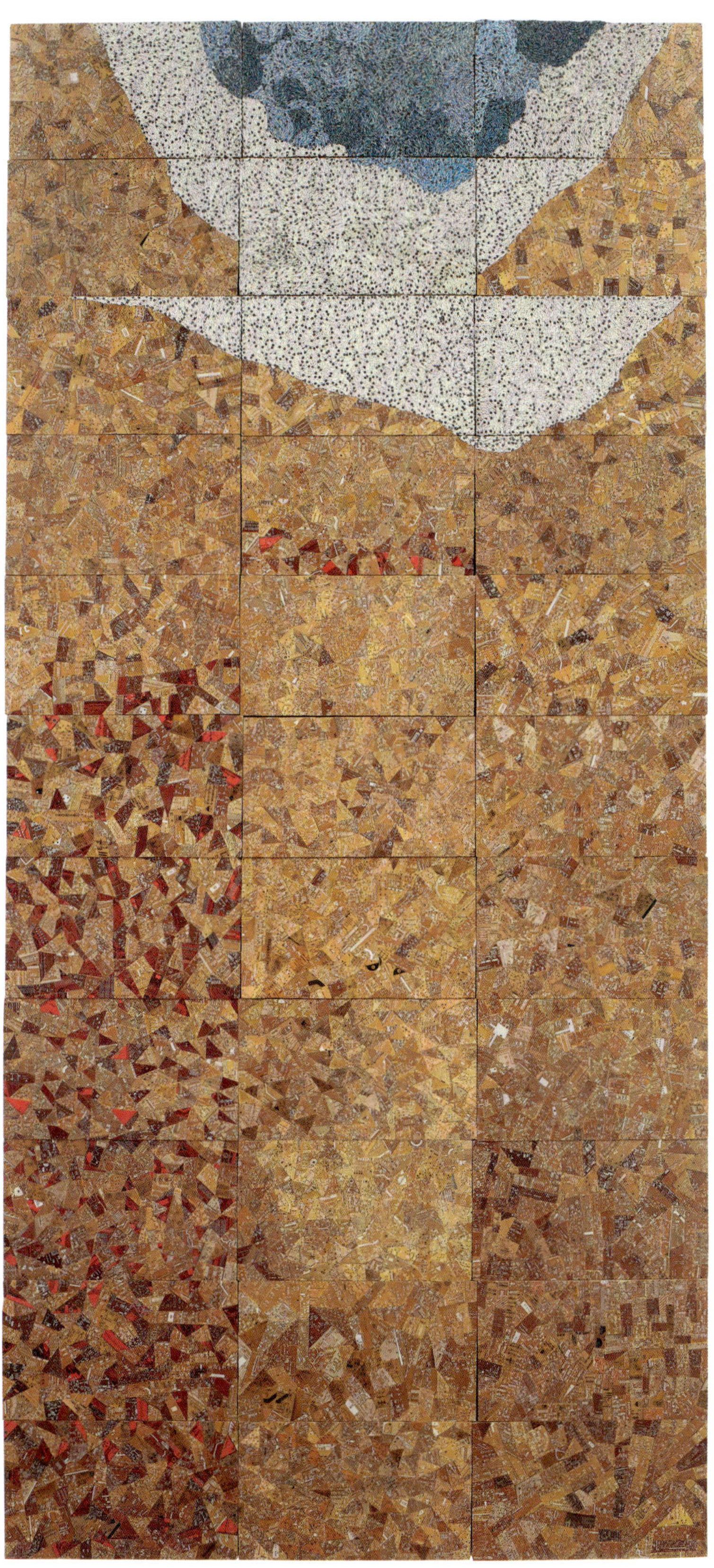

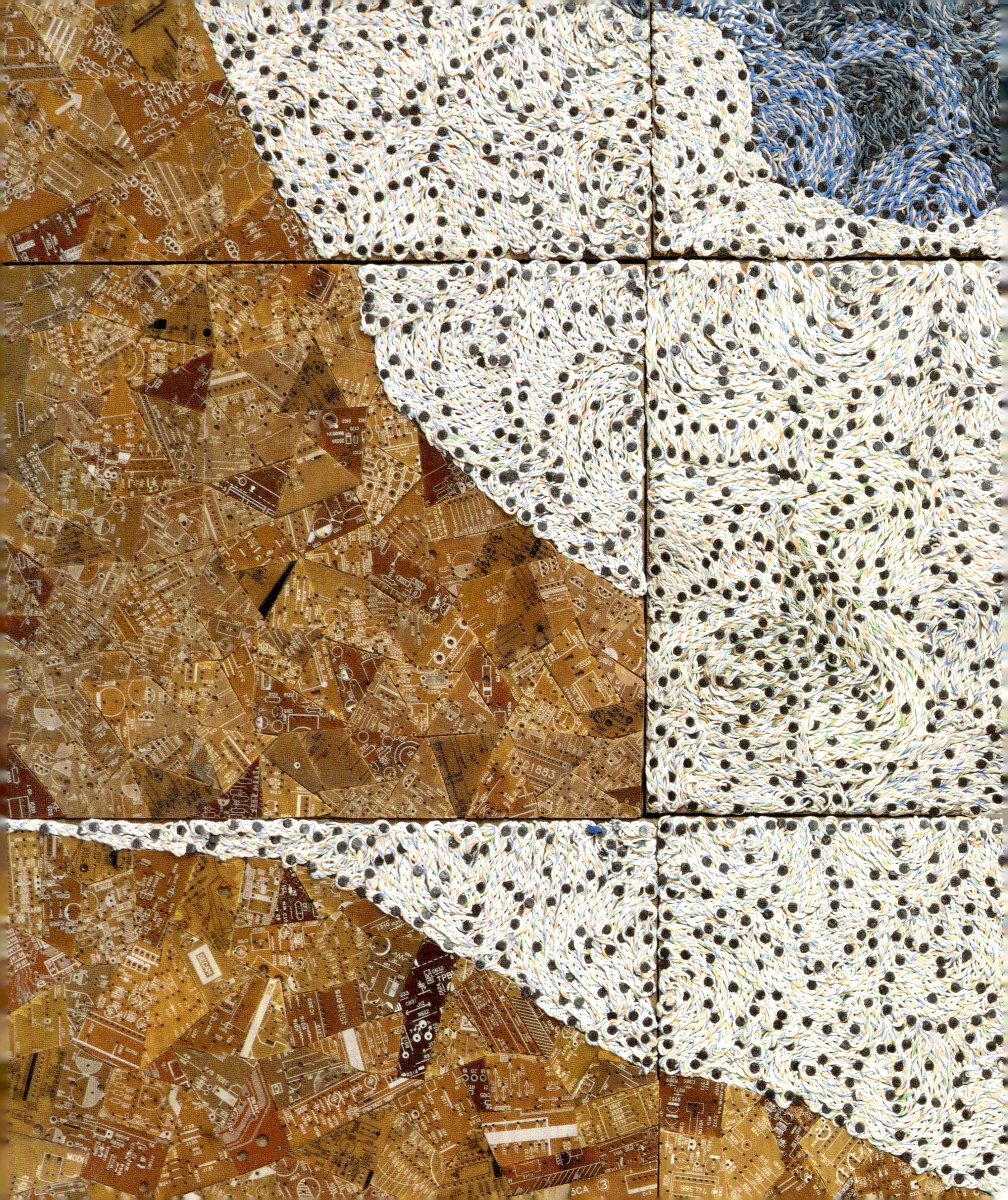

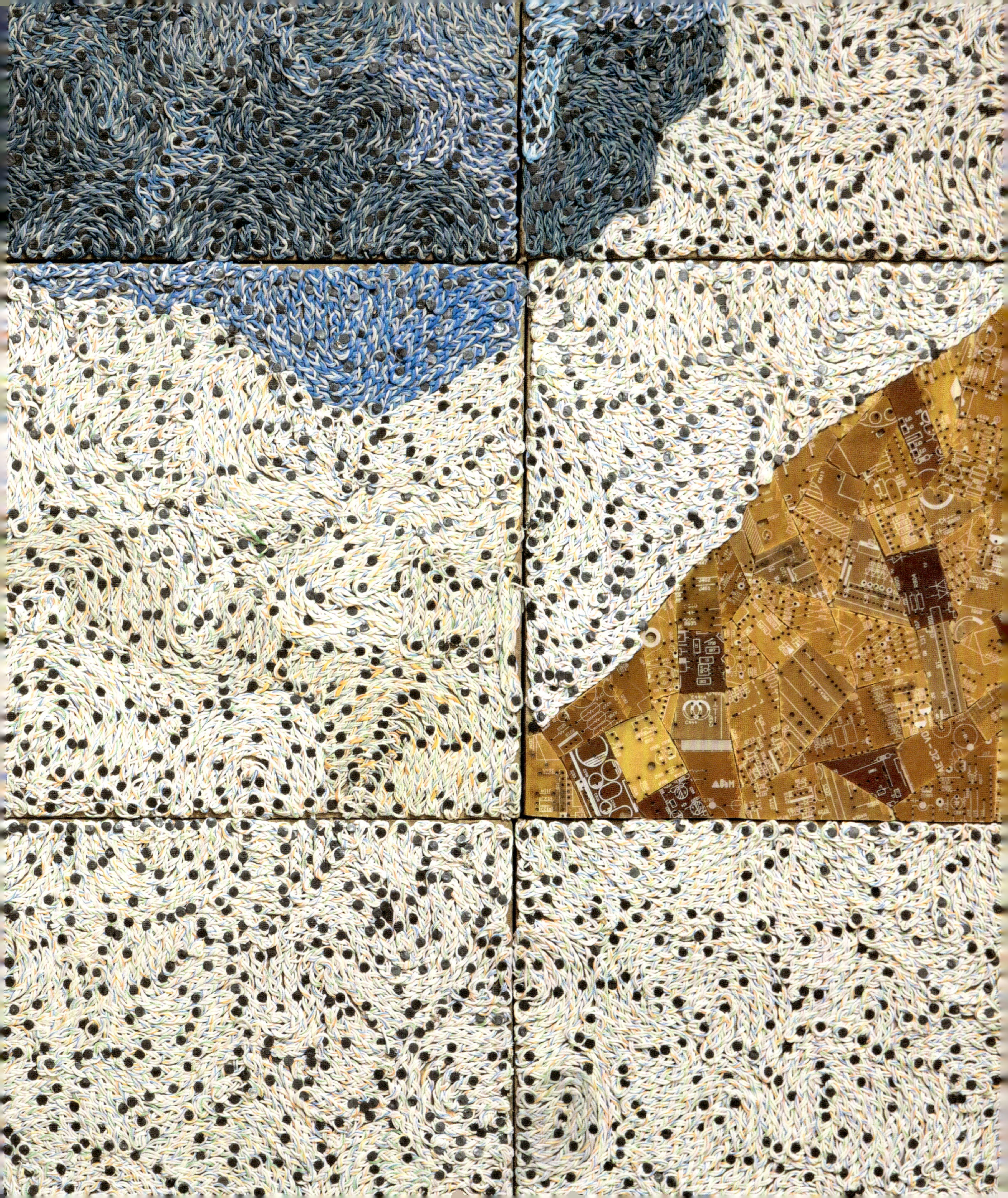

PLATE 28

Tightrope: Silent 1

2019 | Reclaimed electronic components on panel | 72 ½ in. × 10 ft. 6 in. (184.2 × 320 cm)
Courtesy of the artist and James Cohan, New York

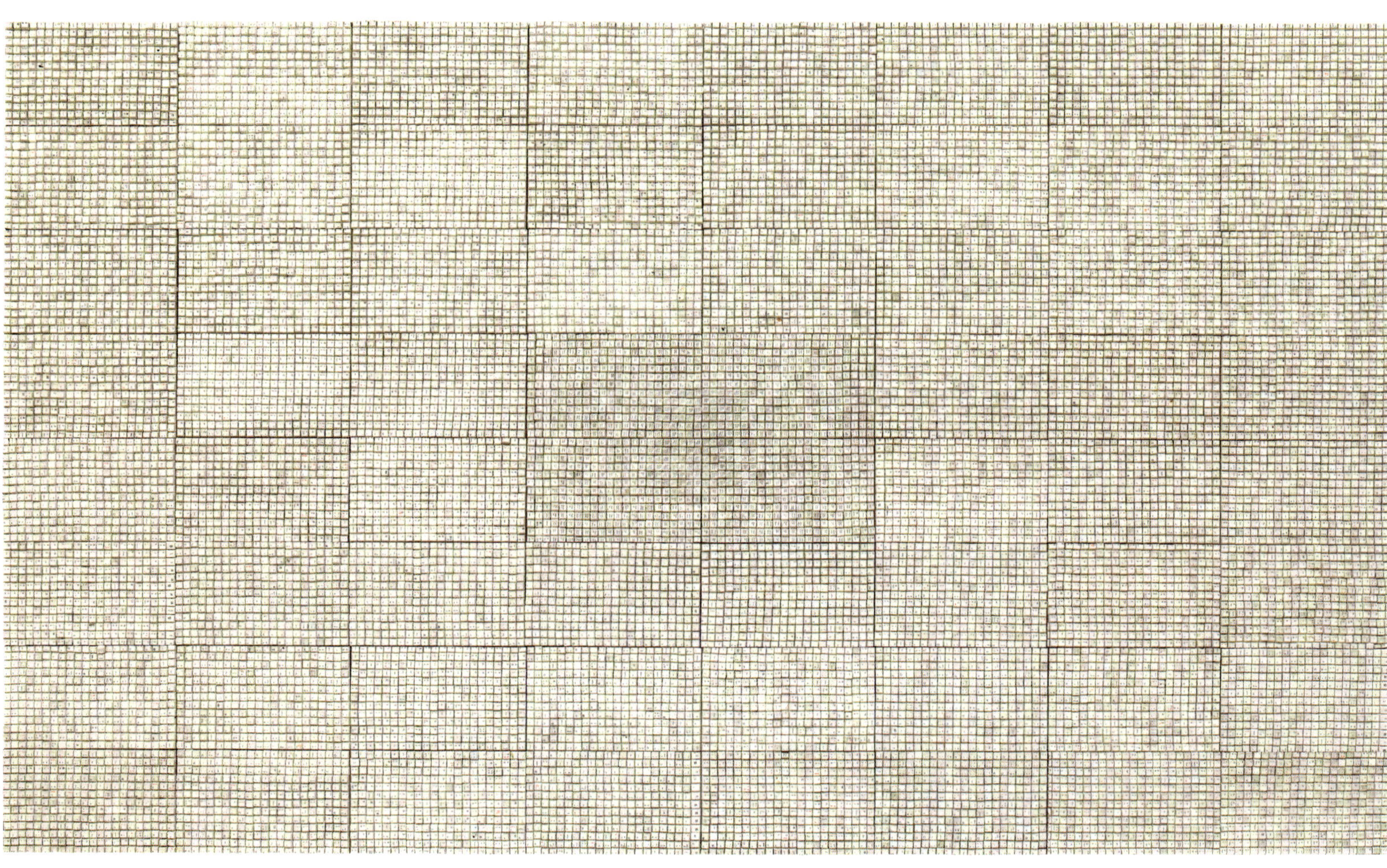

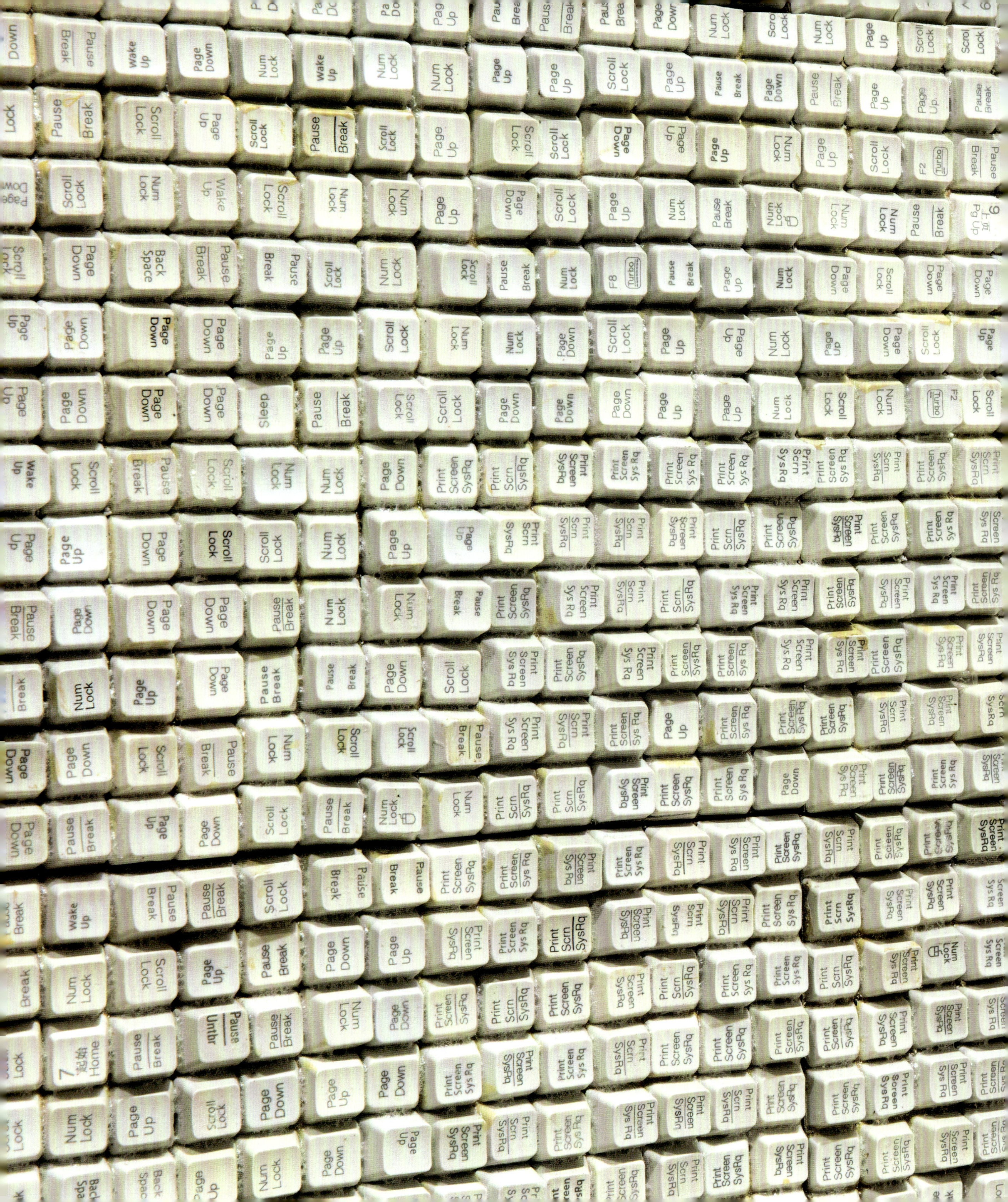

PLATE 29

Tightrope: Silent 2

2019 | Reclaimed electronic components on panel | 72 ½ in. × 10 ft. 6 in. (184.2 × 320 cm)
Courtesy of the artist and James Cohan, New York

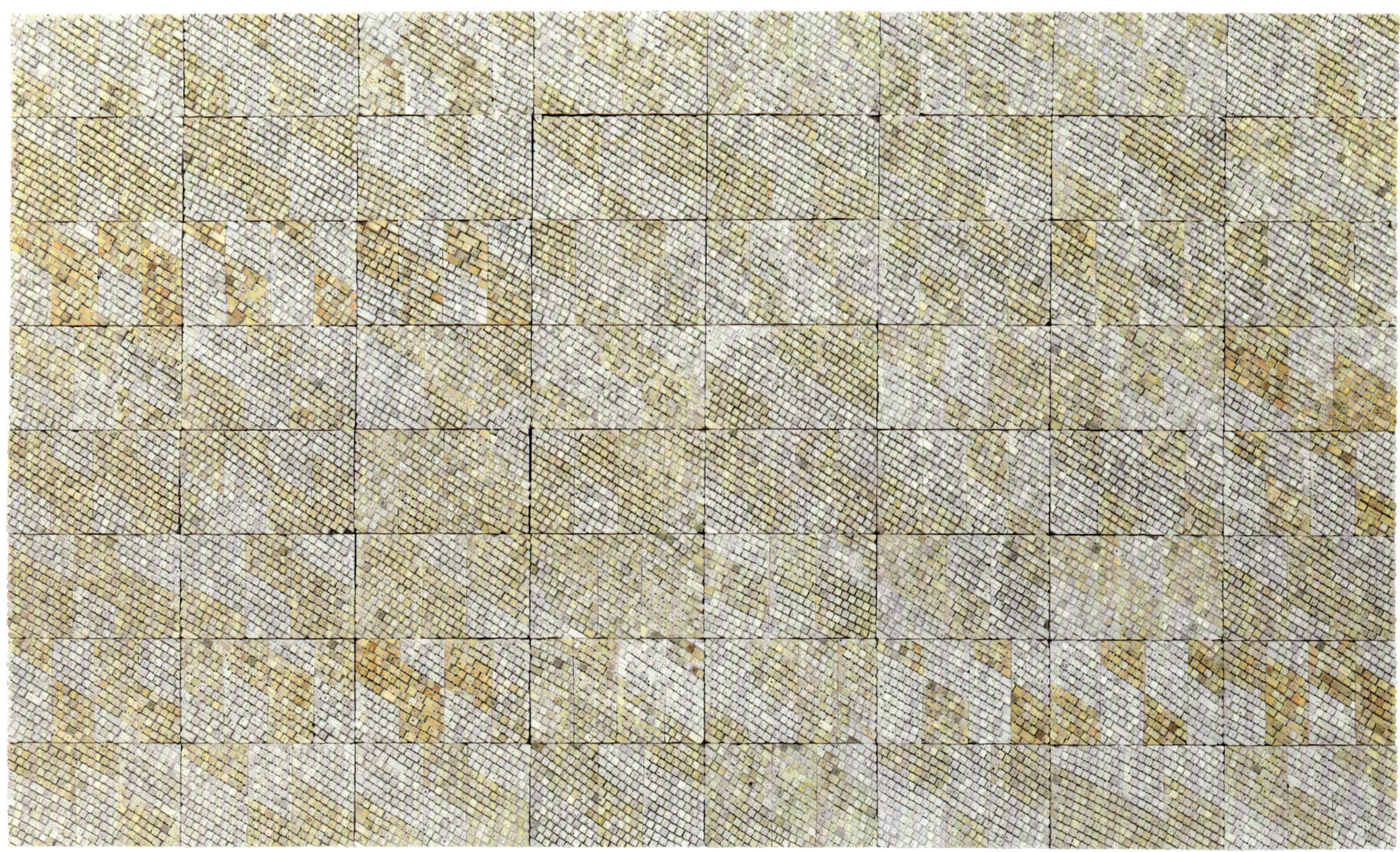

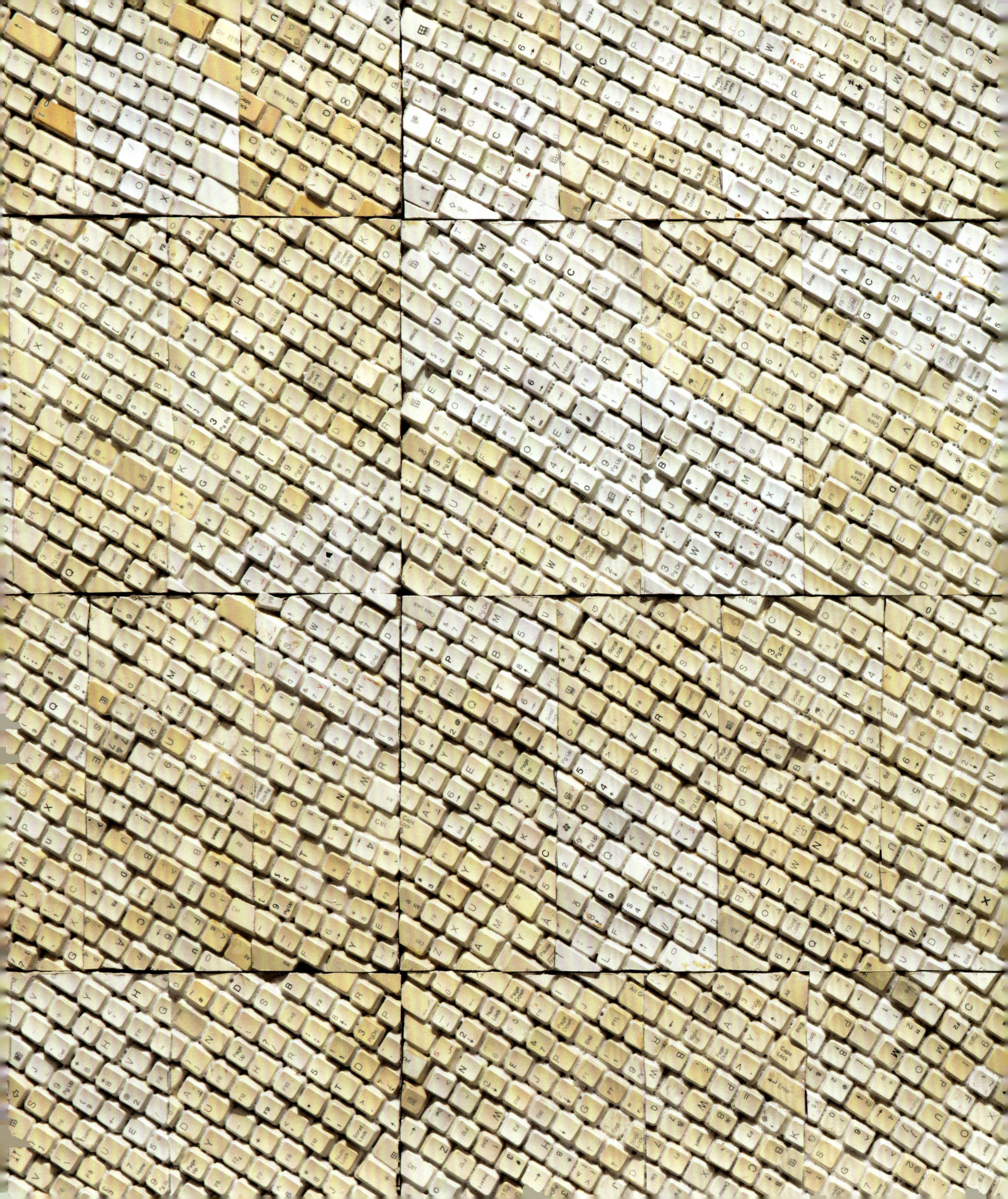

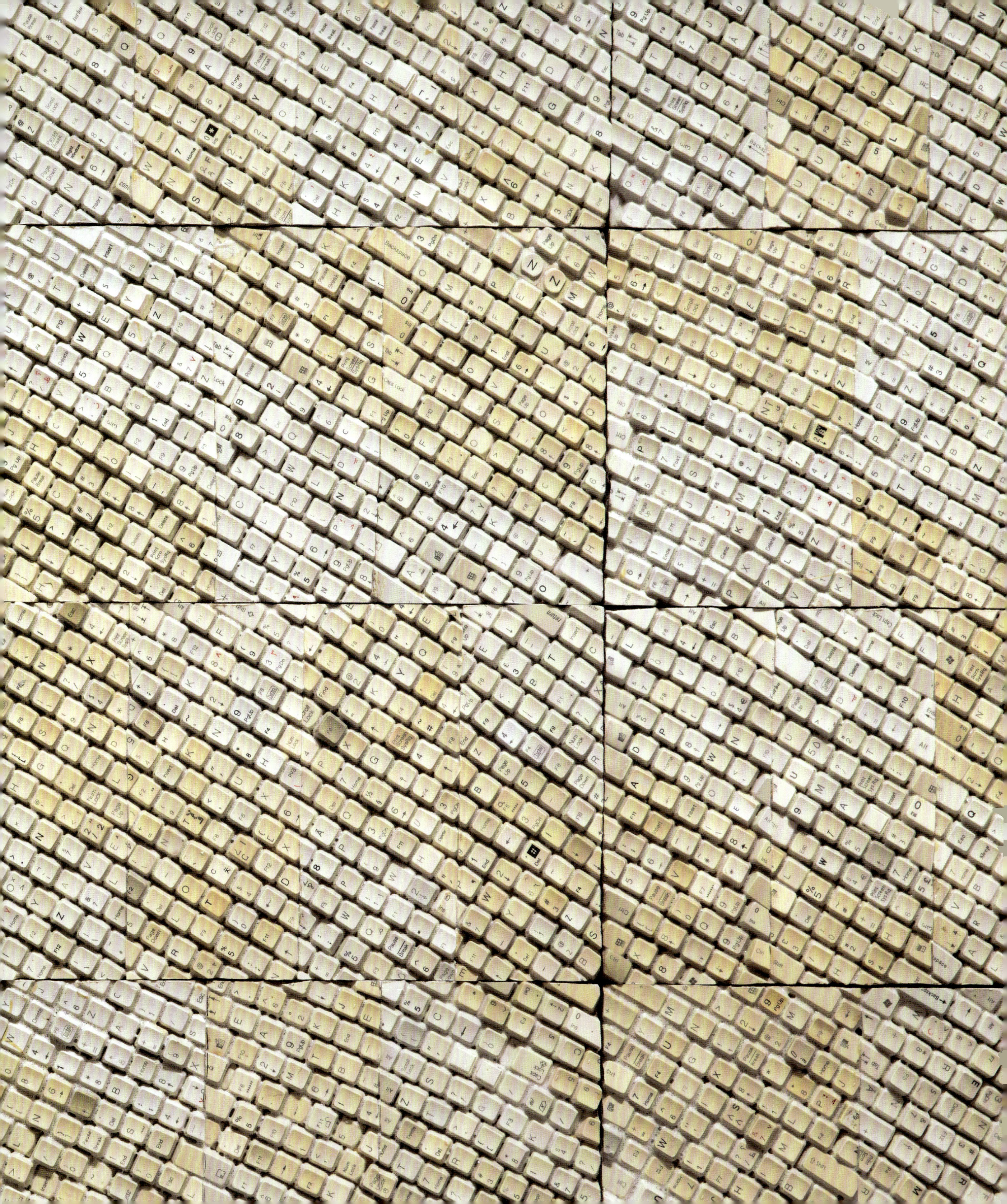

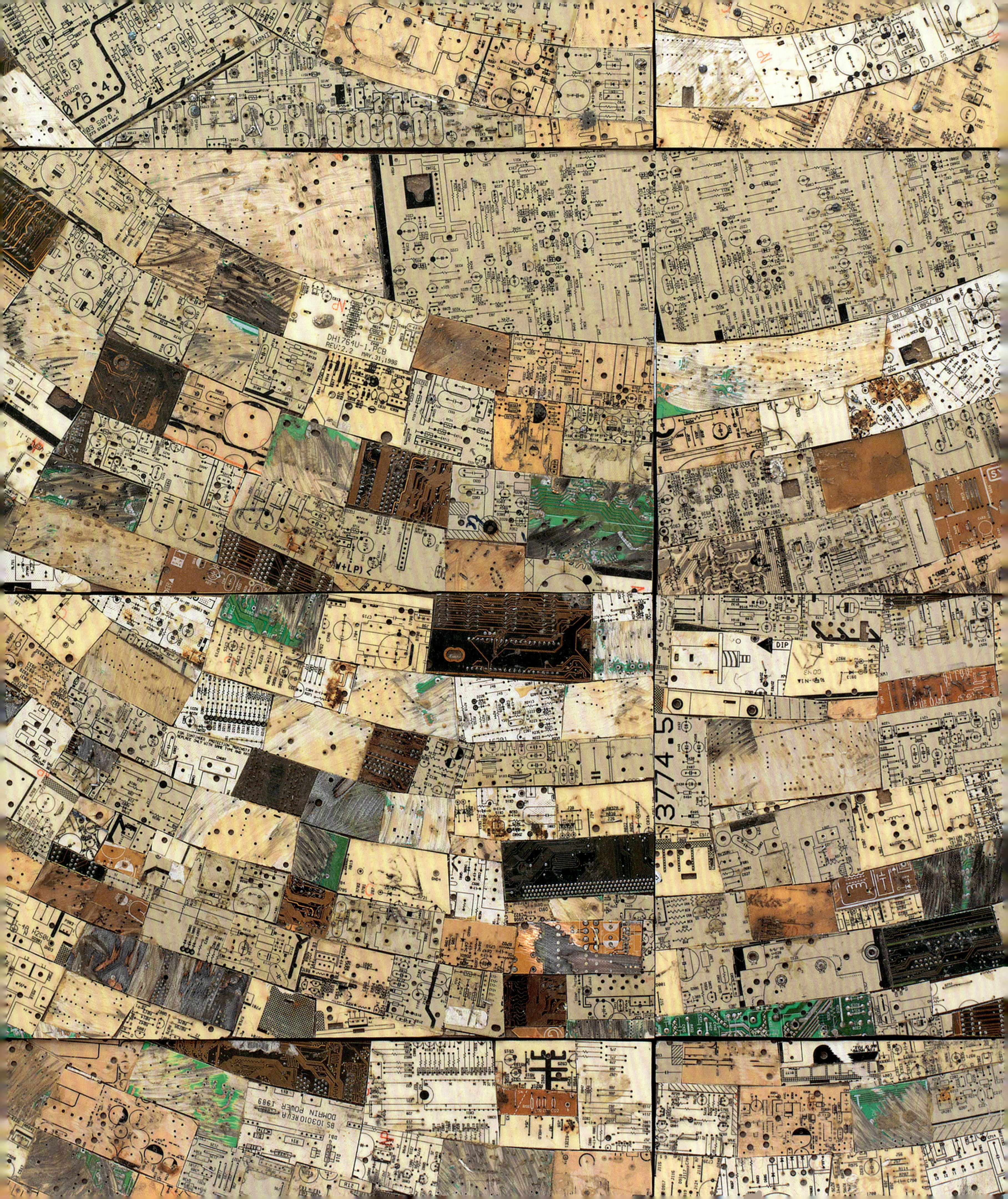

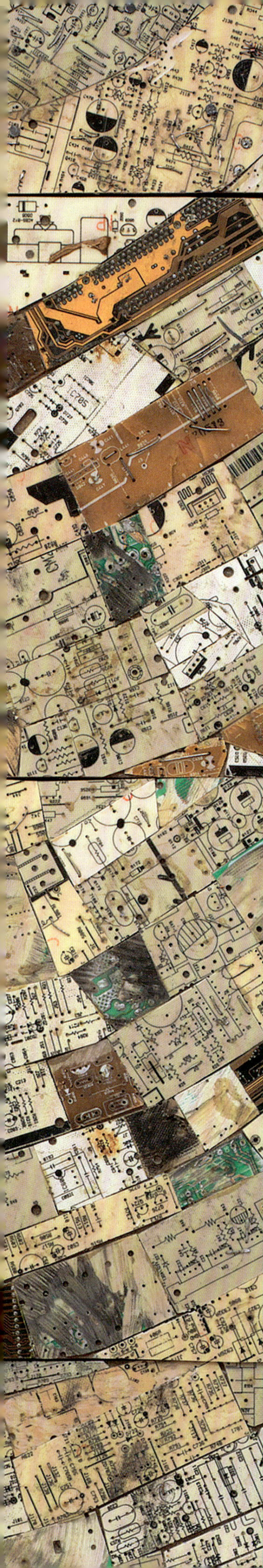

INTERVIEW WITH ELIAS SIME AND MESKEREM ASSEGUED

TRACY L. ADLER

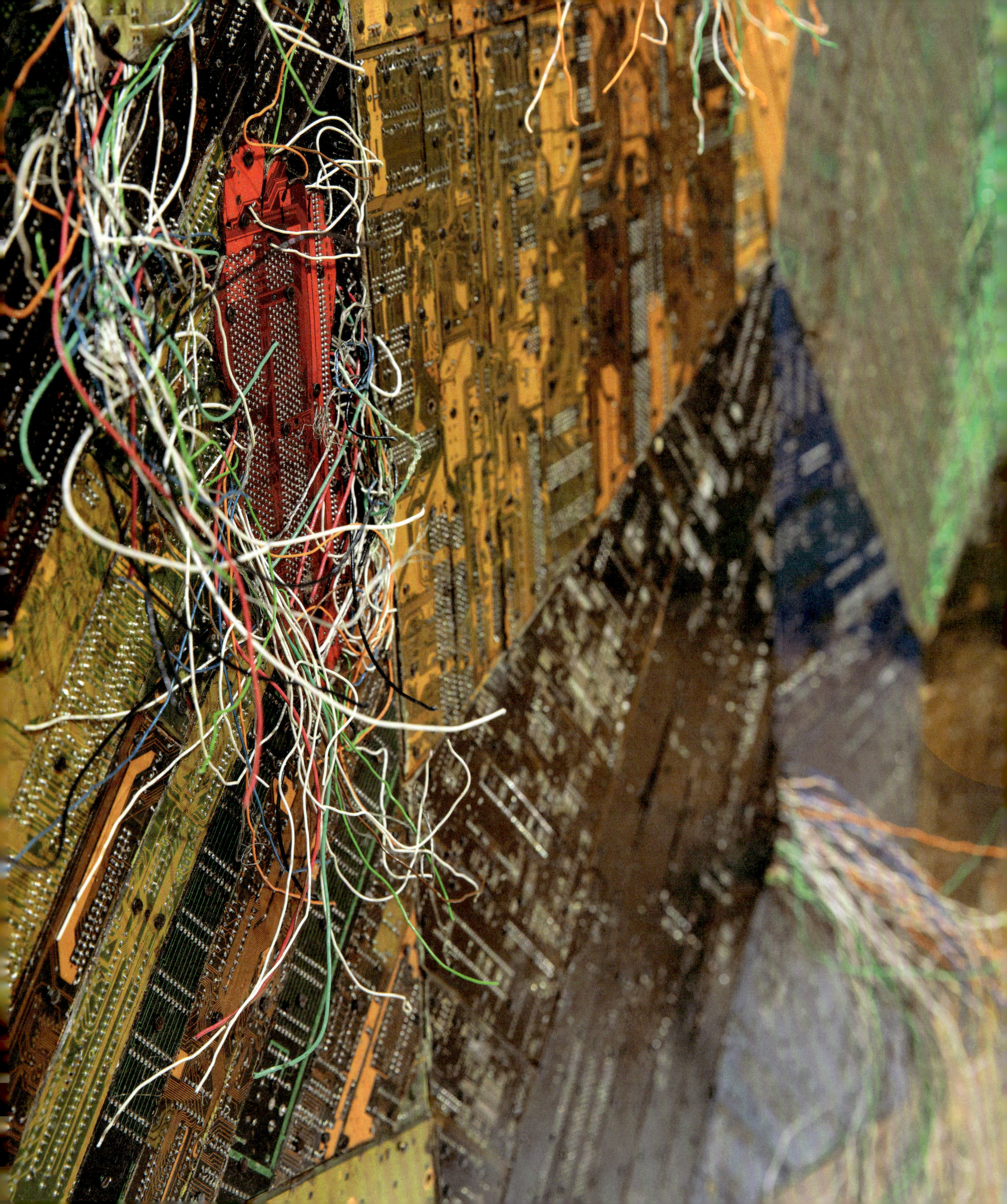

After visiting Elias Sime in Addis Ababa in April 2019, observing him at work in his studio, and spending time with him, Meskerem Assegued, and their staff at the remarkable Zoma Museum, I returned to Hamilton College to continue the work of planning the exhibition for the Wellin Museum. Reflecting on my time in Ethiopia, I found my curiosity piqued as I further probed the artist's inspirations, intentions, and processes. The ensuing interview, conducted over email between May and July 2019, is the fruit of both that curiosity and my subjects' infinite patience.

TRACY L. ADLER: Elias, you have worked with repurposed materials throughout your career. You've mentioned the fact that most of the electronic components, buttons, bottle caps, and other materials have been used before and therefore had a life before you salvaged them. Can you explain why this is an important aspect of your work, both conceptually and materially?

ELIAS SIME: The most difficult and time-consuming part of my art is collecting the material. As soon as a new idea comes to my mind, I make a simple sketch on one of the folded pieces of paper I carry in my back pocket to solidify the idea in my memory. Then, I think about the material that can best express the idea. Sometimes a given material can spark new ideas. In other words, the material and the composition go hand in hand.

Each material I collect has its own story. It has its own language. Every story has a beginning. I think about the first person who thought or dreamed of it and all the people who transformed that dream into a material. I also think about the various people who used and reused the material before it landed in my hands. I never worry about how old or new the material is. My art is not about recycling or repurposing material but about expressing my ideas. For instance, when I first saw a motherboard, it reminded me of a city, of landscapes, as well as of the people in the factory who assembled it. Some of the components I have used in my past work are now antiques. In some ways, my work is a timeline of technology.

TLA: You often use made-made materials to evoke natural elements like landscape. What is the reason for this, and how do you understand our relationship as humans to the natural and built environments?

ES: Humans are introduced to man-made materials at birth. Many infants are introduced to plastic gloves and blankets. Consciously or subconsciously, such materials evoke memories. I use man-made materials to express my thoughts. For instance, the stitched canvases, particularly the ones with small and winding stitches, are meant to express the challenges and hardships Meskerem and I experienced as we traveled both through Ethiopia and through other parts of the world. I wanted to express them not only through colors but also through the careful stitching on the canvas. Humans are the bridge between the natural and built environments. We cannot be separated from either one.

TLA: Meskerem, what kind of challenges and hardships?

MESKEREM ASSEGUED: Elias and I have traveled to many places documenting various rituals still in practice. These travels involved crossing rivers, climbing mountains on foot, riding horseback or muleback for hours and days. There were times when local authorities confronted us, demanding special permits to go deep into the villages for research. There were also times when we misunderstood short journeys and ended up walking for hours and into the evening. Once, we were walking with our local guide to a village of ceramicists in the Gambela region of western Ethiopia. Everyone, including our guide, told us it was a short journey, not more than an hour. Given my experience, I was prepared for a two hours' walk, but getting to the village took more than four hours, in humid weather and strong sun. As soon as we arrived and sat down, I started filming and interviewing. In the midst of it, I suddenly fainted and went into deep sleep, sweating heavily. Apparently, the old ceramicist whom I was filming advised Elias and the guide, who were panicking, not to wake me up. I am not sure how long I slept, but when I woke up, I drank half of the small amount of water I had left and gained enough energy to finish the interview. On our way back, the sun was not as strong, but the humidity was heavy. After about a half hour's walk, we saw a truck and waved our hands. Luckily, the driver stopped and took us to the village where we were staying. Along the way, we learned that he was a smuggler who buys logs from the protected indigenous rain forest. This is an example of the many challenges we have experienced during our field research.

TLA: Elias, there is a graphic quality to your compositions, particularly evident in their intricate patterning, landscapes, and figures. Do you think your early training in graphic design informed this aspect of your work?

ES: I believe that the first thing humans see is light and shadows, which are forms. These forms are graphics. For instance, when you see silhouettes, the first thing you notice is the shades of light and dark. Then, you start to see colors, especially when you are painting. You begin to identify the lights within the lights and the shadows within the shadows. The drawings you make with a pencil are black and white, which is graphic. It is only after making this graphic drawing that you begin to apply colors. This is what I learned academically, and it is what I still apply in my art.

TLA: You've mentioned that you're open to how your work is interpreted, but do you have a particular narrative in mind when you are constructing your compositions?

ES: When viewers interpret my work from their points of view, I enjoy hearing their versions, especially when they are different from mine. However, my art has always been a reaction to whatever I find intriguing or whatever moves me emotionally. My art is often based on my reaction to a certain moment, regardless of its location, time, or circumstances. For example, the sculpture *Flowers & Roots* [pl. 1] was influenced by the peony flowers I saw in the garden [Root Glen] at Hamilton College. I use the stories I hear or anything I see that either evokes a certain memory or gives me a new idea. I am always surprised when writers take the liberty to associate my art with certain political or social views. Whether it's African colonial history, traditional Ethiopian art, or the country's current socioeconomics or politics, that is far from what my art is about.

TLA: When we saw the Saunders peonies that were the inspiration for the site-specific sculpture *Flowers & Roots*, you immediately pointed out the range of tones and how the colors were affected by light and shadow. In your compositions, your palette is wide-ranging, from relatively neutral to vibrant. Can you talk about how you select the colors for each composition and the role of color in general in your work? Since you're often working with preexisting materials, does this limit the range of colors you can use?

ES: I select colors that best express my ideas. I am never short of colors, because they are in every material I use. If a monochromatic palette can express my idea best, that is what I use. The same goes for the vibrant colors. I have never felt limited in terms of color. If I have to improvise, that is what I do. If I have to work with limited colors, I welcome the challenge.

As we were walking through the garden at Hamilton College [that day], I was impressed not only by the flowers' size but also by their colors. The fact that they were hybrids made me think about humanity's endless appetite for expanding boundaries and about the electronic components I use in my art. We not only push the boundaries of materials but also push plants to perform differently. When the professor was crossbreeding his peonies, he would destroy examples he had created but didn't end up liking. I selected the Saunders peony for the sculpture because it demonstrates that bottomless appetite for pushing limits and manipulating nature to conform to our desires.

TLA: When creating works that are site-specific, like the Facebook and Wellin projects, you are inspired by the environment specific to the commission. Can you explain how these places impacted you and how you developed the ideas for the works?

ES: I am a contemporary artist. I make art about my reaction to the moment. When I first saw the peonies, I was impressed, and Meskerem immediately started researching the subject, as we often do. The more I heard about the hybridizing process and Professor [Arthur Percy] Saunders, who cultivated the greatest number of varieties of these flowers in the world, the more curious I became. The same goes for the piece I made for Facebook's headquarters [fig. 12]. Meskerem drove me through a dense forest of redwoods, and we hiked in Jackson State Forest. I was blown away not only by the size of the trees but also by their ability to survive over very long periods of time by reproducing their DNA [i.e., reiterating and fusing to make stronger canopies or trunks]. As an artist, I am very curious, so I want to learn as much as I can about every new place I visit. When I find great stories, I begin to imagine how I can express them artistically.

TLA: Meskerem, your curatorial process and your work as an anthropologist are very much connected. Your research on the Saunders peonies was critical to the making of *Flowers & Roots*. Can you speak about your collaborative process with Elias and your approach to exploring ideas and creating new projects together?

MA: I believe that collaboration is one of the most important ingredients to a successful outcome. I don't remember a time when I have accomplished anything alone. There are many people behind everything Elias and I have done, including my husband, my children, our siblings, friends, and coworkers. One of the beauties of working with Elias is the lack of competition and the respect we have for our differences and similarities. When we both like a new idea that emerges from either one of us, we immediately take action to realize it. If we do not agree, we let it die. This type of collaboration requires trust, which takes time to build.

We also believe that we need to have a clear understanding of whatever project we undertake, which requires research. When we came to the Wellin Museum, the first thing we did was walk through the Root Glen with you and Chris [Harrison, the Wellin's Building Manager and Preparator]. As he has said, Elias was impressed when he saw the peonies. Neither of us had seen such flowers before. That afternoon, Elias and I sat on the museum's patio [Selch Terrace] to brainstorm how to transform this flower into a sculpture. I quickly searched on my phone and translated to Elias, from English to Amharic, a few highlights I found about hybridizing plants as he was sketching the first draft of the sculpture. We learned that the peony is native to Asia, Europe, and western North America and had been crossbred before Saunders. However, he was the first to hybridize it so exhaustively, creating new colors that had never existed before. We discussed the competitive nature of humanity, which sometimes drives people to do whatever it takes to be recognized as the first or the only one in a field. The best way to express this was by making a sculpture of the hybridized flower mixed with motherboards, where the roots connect to electrical wires emerging from large bronze tubes. After we returned to Ethiopia, I continued reading any material I could find about Professor Saunders. I tried to understand as much as possible about the history and science of hybridizing plants. The more I told Elias about my findings, the more he refined the sculpture. We always spend as much time as possible researching until we are both satisfied with a final design.

TLA: How have locations in the United States, Ethiopia, and other countries impacted you as a curator, as Elias's collaborator, and as the cofounder of Zoma Museum?

MA: I see curating as a form of installation art in which the curator makes site-specific art using the work of a given artist. It can also be an artistic collaboration between the artist and the curator. Sometimes, the exhibitions I curate are unrelated to a given venue and its audience, and other times, they are about the place where the venue is situated.

My travels around the world have taught me that humans' emotional reactions to joy and grief are the same. When I was a child, my parents moved from one town to another, and I learned to quickly adapt to new homes and make friends in new schools. I believe these movements may have played a major role in my curatorial practices. In my mind, the differences between the US and Ethiopia or any other country are minimal, if any. I am fascinated by how humans all over the world communicate similarly through body language. We cry when we are sad and laugh when we are happy. My curatorial practice is about the similarities of humanity.

TLA: Meskerem, you've spoken about Alice Waters and her Edible Schoolyard Project as being influential in your approach, particularly at the elementary school at Zoma. Can you address how you've applied some of Waters's methods at Zoma, from teaching about clean water, for example, to growing food? Is running an ecological museum about aesthetics or education or both, and if so, how is that manifested at Zoma?

MA: I met Alice Waters in 2006, when I was curating the exhibition *Green Flame* for the New Crowned Hope Festival in Vienna, directed by Peter Sellars, for Mozart's 250th birthday. But the clean-water system we use at Zoma Museum and at the school is not something I learned from Alice Waters. I learned it from my father, who had large farms, and from my own research and a number of people who taught me over the years. What I learned from Alice Waters was her approach to education. She is a pioneer of teaching children by creating an outdoor classroom in which they plant vegetables, herbs, and fruit trees as well as a kitchen classroom in which they cook what they harvest. Also, one of the elementary schools I attended while growing up in Ethiopia was a Waldorf school, where I also learned about mixed classrooms and hands-on education.

Zoma Museum evolved organically over twenty years of dreaming and perseverance. Creating it took a great deal of risk, but more importantly, we followed up on our instincts with reason and logic. In 2014, after operating Zoma Contemporary Art Center in a smaller space for years, we bought some undesirable land that was being used as a garbage dump in an underserved neighborhood of Addis Ababa adjacent to the Akaki River, where a community of urban farmers distribute their vegetables to the city. As we were clearing the land and renovating the existing mud-and-straw buildings to make Zoma Museum, we knew we were transforming the neighborhood. Most of our employees are young, and a good number are from the neighborhood. We learned as much about farming and animal husbandry from them as they learned from us.

We were able to gradually acquire eight other properties of different sizes next to the original plot of land. One of the properties had an existing school and a dairy barn on it, both in extreme disrepair. Slowly, we transformed the land and the structures into what you see today.

We hired professionals to manage the museum, the school, and the restaurant, including finances, maintenance, and security. Although some of what we do is conventional, we are also flexible and adapt to new challenges as they arise. For instance, Prime Minister Abiy Ahmed's recent visit to Zoma Museum provided us with the opportunity to design and build new landscapes at the Alle School of Fine Arts and Design [at Addis Ababa University] and at the National Palace. This new challenge required a quick adjustment. As the managers at Zoma spread their wings to fill the void created by our absence, Elias and I split ourselves between the palace and the art school. We were able to finish the compound at the school and move all our resources to the palace, where we are currently working.

TLA: Elias, can you speak about the genesis of *Bareness*, the installation of ceramics in the exhibition [pl. 30]? And Meskerem, can you broaden our understanding of the artisan communities in Ethiopia with whom you worked to create it?

ES: There are times I feel empty and vulnerable. This is not unique to me—it is a shared human emotion. The ceramic pieces reflect those moments of vulnerability, of feeling naked, exposed, unprotected, and fragile. They are also about how we will all end up being fragments of the Earth, regardless of our status in life.

MA: Over the years, I have visited ceramicists living and working in many villages in Ethiopia and documented their stories. These ceramicists, who are locally known as *shekla seri*, live near rivers, where they can easily source the clay needed for making the pots, pans, water containers, and such that they sell to middlemen to then sell in the market. Weavers, blacksmiths, and stone carvers also live among the ceramicists. For centuries, these artisans, whom I think are artists, have been living on land owned by others as caregivers of the properties. Usually, they are not landowners. In 2003, Elias and I decided to do a major exhibition in Addis Ababa dedicated to ceramicists in various parts of Ethiopia. In 2011, we exhibited the "Ants and Ceramicists" series, Elias's impressive stitched works [pls. 3, 6, 7], accompanied by short video documentations I had made. The exhibition was about creating awareness of the artisans' stories, their living conditions, and their significant contributions to society. Underappreciation of traditional artisans is not unique to Ethiopia. My travels have taught me that artisans around the world live in similar conditions.

TLA: How did you both work with the artisans to create the works in the show?

MA: In Addis Ababa, there is a community of ceramicists with whom we have been working for many years. Elias, in particular, is very close with them, and they treat him like a member of their family. He gives them a design or sits and works with them in their community. The pieces in the exhibition were made by these ceramicists in Addis Ababa.

TLA: For the Wellin exhibition, Elias, you created two new works, *Tightrope: Silent 1* and *Tightrope: Silent 2* [pls. 28, 29]. Composed solely of computer keys, these works have a pared-down, abstract quality to them. Can you discuss the inspiration for these works and the significance of the subtitle "Silent"?

ES: It took me a great deal of time to collect the keyboards. Keyboards have evolved very quickly—the ones today use a completely different technology from a couple of decades ago. But their colors are monochromatic, which gives an impression of silence. Sometimes, thoughts are expressed through noise, and other times, through silence. The keyboard is not loud, but it is full of symbols. Since my work is often a reaction to what I observe, at the time I made *Tightrope: Silent 1* and *Tightrope: Silent 2*, I wanted to create a calm space in the midst of a lot of activity.

TLA: Can you talk about the meaning the "Tightrope" series holds for you? And can you also discuss the new subcategories "Silent" and "Noiseless"? Why has this theme recently emerged in your work?

ES: When the pieces for "Tightrope" were made, I was thinking about how technology was contributing additional stress to an already competitive and stressful world. Anywhere I go in the world, I notice that lovers in cafés spend more time on their smartphones and barely have an eye-to-eye conversation. Building a lasting relationship between two or more people takes time. It requires sorting out the individual personalities and arriving at consensus. At the same time, technology has solved and simplified many of our problems. "Tightrope" is about the balance required to navigate and adjust to endless demands, rules, and regulations in order to survive. Walking on a tightrope requires years of practice, discipline, and confidence. The slightest mistake can end the tightrope walker's life. On the other hand, a rope that is stretched tight can break. Whenever you pull a string too tight, it breaks.

"Silent" and "Noiseless" are about resistance. When there is a power that keeps trying to push you in a direction that you are trying to avoid, you have two ways to respond. One is by making noise, trying to be heard and understood, and the other is by being silent and staying focused on your ultimate goal. The pieces under the titles "Silent" and "Noiseless" are about the latter.

TLA: Speaking of noise and silence, I feel as if your studio has a sense of quiet as well. Can you discuss your studio practice and the process for creating your work?

ES: My studio is both quiet and loud. It depends on what I am doing. I like making sketches or reading books when the room is quiet. Whenever I change an existing technique or material to something new, I enjoy being alone and without noise. However, when I do physically demanding art, I turn the speaker up, and the loud music gives me energy and helps me focus. I listen to all kinds of music, from traditional Ethiopian to pop or jazz. I also like instrumental music such as flamenco guitar, classical, anything.

TLA: This exhibition focuses on your work of the past decade. Can you speak about your evolution as an artist over that period as well as the direction your work is going?

ES: Whenever I finish a piece of art, I am eager to start the next one with a fresh mind. I rarely look back at my finished pieces. When I see them displayed, I become the audience. I must admit that I enjoy seeing them hanging on walls. When I work on a new piece, I feel like a beginner who is trying to master a new technique. I never worry about what people will say or write about it.

To answer this question, I was trying to imagine what my work was like ten years ago. Quite honestly, my memories are vague. My work is about things that affected me or that I was thinking about at the time I made the art. I have traveled to many different countries around the world, and I am sure that many of my pieces have been influenced by whatever I observed in those places. One thing I know is that the quality of my work has improved. Because my work is mostly about my observation of a particular situation in a particular space and time, it is hard to predict what I will do in the future. One thing, for sure, is that I will continue making art in all shapes and forms as long as I am alive.

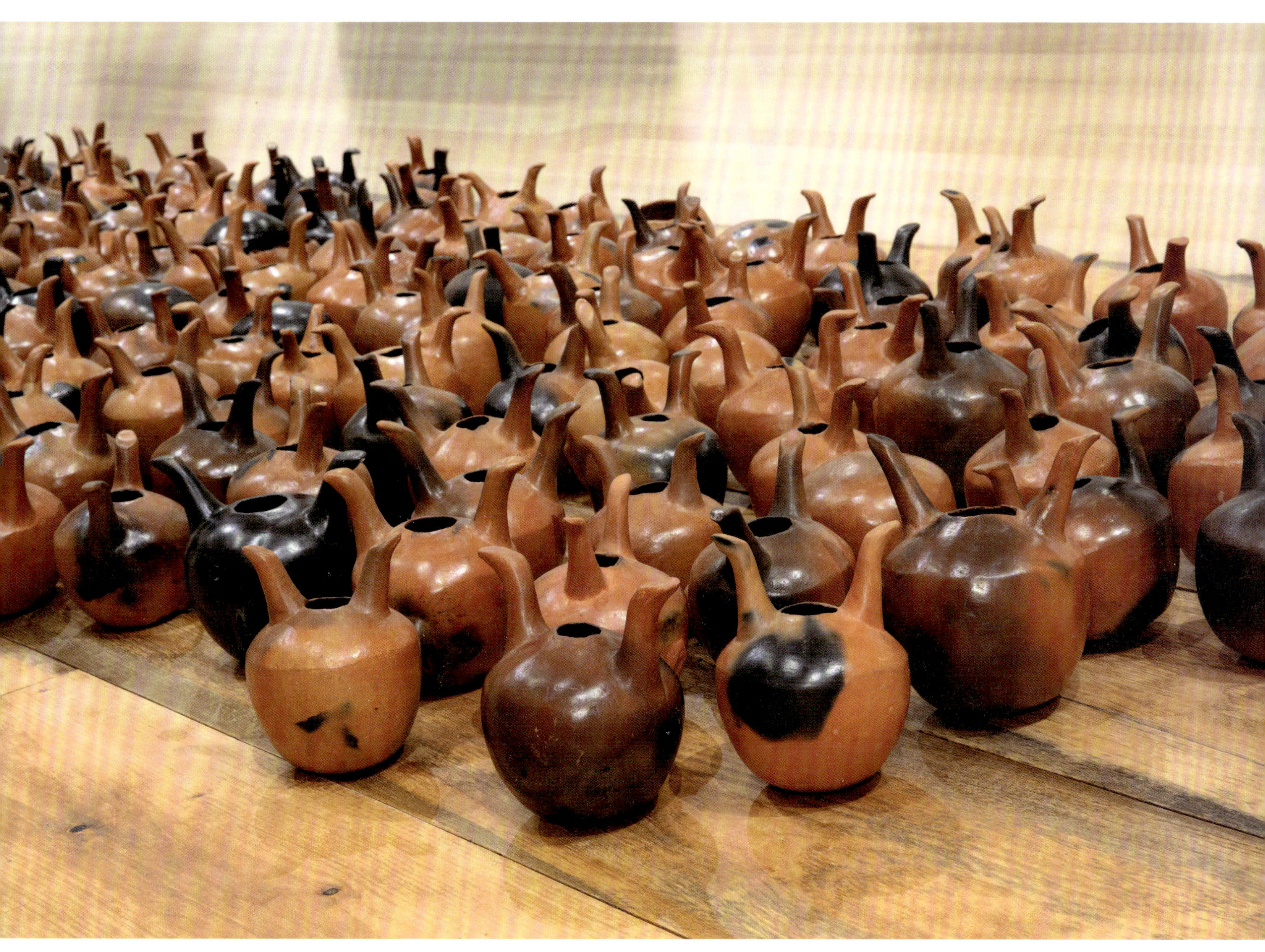

PLATE 30

Bareness

2014 | Fired clay | Installation dimensions variable
Courtesy of the artist and James Cohan, New York

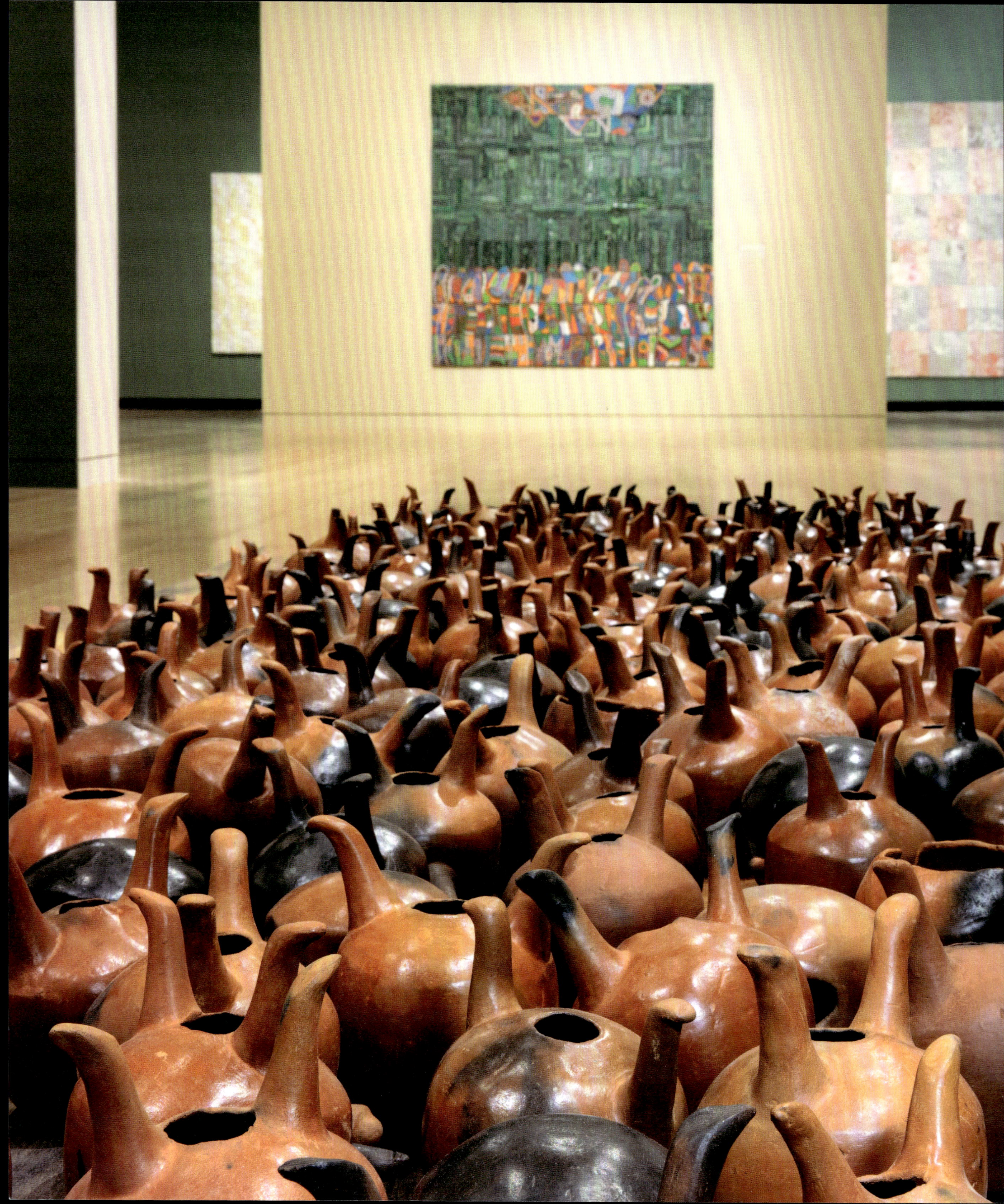

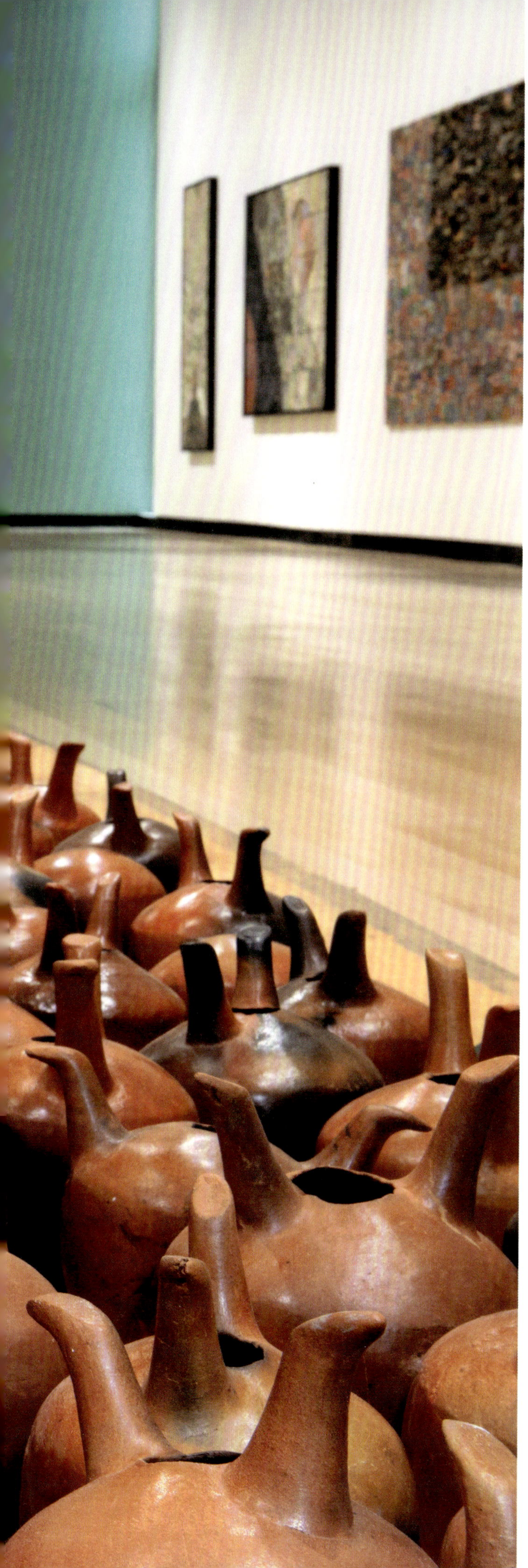

Installation view of *Elias Sime: Tightrope*, Ruth and Elmer Wellin Museum of Art at Hamilton College, Clinton, NY (September 7–December 8, 2019)

EXHIBITION HISTORY

SOLO EXHIBITIONS

2019–21 *Elias Sime: Tightrope*, Ruth and Elmer Wellin Museum of Art at Hamilton College, Clinton, NY, traveling to Akron Art Museum, OH; Kemper Museum of Contemporary Art, Kansas City, MO; Royal Ontario Museum, Toronto

2019 *Elias Sime: NOISELESS*, James Cohan, New York

Elias Sime, Zoma Museum, Addis Ababa, Ethiopia

2018 *Tightrope*, Grimm Gallery, Amsterdam

2017 *Elias Sime: Twisted & Hidden*, James Cohan, New York

2015 *Elias Sime*, James Cohan Gallery, New York

2013 *Tightrope*, British Council, Goethe-Institut, Istituto Italiano di Cultura, and Alliance Éthio-Française, Addis Ababa

2012 *Eye of the Needle, Eye of the Heart*, North Dakota Museum of Art, Grand Forks

2011 *Ants and Ceramicists*, British Council, Goethe-Institut, Istituto Italiano di Cultura, and Alliance Éthio-Française, Addis Ababa

2010 *Oedipus Rex*, Sydney Opera House, Australia

2009 *Oedipus Rex*, Walt Disney Concert Hall, Los Angeles

Eye of the Needle, Eye of the Heart, Santa Monica Museum of Art, CA

Tarat-Tarat, Haunch of Venison, London

2008 *What Is Love?* Alliance Éthio-Française, Addis Ababa

2006 *Metamorphosis*, public mosaic sponsored by European Union and Zoma Contemporary Art Center, Addis Ababa

GOTA Tarat-Tarat, Alliance Éthio-Française, Addis Ababa

2005 *Min Neber?* Istituto Italiano di Cultura, Addis Ababa

2002 *Retrospect Part 1*, part of *Giziawi #1*, Addis Ababa

1999 Hilton Addis Ababa, Addis Ababa

1998 Addis Ababa University, Addis Ababa

1996 United Nations Economic Commission for Africa, Addis Ababa

1995 Organization of African Unity, Addis Ababa

1993 Alliance Éthio-Française, Addis Ababa

GROUP EXHIBITIONS

2020 *Second Careers: Two Tributaries in African Art*, curated by Ugochukwu-Smooth C. Nzewi, Cleveland Museum of Art, OH

Borders, James Cohan, New York

2018 *I Was Raised on the Internet*, Museum of Contemporary Art Chicago

Grids, James Cohan, New York

2017 *Abstract Minded: Works by Six Contemporary African Artists*, N'Namdi Center for Contemporary Art, Detroit, MI

Innovative Approaches, Honored Traditions: The Ruth and Elmer Wellin Museum of Art at Five Years; Highlights from the Permanent Collection, Ruth and Elmer Wellin Museum of Art at Hamilton College, Clinton, NY

2016 *The Distance of a Day*, Israel Museum, Jerusalem

Festival International d'Art Lyrique with Peter Sellars, Aix-en-Provence, France

2010 *Stitches*, Armory Center for the Arts, Pasadena, CA

2008 *The Essential Art of African Textiles: Design without End*, The Metropolitan Museum of Art, New York

Flow, Studio Museum in Harlem, New York

2006 *Green Flame*, New Crowned Hope Festival, directed by Peter Sellars, Vienna, Austria

Goethe-Institut, Addis Wubet, and Zoma Contemporary Art Center, Addis Ababa

2005 *Hidden Talent*, European Union and Zoma Contemporary Art Center, Addis Ababa

Addis Ababa Zare, School of Fine Arts and Design, Addis Ababa University, Addis Ababa

2004 Dak'Art, 6th International Biennale of Contemporary African Art, Dakar, Senegal

2002 *Giziawi #1*, Addis Ababa

2000 Istituto Italiano di Cultura, Addis Ababa

1999 Alliance Éthio-Française, Addis Ababa

1997 Goshu Gallery, Addis Ababa

Joint Dutch-Ethiopian Exhibition, School of Fine Arts and Design, Addis Ababa University, Addis Ababa

1995 National Museum of Ethiopia, Addis Ababa

PUBLIC COLLECTIONS

Carl & Marilynn Thoma Art Foundation, Chicago, IL, and Santa Fe, NM

Chrysler Museum of Art, Norfolk, VA

Des Moines Art Center, IA

Detroit Institute of Arts, Detroit, MI

Hood Museum of Art, Dartmouth College, Hanover, NH

Israel Museum, Jerusalem

Kemper Museum of Contemporary Art, Kansas City, MO

The Metropolitan Museum of Art, New York

Newark Museum, NJ

North Carolina Museum of Art, Raleigh

North Dakota Museum of Art, Grand Forks

Pérez Art Museum Miami, Miami, FL

Pizzuti Collection, Columbus, OH

Royal Ontario Museum, Toronto

Ruth and Elmer Wellin Museum of Art, Hamilton College, Clinton, NY

Samuel P. Harn Museum of Art, University of Florida, Gainesville

Toledo Museum of Art, OH

Virginia Museum of Fine Arts, Richmond

SELECTED BIBLIOGRAPHY

2019 Pilar Viladas, "Ethiopian Artist Elias Sime's First Major Show Goes on View at the Wellin Museum," *Galerie*, November 7, 2019

Hasabie Kidanu, "Spotlight: Tightrope, the First Major Traveling Museum Exhibition of Elias Sime," *Tadias*, November 4, 2019

Gabriella Angeleti, "Review: Elias Sime; Wellin Museum Presents Second Major US Exhibition Devoted to Ethiopian Artist Elias Sime," *The Art Newspaper*, October 11, 2019

Seph Rodney, "Love and Craftsmanship in the Relationship between Machines and Humanity," *Hyperallergic*, September 17, 2019

Zack Hatfield, "Interviews: Elias Sime; Elias Sime on Living and Working with Technology," *Artforum*, September 3, 2019

John Yau, "Mosaics of Motherboards, Keyboards, and Wire," *Hyperallergic*, June 16, 2019

Paddy Johnson, "The Art-Making Trend Outshining Large-Scale Sculpture in New York City's Best Shows," *Observer*, June 10, 2019

Victoria L. Valentine, "Through a Global Lens: Exploring Works on View at the First-Ever Manhattan Edition of 1-54 Contemporary African Art Fair," *Culture Type*, May 9, 2019

Paul Laster, "Painting Portraits: Two Artists at 1-54 Contemporary African Art Fair," *Whitehot Magazine of Contemporary Art*, May 5, 2019

Andy Battaglia, "From the Continent to the Island: 1-54 Contemporary African Art Fair Moves to Manhattan," *ARTnews*, May 2, 2019

Brian Droitcour, "Alternate Timeline," *Art in America*, May 1, 2019

"Elias Sime Set for Major U.S. Museum Shows in NY, Ohio and Kansas," *Tadias*, April 30, 2019

"Noiseless: Elias Sime's New Exhibition," *Tadias*, April 27, 2019

Kate Brown, "'It's All about Life': Ethiopia's Newest Art Museum Doubles as an Experiment in Environmental Sustainability," *Artnet News*, April 22, 2019

Katy Donoghue, "Elias Sime," *Whitewall*, Spring 2019

Guglielmo Mattioli, "Addis Ababa's First Contemporary Art Museum Aims to Revive a Local Architectural Tradition," *Metropolis*, January 22, 2019

2018 Mik Awake, "Ethiopian Enterprise: Artists Build a Future in Addis Ababa and Beyond," *ARTnews*, Summer 2018

2017 Virginia Blackburn, "1-54 Art Fair Returns to London," *Financial Times*, October 5, 2017

Leigh Anne Miller, "Elias Sime," *Art in America*, May 2017

2016 Ginanne Brownell Mitic, "Arts Center in Ethiopia Links Local and Global," *New York Times*, June 16, 2016

Hans-Ulrich Obrist, "Elias Sime," *Pin-Up*, Spring/Summer 2016

"22 Contemporary African Artists Selected by *ArtPremium*," *ArtPremium*, Spring/Summer 2016

2015 Molly Gottschalk, "From Massimiliano Gioni to Alex Gartenfeld, Art-World Insiders Pick Art Basel in Miami Beach's Artists to Watch," *Artsy*, December 4, 2015

Seph Rodney, "Finding Our Way amid the Modern Fatalism of Circuit Boards," *Hyperallergic*, October 14, 2015

Alex Allenchey, "In Sprawling Panels, Ethiopian Artist Elias Sime Recycles the First World's Circuit Boards," *Artsy*, October 1, 2015

Holland Cotter, "Elias Sime Recycles Discarded Objects into Abstract Works," *New York Times*, October 1, 2015

"Elias Sime at James Cohan Gallery," *Arte Fuse*, September 17, 2015

Andrew M. Goldstein, "10 of the Best Artworks of the 2015 Armory Show," *Artspace*, March 8, 2015

2014 Kate Cowcher, "Tightrope: Elias Sime," *African Arts*, Winter 2014

2013 Tibebeselassie Tigabu, "Art Is My Life," *The Reporter Ethiopia*, November 9, 2013

Tibebeselassie Tigabu, "The 'Heart to Heart' from Rome to Addis," *The Reporter Ethiopia*, May 3, 2013

2011 Peter Clothier, "The Art of Elias Sime," *Huffington Post*, May 25, 2011

2009 Quinn Latimer, "Elias Sime," *Frieze*, June/August 2009

"Elias Sime," *BBC World Service*, May 14, 2009

Susan Morgan, "The Talk: Hut Couture," *New York Times*, April 19, 2009

David Ng, "Thrones, Masks and Ethiopia: A Guide to Understanding 'Oedipus Rex' at the L.A. Philharmonic," *Los Angeles Times*, April 16, 2009

David Pagel, "Review: 'Elias Sime: Eye of the Needle, Eye of the Heart' at Santa Monica Museum of Art," *Los Angeles Times*, April 3, 2009

Gloria Goodale, "The Trash of Life Is Elias Sime's Art," *Christian Science Monitor*, March 13, 2009

Scarlet Chenk, "For Elias Simé [*sic*], Every Object Tells a Story," *Los Angeles Times*, February 18, 2009

2008 Meskerem Assegued, "A Retrospective Observation of Elias Sime," *African Identities,* November 2008

Holland Cotter, "Out of Africa, Whatever Africa May Be," *New York Times*, April 4, 2008

CHECKLIST OF THE EXHIBITION

"TIGHTROPE" SERIES

Tightrope 3, 2009–14
Reclaimed electronic components and fiberglass on panel
81 ½ in. × 16 ft. 3 in. (207 × 495.3 cm)
Private collection, New York
PLATE 8

Tightrope 8, 2009–14
Reclaimed electronic components on panel
44 1⁄16 × 70 13⁄16 in. (112 × 180 cm)
Private collection, New York
PLATE 9

Tightrope: Hands and Feet, 2009–14
Reclaimed electronic components and insulated wire on panel
71 in. × 10 ft. 10 ¼ in. (180.3 × 330.8 cm)
Collection of Nancy and Joseph Chetrit, New York
PLATE 10

Tightrope: On the Edge, 2015
Reclaimed electronic components on panel
48 in. × 21 ft. 6 ¾ in. (121.9 × 657.2 cm)
Kemper Museum of Contemporary Art, Kansas City, MO
Bebe and Crosby Kemper Collection, Museum purchase made possible by a gift from the William T. Kemper Charitable Trust, UMB Bank, n.a., Trustee
PLATE 11

Tightrope: Familiar Yet Complex 1, 2016
Reclaimed electronic components and insulated wire on panel
46 × 79 ½ in. (116.8 × 201.9 cm)
Collection of Bill and Christy Gautreaux, Kansas City, MO
PLATE 12

Tightrope: Familiar Yet Complex 2, 2016
Reclaimed electronic components and insulated wire on panel
83 × 87 ½ in. (210.8 × 222.3 cm)
Ruth and Elmer Wellin Museum of Art at Hamilton College, Clinton, NY
Purchase, William G. Roehrick '34 Art Acquisition and Preservation Fund
PLATE 13

Tightrope: Familiar Yet Complex 6, 2016
Reclaimed electronic components and insulated wire on panel
55 ¼ × 79 ½ in. (140.3 × 201.9 cm)
Collection of Jane and James Cohan, New York
PLATE 14

Tightrope: Surface and Shadow 2, 2016
Reclaimed electronic components and buttons on panel
9 ft. ⅝ in. × 17 ft. ⅝ in. (275.9 × 519.8 cm)
Pizzuti Collection, Columbus, OH
PLATE 15

Tightrope: Behind the Beauty, 2017
Reclaimed insulated wire on panel
91 ¼ in. × 10 ft. 7 ¼ in. (231.8 × 323.2 cm)
Collection of Scott Mueller, Cleveland, OH
PLATE 16

Tightrope: In Boxes, 2017
Reclaimed electronic components and insulated wire on panel
64 in. × 11 ft. 10 ⅝ in. (162.6 × 362.3 cm)
Royal Ontario Museum, Toronto
Acquisition made possible by the generous support of the Louise Hawley Stone Charitable Trust
PLATE 17

Tightrope: Internalized, 2017
Reclaimed electronic components and insulated wire on panel
63 ⅜ × 94 ⅜ in. (161 × 239.7 cm)
Private collection
PLATE 18

Tightrope: The Dominant, 2017
Reclaimed insulated wire on panel
81 ⅜ in. × 10 ft. 6 in. (206.7 × 320 cm)
Collection of Erica Tennenbaum and Alex Friedman, New York
PLATE 19

Tightrope: Whirlwind, 2017
Reclaimed insulated wire on panel
9 ft. 1 ¾ in. × 11 ft. 10 ½ in. (278.8 × 362 cm)
Courtesy of the artist and James Cohan, New York
PLATE 20

Tightrope: (1) While Observing . . ., 2018
Reclaimed electronic components on panel
72 ½ × 31 ⅝ in. (184.2 × 80.3 cm)
Carl & Marilynn Thoma Art Foundation, Chicago, IL, and Santa Fe, NM
PLATE 21

Tightrope: (5) While Observing . . ., 2018
Reclaimed electronic components and insulated wire on panel
54 ¼ × 63 in. (137.8 × 160 cm)
Collection of Chris and Heather Kempczinski, Boston
PLATE 22

Tightrope: (8) While Observing . . ., 2018
Reclaimed electronic components and insulated wire on panel
86 ¾ × 46 ⅝ in. (220.4 × 118.4 cm)
Courtesy of the artist and James Cohan, New York
PLATE 23

Tightrope: (9) While Observing . . ., 2018
Reclaimed electronic components and insulated wire on panel
94 ⅜ × 63 ⅜ in. (239.7 × 161 cm)
Collection of Robert and Karen Duncan, Lincoln, NE
PLATE 24

Tightrope: Noiseless 2, 2019
Reclaimed electronic components and insulated wire on panel
8 ft. 5 in. × 13 ft. 2 in. (256.5 × 401.3 cm)
Courtesy of the artist and James Cohan, New York
PLATE 25

Tightrope: Noiseless 12, 2019
Reclaimed insulated wire on panel
9 ft. 9 in. × 63 ½ in. (297.2 × 161.3 cm)
Des Moines Art Center, IA
Purchased with funds from the Edmundson Art Foundation
PLATE 26

Tightrope: Noiseless 23, 2019
Reclaimed electronic components and insulated wire on panel
8 ft. 4 ½ in. × 46 ¾ in. (255.3 × 118.7 cm)
Collection of Charles Banta, Buffalo, NY
PLATE 27

Tightrope: Silent 1, 2019
Reclaimed electronic components on panel
72 ½ in. × 10 ft. 6 in. (184.2 × 320 cm)
Courtesy of the artist and James Cohan, New York
PLATE 28

Tightrope: Silent 2, 2019
Reclaimed electronic components on panel
72 ½ in. × 10 ft. 6 in. (184.2 × 320 cm)
Courtesy of the artist and James Cohan, New York
PLATE 29

CERAMICS

Bareness, 2014
Fired clay
Installation dimensions variable
Courtesy of the artist and James Cohan, New York
PLATE 30

STITCHED CANVASES

Cactus 2, 2003–4
Yarn and buttons on canvas, signed with bottle cap
56 ¼ × 29 ⅛ in. (142.9 × 74 cm)
Collection of Beth Rudin DeWoody
PLATE 2

Aremoch, 2004
Yarn, bottle caps, and fabric on burlap,
mounted on canvas, signed with bottle cap
35 ⅝ × 51 ½ in. (90.5 × 130.8 cm)
Collection of Tony and Sandra Tamer
PLATE 4

Splash of a Pebble in Muddy Water, 2006
Yarn on canvas, signed with bottle cap
9 ft. ½ in. × 74 ½ in. (275.6 × 189.2 cm)
Collection of Bill and Christy Gautreaux, Kansas City, MO
PLATE 5

Ants and Ceramicists 6, 2009–14
Yarn on canvas, signed with bottle cap
61 × 33 in. (154.9 × 83.8 cm)
Courtesy of the artist and James Cohan, New York
PLATE 6

Ants and Ceramicists 10, 2009–14
Yarn and found objects on canvas, signed with bottle cap
61 × 33 in. (154.9 × 83.8 cm)
Collection of James Zang, Portugal
PLATE 7

Ants and Ceramicists 11, 2009–14
Yarn on canvas, signed with bottle cap
73 ⅜ × 51 ⅝ in. (186.4 × 131.1 cm)
Collection of Erica Tennenbaum and Alex Friedman, New York
PLATE 3

SITE-SPECIFIC SCULPTURE ON PATRICIA BAKWIN SELCH TERRACE

Flowers & Roots, 2019
Reclaimed electronic components, insulated wire, bronze sheeting, and custom-dyed fiber-cement composite
9 ft. 3 in. × 17 ft. 5 in. × 12 ft. 10 in. (282 × 530.9 × 391.2 cm)
Produced by the Ruth and Elmer Wellin Museum of Art at Hamilton College, Clinton, NY; supported by the Daniel W. Dietrich '64 Fund for Innovation in the Arts
PLATE 1

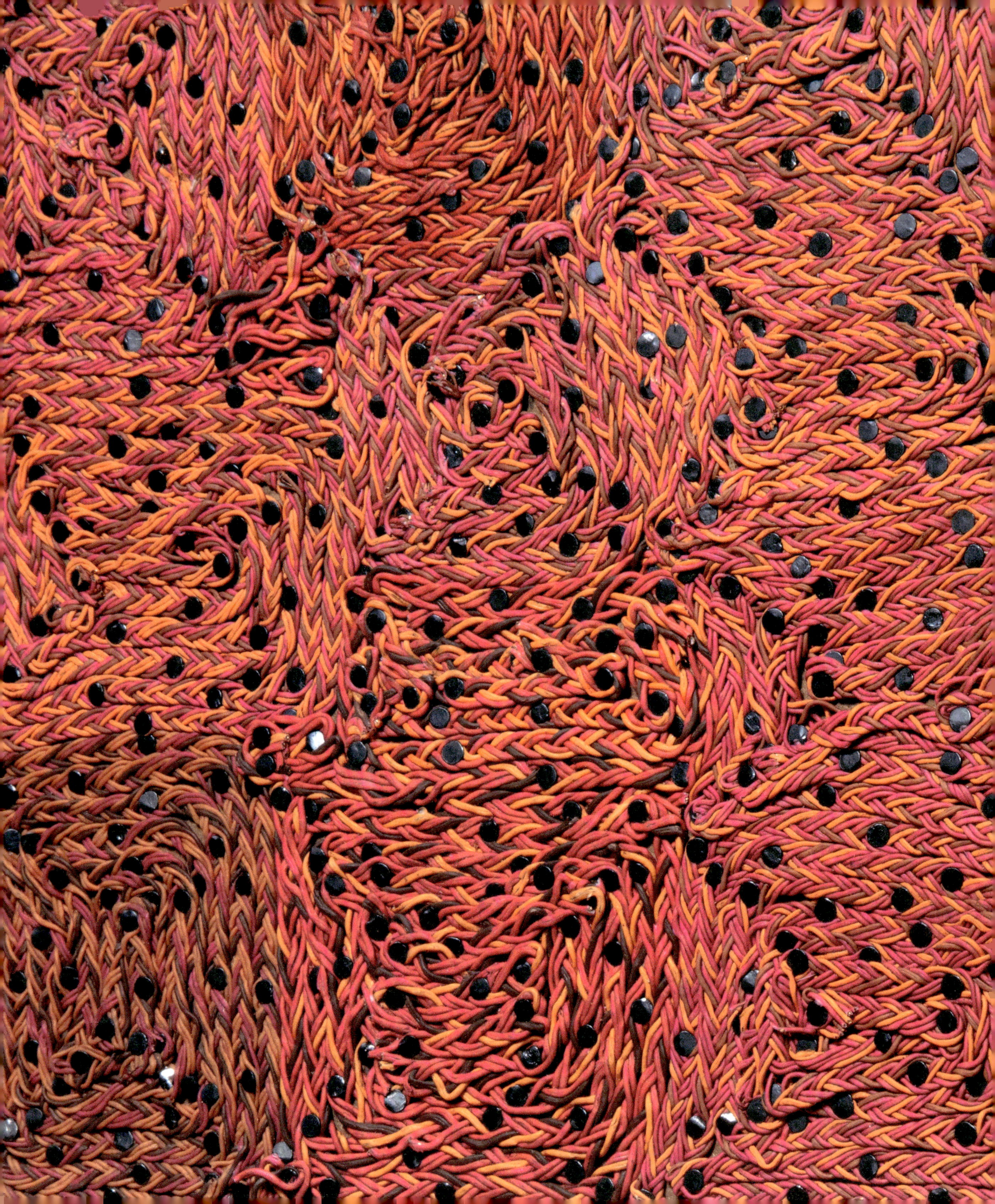

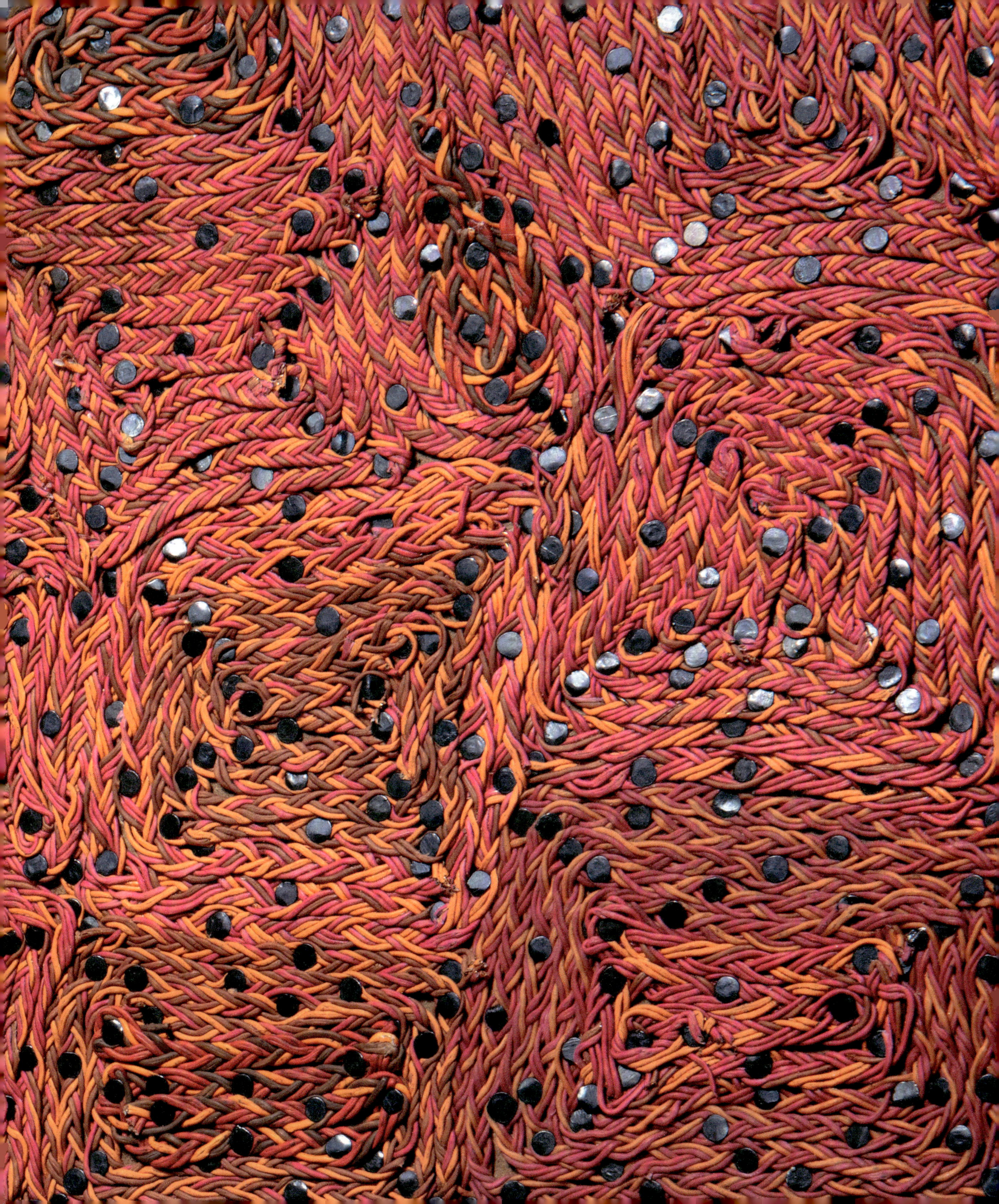

Ruth and Elmer Wellin Museum of Art at Hamilton College

Tracy L. Adler
Johnson-Pote Director

Katherine D. Alcauskas
Collections Curator and Exhibitions Manager

Alexander D'Acunto
Security Manager

Christopher Harrison
Building Manager and Museum Preparator

Marjorie Johnson
Museum Educator and Docent Program Supervisor

Emma Pfeifer
Office Assistant

Michelle Reynolds
Curatorial and Academic Programs Specialist

Amy Sylvester
Office Administrator

The Ruth and Elmer Wellin Museum of Art's programs and publications are made possible, in part, by the Daniel W. Dietrich '64 Arts Museum Programming Fund; the Johnson-Pote Museum Director Fund; the John B. Root '44 Exhibition Fund; the Edward W. and Grace C. Root Endowment Fund; and the William G. Roehrick '34 Lecture Fund, as well as private contributions. Additional support for *Elias Sime: Tightrope* has been provided by the Daniel W. Dietrich '64 Fund for Innovation in the Arts; the Gautreaux Family Foundation; the Carl & Marilynn Thoma Art Foundation; and private contributions.

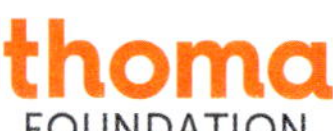

This book is published in conjunction with the exhibition *Elias Sime: Tightrope*, organized by the Ruth and Elmer Wellin Museum of Art at Hamilton College.

Ruth and Elmer Wellin Museum of Art, Clinton, NY
September 7–December 8, 2019

Akron Art Museum, Akron, OH
February 29–May 24, 2020

Kemper Museum of Contemporary Art, Kansas City, MO
June 11–September 13, 2020

Royal Ontario Museum, Toronto
October 24, 2020–February 21, 2021

Published in 2019 by the Wellin Museum of Art and DelMonico Books•Prestel

DelMonico Books, an imprint of Prestel, a member of Verlagsgruppe Random House GmbH

Prestel Verlag
Neumarkter Strasse 28
81673 Munich

Prestel Publishing Ltd.
14-17 Wells Street
London W1T 3PD

Prestel Publishing
900 Broadway, Suite 603
New York, NY 10003
www.prestel.com

Designed by Tim Laun and Natalie Wedeking
Copyedited by Jennifer Bernstein, Tenacious Editorial
Printed and bound in Italy by Graphicom

Library of Congress Control Number: 2019954837
A CIP catalogue record for this book is available from the British Library.

ISBN: 978-3-7913-5881-9

Cover (front and back): *Tightrope: Familiar Yet Complex 2* (details of pl. 13)

Uncaptioned Images (page numbers in bold)
2–3, 154–55: *Tightrope: Noiseless 2* (details of pl. 25). **4–5, 114–15:** *Tightrope: Surface and Shadow 2* (details of pl. 15). **6–7, 8, 10–11, 22–23, 106–7:** *Tightrope: Familiar Yet Complex 2* (details of pl. 13). **14, 134–35:** *Tightrope: Whirlwind* (details of pl. 20). **18–19, 71:** views of Zoma Museum, Addis Ababa. **26–27, 126–27:** *Tightrope: Internalized* (details of pl. 18). **36–37:** views of *Flowers & Roots* (pl. 1). **38–39, 90–91:** *Tightrope 8* (details of pl. 9). **50–51:** *Ants and Ceramicists II* (detail of pl. 3). **58–59:** *Aremoch* (detail of pl. 4). **62–63, 166–67:** *Tightrope: Silent 1* (details of pl. 28). **64:** Elias Sime at work in Addis Ababa, with details of his materials. **74:** *Tightrope: Zooming In* (detail of fig. 20). **76:** view of the Merkato, Addis Ababa. **82–83, 122–23:** *Tightrope: In Boxes* (details of pl. 17). **86–87:** *Tightrope 3* (detail of pl. 8). **94–95, 174:** *Tightrope: Hands and Feet* (details of pl. 10). **98–99, 192:** *Tightrope: On the Edge* (details of pl. 11). **102–3:** *Tightrope: Familiar Yet Complex 1* (detail of pl. 12). **110–11:** *Tightrope: Familiar Yet Complex 6* (detail of pl. 14). **118–19:** *Tightrope: Behind the Beauty* (detail of pl. 16). **130–31, 188–89:** *Tightrope: The Dominant* (details of pl. 19). **138–39, 172–73:** *Tightrope: (1) While Observing . . .* (details of pl. 21). **142–43:** *Tightrope: (5) While Observing . . .* (detail of pl. 22). **146–47:** *Tightrope: (8) While Observing . . .* (detail of pl. 23). **150–51:** *Tightrope: (9) While Observing . . .* (detail of pl. 24). **158–59:** *Tightrope: Noiseless 12* (detail of pl. 26). **162–63:** *Tightrope: Noiseless 23* (detail of pl. 27). **170–71:** *Tightrope: Silent 2* (detail of pl. 29)

Photograph Credits (page numbers in bold)
Tracy L. Adler: **71.** John Bentham: cover (front and back), **2–8, 10–13, 22–27, 34–39, 58–63, 72–73, 82–83, 86–87, 90–91, 96–99, 102–3, 105–7, 110–11, 114–15, 118–23, 125–27, 130–31, 134–35, 137–39, 142–43, 146–47, 150–51, 154–55, 158–59, 162–63, 165–67, 169–74, 181–83, 188–89, 192.** Courtesy of Bonhams: **47.** Christopher Burke: **14, 79** (fig. 26), **133, 141, 145, 153, 157.** Phoebe d'Heurle: **54.** Karen E. Milbourne: **64, 68, 76–77.** Aida Muluneh: **52** (fig. 10). Adam Reich: **49–51, 84–85, 89.** Janelle Rodriguez: **32.** E. G. Schempf, 2019: **96–97.** Michel Temteme: **16, 18–19, 55** (fig. 13), **70.** Mariah Tiffany, courtesy of Facebook Artist in Residence (AIR) program: **55** (fig. 12). Helen Zeru: **52** (fig. 9)

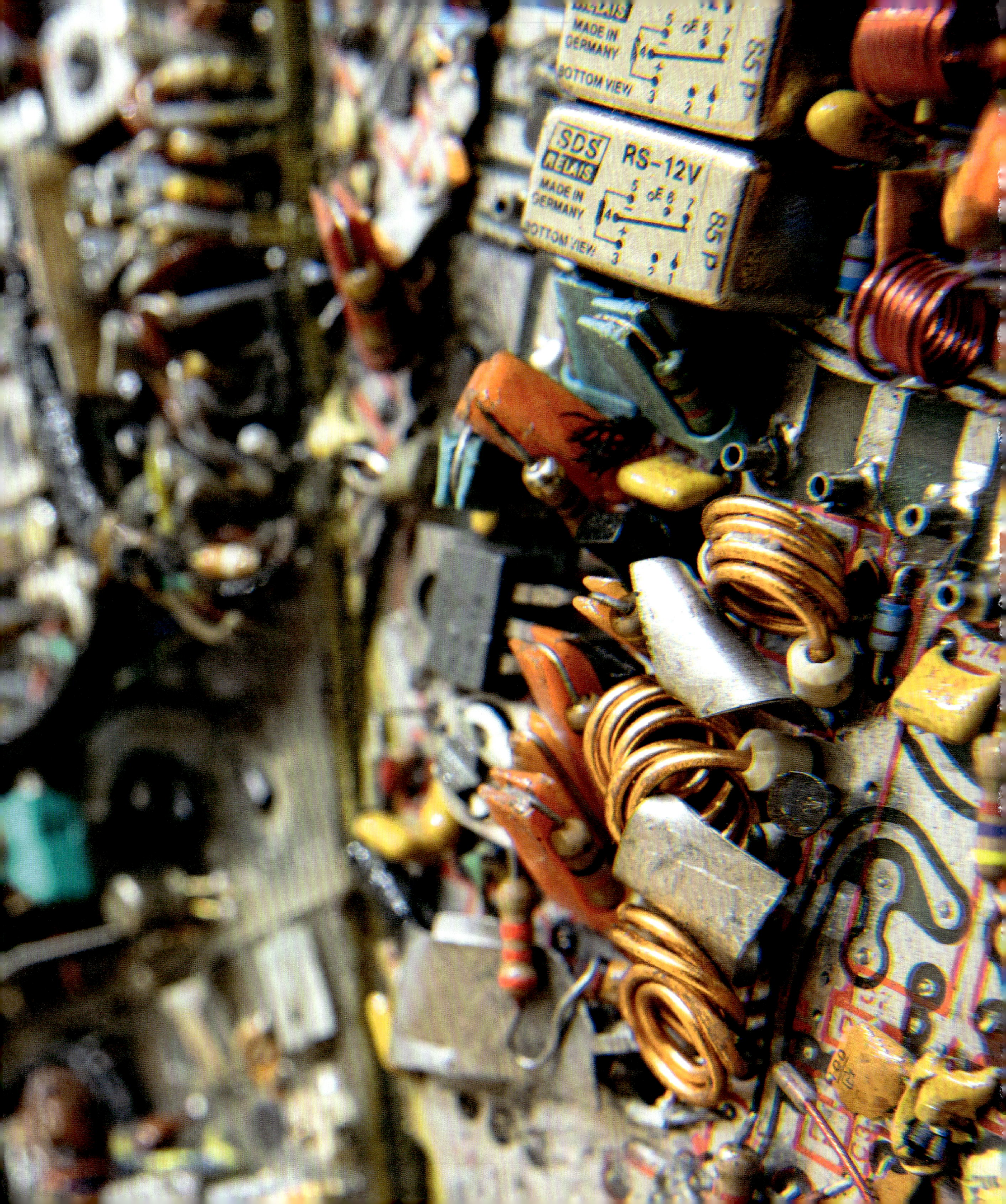
RELAIS
MADE IN
GERMANY
BOTTOM VIEW
85 P
SDS
RELAIS
RS-12V
MADE IN
GERMANY
BOTTOM VIEW
85 P